little boy Blue

little boy Blue

A puppy's rescue from death row and his owner's journey for truth

BY KIM KAVIN
Foreword by Jim Gorant

BARRON'S

All Inquiries should be addressed to:
Barron's Educational Series, Inc.
250 Wireless Boulevard
Hauppauge, NY 11788
www.barronseduc.com

Some names have been changed in this book to protect
the privacy of the individual/organization involved.

ISBN: 978-0-7641-6526-9

Library of Congress Catalog Card No: 2012012685

Library of Congress Cataloging-in-Publication
    Kavin, Kim.
        Little boy Blue : a puppy's rescue from death row and his
    owner's journey for truth / by Kim Kavin; forward by Jim
    Gorant.
        p. cm.
        ISBN 978-0-7641-6526-9 (alk. paper)
        1. Dog rescue—United States. 2. Animal shelters—United
    States. 3. Euthanasia of animals—United States. I. Title.
    HV4746.K38   2012
    636.08'32—dc23   2012012685

Printed in the United States of America
9 8 7 6 5 4 3 2 1

For the ones who can still be saved.

"Our values are defined by what we will tolerate when it is done to others."
—William Greider

~

"Nothing is inevitable unless our inaction makes it so."
—Ronald Regan

Contents

Foreword

~

The first time I walked in on my wife I think we were both a little embarrassed. I had arrived home early from work and stepped into the kitchen without making much of an entrance. When she finally heard me, she turned quickly, a shocked look in her eyes and a forced smile on her face. She used her body to shield the computer screen from view, and I had the creepy feeling that I'd just walked in on someone surreptitiously surfing for porn.

I had, although there was a twist. This was doggy porn. The URL on the browswer was that of Petfinder.com and on the screen was a full-body shot of a coquettish little Labradoodle who looked back over her shoulder with a mischievous glint in her eye. "Isn't she cute?" Karin said, and I nodded in a way that signaled assent without commitment. "Wait," she said. "Look at this one," and began navigating across the site with an ease that made it clear she'd been at this for a while and it wasn't her first time. At that moment one thing became abundantly clear: We were getting a dog.

The possibility didn't exactly come as a surprise. It had been a topic of conversation around our house—sometimes relentlessly so—for going on two years. Upon turning nine, our daughter had embarked upon an all-out campaign to bring a little furry enthusiasm to our family. The program consisted of continual asking, alternating promises of both doggy upkeep and household diligence, bartering, pleading, stomping, and the occasional moment of used-car-lot dissonance when she would look across the table and say, "Okay, what's it gonna take to make this happen?"

When we had recovered from the image of our little girl some day hawking Gremlins and Pacers in a gravel lot next to a strip mall, Karin and I could empathize. We loved dogs. We'd each had them growing up, and part of us wanted to get one now. Part of us didn't.

We both have busy jobs, we live in an old house that requires a lot of attention, and our two children have active lives that demand our participation. It's a great life (no complaints here), but it's a pretty fast-spinning carousel of train schedules, car pools, pickups, drop-offs, laundry, dinner, practices, games, Home Depot runs, doctor, dentist and orthodontist appointments, book reports, and so on.

As much as we liked the idea of a dog, we knew the reality of it would only add to the insanity. The kids insisted that they would take care of everything, walking and feeding and cleaning up the poop in the yard. Friends of ours suggested that it would teach them responsibility. We weren't buying that. For starters, we'd both been on the other side of that exchange. We'd made those promises as kids and the dogs that our parents had bought us suffered at our lack of follow-through. We knew that if we got a dog, we were taking the responsibility. If the kids helped out great, but we weren't going to count on it.

Our conversations on the topic always led to a place where we agreed it would be nice but probably not smart. "If you really wanted to, I would do it," Karin would say. To which I would say the same thing. And there the issue sat.

Except for one thing. At the end of 2008 I wrote a story for *Sports Illustrated,* the magazine for which I work, about the dogs rescued from Michael Vick's fighting operation. The story wound up on the cover, and I was soon approached about turning it into a book. I finished the manuscript in January 2010 and let Karin read it before turning it in. The book, *The Lost Dogs: Michael Vick's Dogs and Their Tale of Rescue and Redemption,* exposed the brutality of dog fighting but was largely an account of resilience and compassion that highlighted the connection between dogs and people.

It was shortly after Karin read the rough draft that I started to catch her looking at dog listings online. Our daughter's campaign hadn't abated, and sometimes I'd come home and find the two of them sitting in front of the computer together looking through the listings. "Have I shown you the pictures of Fluffy— or Lucky or Baby or Stumpy?"—became a regular question around our house. Somehow, though, our debates about the topic led to the same conclusion.

Until they didn't.

Finally, in early spring Karin admitted what had already become increasingly clear to me: She wanted a dog. After the book I had written there was no doubt we would get a rescue. But if my research and talks with so many in the animal-rescue community taught me anything, it was that most adoptions go wrong at the start, because people either set their heart on a breed that isn't right for them or they devote one day to the job and come home with the first dog that touches their heart.

For us, the process wasn't about finding *a dog*, but about finding *the dog*—which meant the one that was the best fit for our family. We made up a list of ideal attributes: adult, housebroken, low- to medium-energy level, and ideally a non- or low-shedding breed. And while we didn't want a big dog, we didn't want one of those bedroom slippers with legs, either. I felt a bit like the Goldilocks of dog rescue, but I figured that was better than being Little Red Riding Hood.

We started looking in earnest. We attended adoption days at pet stores within a thirty-mile radius. We visited shelters. We continued to comb Petfinder, filling out applications and sending e-mails about dogs that seemed like they might be right for us. We came close a few times, but for one reason or another we couldn't make a connection. With our daughter heading off to camp and a family vacation to follow, we suspended our search for the summer.

In September, my book came out and became a *New York Times* best seller. The flurry of interviews that came along with the success inevitably included the question: "So what type of dog do you have?" An awkward pause followed while I explained that we didn't have a dog, but we were working on it.

About a month later we identified a spunky-looking Schnauzer mix at a rescue called For the Love of Dogs about an hour away in Westchester County, New York. He had a lot of the qualities we were looking for, although at six he was a little old. Karin and I filled out the online forms, and after we'd been approved we drove up to visit.

His name was Chester, and he was gray and black, about twenty-five pounds and one of his bottom teeth stuck out, so that even when he closed his mouth the fang poked out between his lips. The snaggletooth made him look like a rough-and-tumble street urchin, and that seemed to go with his personality. On his walk he charged ahead, pulling on the leash, huffing and grunting at the restraint. He rolled on the ground as if he were John Belushi doing the Gator in *Animal House*. He pawed at the earth like an angry bull. We liked his spirit but wondered if he was a bit too much.

We went home. We thought about it. We loaded the kids in the car and went back a second time. They loved him, and watching him with them I could see that he was friendly and energetic, but also responsive and patient. After one more visit, we adopted him.

In the year since we've brought him home he's been wonderful. He's fun and sweet and he'd clearly lived in a house before because he has great manners. There are a million stories, but I'll leave it at this: Since we got him, two of our neighbors and Karin's brother have been so charmed by him that they have started looking to adopt—Chester is the kind of dog who makes people want a dog.

When we stopped to think about these things we couldn't help but wonder where he came from and how he ended up with us. We knew only the basics. His previous owner had turned him in to a high-kill shelter in South Carolina. He was on the short list to be put down; dogs who are turned in are often put down sooner than others because the shelter knows that no one is going to show up to make a claim, so they don't have to wait. The rescue group in Westchester, For the Love of Dogs, found him online and claimed him and eight others. No one knows exactly when, but within a few days it would have been all over for him.

Instead, he spent two weeks in a boarding facility to make sure he didn't have any infections, and then he was crated, loaded into the back of a van, and hauled from South Carolina to New York overnight by a courier hired specifically for the task. There's a photo taken of him upon his arrival that still shocks. He looks like a different dog—a different species, actually—smaller and scared, his hair matted and wet and dirty. If I didn't know otherwise I'd guess that he'd just emerged after crawling through a mile-long sewer pipe. The only recognizable feature of the dog I know today are his bright eyes.

Sometimes when I see him running in the yard or lying on his bed chewing on his favorite toy—a stuffed penguin that makes an infernal high-pitched squeak—I want to know more. I want to know who turned him in and why and how such a great dog could be given almost no chance to find another home. At other moments, I don't want to know any more than I already do. It's too mind-bending and sad to consider.

But at the end of the day I know that knowledge is better. Shortly after *The Lost Dogs* came out I attended a book signing not far from where I live. It was a beautiful fall day, so not many people showed up, but Kim Kavin did. I was happy to see her. I had met Kim about ten years earlier, when we were both working at magazines that catered to boaters and were members of an organization called Boating Writers International. About eight of us had gathered to discuss an update to the rules and bylaws and standards of professional conduct.

What became clear very quickly was that Kim was among the sharpest people in the room, and I don't think anyone who was there that day would disagree, the best pure journalist. I moved on from the boating gig shortly thereafter, but I stayed in touch with Kim over the years and continued to enjoy her work. When she told me the tale of her boy Blue and what she'd uncovered about his history I was reminded of her talents all over again. Even more so than Chester, he'd been on the verge of a needless death and only through the efforts of a selfless multitude did he somehow defy the odds and survive.

Here, I'd been using Petfinder for months, sending e-mails inquiring about dogs as far away as Kansas, but never did I ask the questions any good journalist should, including "How the hell will those dogs get here?" Kim had asked, and as a reward she had uncovered a secret world that few of us could even imagine existed. I knew immediately she was onto a great story—not only in the sense that it would be a fascinating one to read but also in that it would be an important one to tell.

As with dog fighting, the best way to change the bad and encourage the good is to shine a light on each. The story of the cruelty and unfairness of high-kill shelters and the lifesaving relief of the Petfinder revolution, including the people who labor so hard behind the scenes to make it work, needs to be told. We'll all be better off for having heard it. You, me, and the Chesters of the world.

Lately another theory has arisen around our house: Wouldn't it be nice if Chester had a playmate? When we talk about it honestly, we know that it's not the smart thing to do. We also know that there are fantastic animals out there who need a chance. I imagine that one of these days I'm going to come home and find my wife and daughter huddled around the computer making those prolonged "awwwing" sounds. I listen for it every time I come through the door.

Jim Gorant

The First Bread Crumbs

~

I'm the oldest child in my family, but I wasn't the first to be cradled and loved. My parents' black Scottish Terrier enjoyed hugs and kisses galore, had all the toys he wanted, and was as spoiled as any kid might be. It's no surprise that my first word was not "Daddy" or "Mama," but instead "Mac." He was my first best friend. It was fated that I would grow up to love my dogs the way most other people love their children.

Countless photos in our family album show Mac planted firmly by my side. There's Mac sitting next to my crib, next to me in my baby carrier, next to me on a hand-crocheted, pink and white afghan atop the summer's green grass. I'm sure a few of the portraits would embarrass Mac were he still around today—especially the one where he's propped up against a 1970s swirl of orange and yellow, as if he were on some kind of disco-inspired acid trip—but I think he'd like the ones of us two just as much as I do, because we were practically treated like brother and sister. We both got presents under the Christmas tree. We both went for the same walks in the park. In the photo I like best, Mac and I are sitting side by side on the diving board at my grandfather's lake house, and I'm giving him a huge hug. This isn't your average embrace. It's the kind where a child wraps her arms around the neck of somebody she adores and squeezes so tightly that you know she'll never be able to let go, at least not in her own favorite memories. When I look at that photo today, I don't just see the happiness of a girl and her first dog. I see the heart of a dog lover learning how it feels to overflow with joy.

Even now, more than thirty years later, there are more photos of dogs on the walls of my parents' home than there are photos of people. My mom's favorite sweatshirt reads "Ask Me About My Granddog." My father keeps a fuzzy orange gorilla, the favorite toy of another now-gone family dog, in the china cabinet where other folks might display a sports trophy or retirement plaque. I have precious few memories of our family home without a dog in it. After Mac came the Doberman named Tallen. After Tallen came the West Highland White Terriers Brandy and Corky (their official papers read Brandywine Mist and Kavin's Colonel Corker III). When they died, we welcomed the Doberman Tanner. When he left us, his look-alike Quincy joined our pack, as did my sister's black Labrador, Sadie May, whom I fondly call my niece. I've liked some of these dogs better than others over the years, but I've also adored every last one the way other little girls love their favorite dolls. The thought of going to sleep at night without a dog in the house is as foreign to me as the thought of letting a trained dog sleep anywhere but in the bed at my feet—and under the covers if it's cold during the winter, of course.

When I graduated from college, the first thing I did was get my own dog. It didn't dawn on me that I might consider living without one. And though I'd always been raised alongside my parents' purebreds, I was okay with having a mutt. I figured they needed good homes, too. My fiancé and I found the beagle mix by way of an advertisement in the newspaper's classified section. This was circa 1994 in Cedar Rapids, Iowa—a heck of a long way from my New Jersey hometown, but the only city that offered us both jobs in the news business right out of college. The puppies were on a farm in Central City, less than an hour's drive away. We arrived to find a beagle tending to her pups in the shadow of a ticked-off farmer. He desperately wanted the name of the neighborhood tramp who had knocked her up, because the mixed-breed puppies commanded a lower selling price than purebreds.

"What will you do if there are some puppies you can't sell?" I asked the farmer as I played with the floppy-eared pups in the grass.

"I'll drown them in that river over there," he deadpanned, "in a bag full of rocks."

It might have been a sales pitch, it might have been reality, but whatever the case, I scooped up the puppy with the raccoon-mask face and cradled him in my arms like a refugee. Floyd would survive not only the farmer, but also my relationship with the fiancé (when we broke up, I kept the TV, the VCR, and the dog—my three most prized possessions). That dog would be my daily companion for nearly sixteen years to come. He would move with me back to the Northeast, adjusting without complaint to five different apartments, rented basements, and condos as I traded up to better and better jobs at newspapers and magazines in New York, New Jersey, and Connecticut. He would sit under my desk at the office, by my side at company softball games, and on my lap at night on the couch. He'd even make room on that couch for the man I would eventually marry—though only after a few grumbling go-arounds in which Floyd made it clear he was still the number one male in my life.

When Floyd turned eleven, I bought a house on five and a half acres of woodland in west-central New Jersey, right between New York City and Philadelphia, in a place where deer still roam in herds and the occasional cow takes a morning stroll up the street. My husband had gotten a job nearby, and my savings had allowed us to trade up from the two-bedroom townhouse where we'd been living into a four-bedroom colonial on a cul-de-sac. The backyard must have looked like a football field to Floyd after all those years of apartment and condominium life, and I took my veterinarian's suggestion to encourage him to run around by bringing home a playmate.

This time I logged onto Petfinder.com. The year was 2005, and Petfinder had been live since 1996, when Floyd was just two years old. I can't remember seeing any publicity about it, but somehow I had internalized the idea that this website had replaced the local classified ads as a nationwide billboard for pets in need of homes. I was far from alone in my thinking. By 2008,

Petfinder would claim more than sixty million visitors each year. That's a heck of a lot of people. It's more than fifteen times the number of fans who attended a game in 2010 at Yankee Stadium, which was the best-attended venue in all of Major League Baseball. It's about the same number of people who receive Social Security—the largest federal program in the United States. It's about three times the number of people in America's six largest cities, if you combine the entire populations of New York, Los Angeles, Chicago, Houston, Philadelphia, and Phoenix. Petfinder quickly grew into the largest website of its kind, with some thirteen thousand rescue groups and shelters uploading photos of adoptable animals every day. Since its inception in 1996, the website has helped to connect an estimated seventeen million animals with new homes.

Mine was about to become the next one. I typed in my New Jersey zip code and the word "hound," figuring that Floyd would want a friend who could understand him when he sang out one of his big, bellowing bays.

A brown face with a white lightning bolt caught my attention immediately. She was listed as a Pointer/Labrador, about twelve weeks old, and less than a half hour away. I clicked on the link and was asked to fill out a three-page form detailing our intentions for the dog's training, the status of our yard's fencing, and the number of hours my husband and I spent away from home at work. I half expected to offer a blood sample and submit to a drug test. It felt like winning a reprieve from a tax audit when Rawhide Rescue invited us to meet the pup in Plainfield, New Jersey, and pay $250 to bring her home. What a difference from the farmer who had wanted thirty-five bucks to take a "damn mutt" off his hands. The act of acquiring a puppy in America, it seemed to me, had changed substantially during the past decade.

We decided to call her Stella because, well, it was fun to shout her name like Marlon Brando in *A Streetcar Named Desire*. We of course loved her instantly, but we wouldn't realize for nearly a year that Stella is no Labrador at all. Most likely, according to the breeders, veterinarians, and trainers I consulted, she's a combination of Foxhound, Pointer, and American Pit Bull Terrier—not to mention a sixty-pound alpha female with aggression tendencies that would require a $100-per-hour private trainer for us to learn how to manage. I had always enjoyed my daily walks with Floyd, but Stella's insatiable energy required me to become a jogger, with runs as long as five miles simply to help her work out her excessive intensity. She broke her kneecap trying to jump over our four-foot-tall split-rail fence to chase a deer. She figured out how to open the spare bedroom door and ate enough Gorilla Glue to require an expensive chiseling of her stomach. She worked her way past the downstairs doggy gate and shredded our newly reupholstered sectional sofa. Not just the cloth and cushion stuffing, mind you, but also the wooden frame.

Floyd liked Stella for maybe the first three days. Though he would live to be nearly sixteen, he was already old at eleven, and the daily tornado that Stella became was just too much for him to bear. They'd make their peace after about a year, when Stella finally stopped nipping at him, but by then her favorite game had become getting her face as close as she could to his, like a bratty kid who insists, "But I'm not touching you!" And that was better than the countless times when he'd be sitting in the kitchen, an old man content merely to be breathing, and she'd wander by, line her butt up alongside his head, and whap him onto the floor with a flick of her hip. The word bitch most certainly applied.

I was surprised by how lonely Stella seemed after Floyd died. She was never one to sit by my feet as I typed magazine articles and books on my keyboard, but once he was gone from his favorite pillow beneath my desk, she peeked through the door to my home office more often than usual. It was Stella who stood next to me for a solid ten minutes on the day I emptied the dryer's lint trap, found it full of Floyd's black hair, and began to bawl. I'm not sure whether she actually missed him, too, or whether she just knew that I was devastated, but I felt sure that she wanted another dog in the house just as badly as I did. My husband, too, could tell my heart was aching. Stella was my girl, but Floyd had been one of my soul mates.

By now it was 2010. Stella was five years old and I was back on Petfinder.com, scrolling along with millions of other people through the puppy pictures. A male brindle listed as a Labrador/Plott Hound, only a half hour away in Pennsylvania, caught my eye. This time the form was not three but five pages long, and a volunteer named Jane Zeolla from Lulu's Rescue actually showed up to inspect the house instead of just asking me about it. She spent half an hour interviewing me, nosing around for anything that might be dangerous to a dog, and, in general, sizing me up as a potential puppy adopter. I actually felt nervous, despite my nearly forty years of having lived with dogs as my housemates. I took Stella for a long walk and gave her a bone filled with peanut butter just before Zeolla arrived, hoping my beloved maniac would somehow instantly transform into an accomplished graduate of New England's finest finishing schools.

Zeolla said she thought our home would be ideal for the pup in question. I had carefully selected him after more thought and research than I allowed for my own wedding gown. I knew I needed just the right dog as Stella's everyday pal, lest she turn him into a chew toy. I required a young, nonthreatening male with some kind of hunting hound in him, and with a history of fearlessness when playing with dogs at least twice his size. Nobody knew this particular puppy's origins, but I was told he'd spent his most recent days on a foster farm playing with lots of other dogs, including a seventy-pound Labrador/pit bull mix. That, plus his achingly adorable face, led me to believe he was our boy.

I asked if I could meet him to see if he was "as advertised." As much as I'd grown to love Stella, I also liked the new sofa. I didn't need another reenactment of *Jaws* being played out in my den.

That's when I learned the puppy wasn't in our part of New Jersey, or even in our region of the United States. He was in rural North Carolina, somewhere north of Durham.

"But the Petfinder site said just over the border in Pennsylvania," I blurted, utterly confused. I had specifically searched for pups within a hundred miles of our home, so I could check them out before committing.

Zeolla explained that rescue groups up North now put their own zip codes onto sites like Petfinder.com so people like me will find dogs who are far away, but dearly in need. "There are so many unwanted dogs in the South that they don't know what to do with them," she said. "The people don't spay and neuter. In the shelters up here, all you find are pit bulls from the inner cities. They're not likely to be adopted because so many people are unfairly biased against the breed. But down South, you find all kinds of adoptable, healthy dogs who are being killed because they don't have homes. So we work with a network of volunteers to bring them up here, and we use our own address to get them adopted locally."

It was my first hint that this puppy's story was somehow larger, the first bread crumb on a trail that I could not even imagine while sitting at my kitchen table that sunny spring afternoon.

My new boy, she told me, would most likely be brought by "ground transport," assuming she could get him a spot on one of the RVs that volunteers drive from as far south as Florida to as far north as Maine every weekend, often carrying dozens of dogs at a time. There was also a chance he could arrive on a private plane, which was sometimes an option if all of the ground transports were full.

I nodded as if I understood, and I nonchalantly offered to refill her glass of iced tea. All the while, I was thinking, *A private plane for a shelter dog? Are these rescue people from the Twilight Zone?*

Her description turned out to be spot on. Three days later, I found myself driving to a shopping center on the New Jersey–

Pennsylvania border. In its parking lot, I met a perfectly pleasant, if entirely exhausted, couple who had driven through the
night in their RV full of rescued dogs from the Carolinas. It was
about 9:30 A.M., and the shopping center was their third stop
already that morning. I knocked on the RV's driver-side window.
The husband motioned for me to go around to the side door.

Out came the wife. I didn't hear any dogs barking, and I didn't
see any dogs right away. "You must be Kim," she said with a
weary smile.

"I am," I replied. I felt the way drug addicts probably do
when they try to score a dime bag on the side of the road. "How
do we do this?"

She and her husband, I'd learn, had done this countless times
before. They charge ninety-five dollars per dog and sometimes
transport more than a dozen dogs every weekend. She disap-
peared back inside the RV while I stood on the curb, fumbling
with the swanky new collar and leash I'd bought the day before. I wondered how the new puppy would like the name we'd
picked out for him. Although Stella's name had come from one
of my favorite Academy Award-winning theatrical releases, this
dog's name had come from one of my husband's recent finds. It
was from the movie *Old School,* when Will Ferrell shouts over
the coffin of a fraternity pledge who dies of a heart attack during
a jelly-wrestling match, "You're my boy, Blue!"

A few moments later, the woman reemerged holding a twenty-
pound puppy whose face looked exactly like the photograph I'd
seen online. With the fluid motion of a nurse in a delivery room,
she handed him to me and stood back to watch my reaction.

Blue was no more a Labrador than Stella, despite their similar advertisements by rescue groups doing their best to guess at the breed mixes involved. He was already four or five months old based on the adult teeth that had come in, and he was about the size that a beagle would be at that age. His face shape and ears looked beagle-ish, too, albeit with eyes and a forehead that could easily have been genetic hand-me-downs from a pit bull. He had an exceptionally long torso, like some coonhounds native to the South or, perhaps, a Dachshund. His brindle coat reminded me a great deal of Boxers I've known, a rich caramel brown with black tiger stripes. And he had a white "tuxedo shirt" on his chest, plus white bands around all four paws where a gold toe might be on a sock. He was not precisely what I'd expected, but he was, in a word, gorgeous. If he hadn't been a mutt found in a shelter, he might have passed for some new and strangely named designer dog breed, like a Puggle.

He seemed shell-shocked—as any baby would be after riding five hundred miles in a cage in an RV in the middle of the night—but he let me hold him, and he gave me a kiss, and he looked up at me with big brown eyes that said, "Trust me, I'm a survivor." I handed over a check for nearly $400 that included the transport fee—*four hundred dollars for a shelter dog*, I thought—and placed Blue in the Jeep for our ride home. The couple in the RV continued about their business, I suppose shifting dogs from crate to crate before driving onward to their next stop. I didn't even catch their names before I said goodbye. It never occurred to me that I might want to find them again in the near future.

Much to my delight, Blue's first steps on the grass of New Jersey included walking up to Stella the way a featherweight contender approaches a heavyweight champ. He was absurdly outclassed in size, easily at a forty-pound disadvantage, but he wasn't afraid as the two of them sniffed one another on the neutral turf of my neighbor's backyard. Blue knew not only how to avoid a fight, but also how to create an ally. He rolled on his back to let Stella know she could be the boss, then hopped right back up to show her that he wanted to play at her level. Stella tried to wrestle with Blue, but realized he was too small. She tried to play tug with him, but figured he was too weak. Just when my favorite little headache was probably thinking, "This dog's only use is as a punching bag," Blue broke into a sprint and encouraged her to give chase. It was their favorite game by dinnertime that night, and they've played it every day since.

Blue is asleep at my feet as I type this, tired from his morning walk and using Stella's backside as a pillow on a floor littered with squeaky toys, tennis balls, and chew bones. He is an absolutely wonderful puppy. He's a fast learner—he knew his name, "sit," and "lie down" inside of four days, and he set a world record of only three accidents before figuring out how to use the doggy door. He can never replace Floyd in my heart, but he sure does help to supplant the overwhelming sense of loss and sadness with pure, unadulterated joy. He bounds at me with puppy love practically flying off the tips of his flapping ears, jumping into my arms several times a day simply because he's so happy. And I get stopped at least three times a week at the local parks by people asking what breed he is, with his gorgeous brindle coat standing out in a suburban desert of yellow Labradors.

The more I considered Blue's personality, the more I realized how different from Stella he was. I began to see how somebody might have called Stella "damaged" or "unadoptable" because she needed so much training, so much exercise, and so much patience during the first couple of years. A lot of people would have given her right back to a shelter with less thought than they give to returning a dented baking pan at the grocery store. I most definitely do not agree that Stella was unworthy of saving, but I can see the argument arising, especially in towns where any puppy who even remotely resembles a pit bull is considered dangerous. She's lucky she didn't get the needle before being given a chance to grow into the terrific adult dog that she is, one who will perform on cue not only "sit" and "stay," but also "high five," "jab," and "left hook."

Blue, though, is an altogether different kind of puppy. He has not presented a single major challenge, unless you count the fact that he wants to be cuddled twenty-four hours a day without breaks for a good night's sleep. He's a lifetime companion in the making, just like Floyd was from the first days that I knew him.

When I started to think about how Blue had to be driven hundreds of miles in that RV to find a happy home, I was baffled. He struck me as a truly awesome boy, and I couldn't imagine why it would require such effort to find him a family. The only indications Blue showed that first day of having endured anything strange were the healed-over scabs and tiny, hairless spots that I found from his face all the way to the middle of his back.

They weren't big or disgusting, but the more I petted him, the more spots I found beneath the patches of hair that were already growing back. He didn't scratch at them, and he didn't wince when I touched them, but they gave me enough concern that they became the number one thing I decided to mention when I took him to my veterinarian for his initial checkup.

It was there that I would get my first real insights into the place where he'd started his journey, along with my first inklings that something about his situation had been horribly, horribly wrong.

Quarantine and Questions

~~~

No children live in my house, but kids are always underfoot. My property sits on a cul-de-sac where neighborhood pickup games often result in a wayward kickball or baseball rolling across my front yard. Whichever kid runs down the hill to retrieve the lost ball inevitably sees my dogs staring like bleacher creatures out the front door, lacking only for official scorecards and the opposable thumbs required to fill them in. Once word spread among the elementary- and middle-school kids that there was a new puppy sitting just beyond my welcome mat, I heard a knock at my door at least once or twice a day.

I wanted Blue to know youngsters of all ages while he was still a puppy, so he'd learn to behave properly around them whether they were gently rubbing his ears or mischievously pulling his tail. So it was that Blue's first playmates included my neighbors Erika and Andrew. Erika was about to graduate from high school, and Andrew was a couple of years younger. They'd grown up around dogs and had always done well with the dogs at my house, and they're smart kids whose parents are generous. They eagerly volunteered to be the guinea pigs as we tested Blue's reaction to older kids, with their mother, Stacy, and me standing cautiously next to them in their backyard.

I let Blue off his leash once he was safely inside their fence, and he stood for a few moments getting the lay of the land. Both kids were desperate to play with the puppy, but Blue took his time, sizing them up the way a blackjack player seeks out a friendly-looking dealer at a casino. After a few minutes, my all-too-typical little man decided that he first wanted to meet Erika, who happens to be an attractive blonde. She knelt down at his level and cooed so instinctively at his cuteness that we thought her heart might actually be melting with love. He didn't so much walk up to her as he did a belly crawl, inching his way across the grass in a posture so submissive you'd think he was yet another shy high-school boy angling to ask her for a date. When Erika reached out to pet Blue, he rolled onto his back and exposed his tummy to her. She rubbed it gently for a few seconds before he flipped himself and sprang to his feet, wagging his tail faster than a hummingbird flutters its wings. Erika's smile was as bright as the sunshine that afternoon, and Blue's demeanor was just as warm.

I felt the muscles in my hand relax as I unclenched my knuckles from around the leash I'd been gripping at the ready. Stacy looked on with unabashed approval, saying, simply, "What a cute little dog."

Andrew next moved toward Blue with the lanky lope of just about every adolescent boy I know. Blue wasn't as comfortable with Andrew's approach as he had been with Erika's, and he darted backward, scampering with his tiny puppy toes until he was well out of Andrew's reach. Blue tucked his tail between his legs and let his ears droop in what looked to us all like an unquestionable sign of fear. It wasn't like with so many puppies who get nervous or uncomfortable if you approach them from overhead instead of reaching toward their bellies. It also wasn't something that happened quickly, as with most puppies who then bounce right back to cheerful play. Blue's cowering and retreating lingered like an unwelcome stench in the air, in a way that made it obvious he had learned the hard way to be leery. He wasn't looking at us with the curious eyes of a puppy who was momentarily startled. He was looking at us with the eyes of a survivor who knew far more about the harsher side of human nature than any dog ever should.

Andrew felt so bad that he stopped moving entirely, even skipping a breath or two. Then he sat down in the grass and waited until Blue was ready to come to him. Again, Blue belly-crawled across the lawn. His posture showed friendliness, but also wariness until he felt sure that he was safe.

Mental note, I thought. *Blue is a sweetheart, but he seems unusually timid for a puppy. Somebody has taught this dog not to trust some people until they prove themselves friendly.*

With Erika and Andrew now proudly counting themselves among Blue's best friends in the entire world, I walked him home just in time to greet another friend who'd dropped by to

meet him. I kept Blue on his leash in the driveway as Brandi unloaded the car seat that held her infant daughter, Avery. We let
Blue sniff the car seat itself, and then Avery's itty-bitty baby
feet. While Brandi and I were both at the Defcon One stage
of alert, Blue and Avery alike seemed remarkably nonplussed.
Blue was more interested in saying hello to Brandi, who happily swapped newborns with me and took Blue into my backyard to play.

Blue was shy with Brandi, just as he'd initially been with
Erika and Andrew, but she lured him with a welcome-home
chew toy wrapped inside soft animal hide that is apparently
as delicious to dogs as black truffles are to connoisseurs of
French cuisine. Blue went crazy for the thing, and of course
then crazy for Brandi, this mysterious new human being who
was the bearer of exciting things to gnaw. Once he felt comfortable with her, he let her hold him and pet him and hug
him, and she fell in love with him just as quickly as everybody
else who'd met him. Blue seemed to have more than the usual
allotment of natural puppy charm. Something about the way
he tested people before trusting them made everybody want to
cuddle him that much more.

I was expecting a similar reaction when I brought Blue to
my veterinarian a few days later for his first checkup. Dr. Allison Milne and her staff at Mendham Animal Hospital had
been outstanding with Floyd and Stella alike, and I knew I
could trust them implicitly with Blue's care, no matter what
he ended up needing. When Floyd, around age ten, had de-
veloped benign tumors that grew so large that they impeded

his ability to walk, Dr. Milne had put his quality of life before his age and done surgery that some other vets would have refused the old man, but that ended up giving him five additional years of comfortable walks at the park. Stella was known as a frequent flyer in the office thanks to her Velociraptor-like tendencies to puzzle her way into all kinds of bones fractured and items swallowed, and Dr. Milne and her staff always welcomed her with hugs and treats, as well as with bandages and stitches. Maybe the staff really liked my dogs, or maybe they really liked the way my countless visits were providing serious funding for the office mortgage. Either way, I couldn't wait to introduce the squad to Blue.

He had arrived on the RV without a shred of paperwork, so the folks at Lulu's Rescue had spent a few days tracking down what they could while I was settling Blue into his new life. They'd e-mailed me a few files that morning, and I'd printed them out to bring to Dr. Milne without actually having time to read them myself. Only after I was in the exam room with Blue sitting on the table, with a veterinary technician holding him in place and Dr. Milne listening to his lungs with her stethoscope, did I finally have a chance to look over the four sheets of paper. They weren't much, but they contained all the information that had been recorded about Blue during his first five months of life.

One sheet of paper was just that, a plain piece of standard white with only three lines of handwritten notations. They indicated the dates that Blue had received his second and third doses of puppy booster shots for parvovirus, distemper, and parainfluenza, as well as a dose of Heartgard, which many dogs take once a month to prevent heartworm. It was standard stuff in terms of veterinary care, albeit recorded in a thoroughly homespun way.

The second sheet was an official-looking certificate from Roxboro Animal Hospital in Roxboro, North Carolina, a city that I would later learn has fewer than ten thousand residents and that is the seat of Person County. This sheet described Blue as a Boxer/Hound mix and noted the date of his first rabies vaccine. His owner was listed as an alphabet soup of letters that I guessed was a generic acronym for some kind of animal-rescue group.

Third was a sheet that bore the same date as Blue's rabies vaccine, from the same animal hospital in Roxboro. The computer-generated form stated that he'd received a physical exam, a round of puppy booster shots, a supply of Heartgard to prevent heartworm, and a supply of Frontline for fleas and ticks. It looked very much like the receipts that I get from Dr. Milne's office after my visits, itemized with standard information that I recognized from my own dogs' care. At the bottom, someone had handwritten reminder dates for when Blue needed his next doses of everything. *All on the up-and-up*, I thought.

The fourth and final sheet was also computer generated, but from a different source. The top read "POP-NC" beneath the line "Pet Overpopulation Patrol—Mobile Spay/Neuter." There, Blue had received a physical exam that showed almost everything about him to be normal. He'd been neutered and given pain medication for any post-operation discomfort, and his surgery was listed as "uncomplicated."

There was, however, one line on that fourth sheet that gave me pause. Under "skin/hair/nails," the POP veterinarian had listed Blue as abnormal. She had handwritten "circular dermatitis on chest—recommend culture for ringworm." Beneath that note was another one, left by someone with different handwriting. It was an asterisk followed by three words: "treated for ringworm."

I was about to hand the information to Dr. Milne when she asked me about the little scabs running from Blue's face all along his neck and onto his upper back. She was going to do a scraping for mange to be sure that's not what had caused them.

"It says here that he was treated for ringworm," I told her as I handed over the paperwork. "None of my dogs have ever had ringworm. Is that some kind of rash? He was advertised as healthy, so maybe they're just scabs that are still healing from the treatment."

Dr. Milne immediately stepped away from Blue and began to read the papers, scouring them the way a divorce attorney reviews bank records for signs of hidden money. The veterinary technician who had been holding Blue on the exam table threw her arms into the air and stepped back, as if my precious pooch were a ticking nuclear bomb. Blue himself sat freakishly still, no doubt sensing the sudden change in mood. I walked over and put my arm around him to comfort him, just as I had countless times during the past few days.

Ringworm, I would learn, is not actually a worm, but instead a fungus. It creates a highly contagious, hard-to-kill skin infection that can be passed from dogs to dogs, and from dogs to humans.

Most of the vet techs in the office had suffered with it before—itchy, red, scaly patches that can blister and ooze—and the one who had just been holding Blue didn't want any part of having it again. Dr. Milne asked me to wait while the vet tech went and found one of her colleagues, who seemed to be immune to ringworm and was not concerned about becoming infected.

Dr. Milne herself, having now read all four sheets of paper, shook her head in disgust. She let out a sigh, and then for the first time in the five years I'd known her, she raised her voice.

"You know," she hollered, "I get that they're trying to rescue dogs out of shelters, but there is a difference between saving dogs on a shoestring and giving proper medical care! What do these notes even mean? Was this dog ever actually tested for ringworm? Did they verify that it's cured? How can these people adopt out a dog who might be infecting every other dog and person who touches him?"

My mind immediately flashed to Erika. And then to Andrew. And then to baby Avery, who was just a few months old. The hair on her head hadn't even grown in all the way yet. Her mom and I had been so excited about the new puppy that we'd passed Blue and Avery back and forth without even thinking to wash our hands.

"Can babies get this?" I asked with an overwhelming sense of dread.

"Not only can they get it, but it can be very difficult to clear up," Dr. Milne answered. "It's not common, but it is possible. Anybody who touched this dog and then held a baby could have transferred it."

I sat down on the chair in the exam room and took a deep breath. It felt like a hamster was running loose inside my intestines.

Dr. Milne walked stoically out of the exam room. She returned a moment later with a piece of scrap paper and a pen. She said that Blue would need a ringworm test and two full weeks of quarantine at my house until the test results were confirmed, and that she would prefer not to release him from her office at all until we could get at least a few basic questions answered.

"We don't want to spread this problem any further than it has already gone," she said. "We're now in a situation where we're dealing with public health, not just a puppy's rash."

Some people may think she was overreacting, but the truth is that she was right to be concerned. I would later learn that some states have gone so far as to pass quarantine laws to prevent dogs from being transported with diseases like ringworm. Dr. Milne wasn't upset so much because of the rash itself, but instead because I may have gotten Blue from what appeared in that moment to be an irresponsible rescue.

On the scrap paper, Dr. Milne wrote the four questions that she said needed immediate answers. Number One: How was it determined that Blue had ringworm—were actual ringworm cultures taken, or were they just recommended? Number Two: What kind of treatment had Blue received, specifically? Number Three: How long was he treated? Number Four: Was he retested for ringworm after the treatment was completed?

"They're all important," she told me, "but that last one is really important. The standard of care for ringworm includes doing a test to confirm that the fungus is present, and then doing the same test a second time, after the treatment, to make sure it's actually gone. Sometimes it requires multiple rounds of treatment before the fungus is killed all the way."

I looked over at Blue, who was now lying instead of sitting on the exam table. His big, brown puppy eyes drooped with exhaustion. It had been a long day for him on the heels of a long week. I asked Dr. Milne to leave us the room and the records. As Blue faded into a nap, I took out my cell phone and began calling every number on those four sheets of paper.

Mostly, I got hold of office workers who could only confirm what the papers already stated. Then one telephone number led me to a feed store in North Carolina, a place where a van apparently shows up every week or so to offer inexpensive spaying and neutering services. I asked the feed store guy for any help he could give me, and he asked me to hold on while he grabbed his phone book to get the number for the people he knows from the van. The woman who answered my call to that number didn't know anything about Blue, but she did recognize the alphabet soup that I read off the paper identifying Blue's owner at the time of his surgery.

"That's the Canine Volunteer Rescue of Person County here in North Carolina," the woman said, so quickly that she might as well have been recalling her own home address. She was kind enough to look up the group's phone number for me before adding, "You want to talk to a woman there named Annie Turner."

It surprised me that this woman knew the rescue worker by name. A week earlier, I'd clicked on a photograph of a puppy listed within an hour of my home and offered to adopt him. I'd been told that he was homeless, saved from a shelter, and had no known origins. Now I was on the phone to a place hundreds of miles away where the people involved in Blue's earliest days seemed to all know one another by name. It felt weird to me, perhaps because I live in a New Jersey county that is home to nearly a half million people, most of them strangers to one another in the suburbs of the even-bigger New York City. I had the immediate sense that I was calling a part of America that was much smaller and much different, a place where I was somehow inserting myself into a group of people who knew each other really, oddly well.

I thanked the woman for Annie Turner's phone number and asked her if she could tell me anything more about the type of treatment the spay/neuter veterinarian would have given Blue for ringworm.

"Oh, we don't treat things like that," she said. "We would have only recommended that he get a ringworm culture done, that some kind of follow-up be done at the local veterinarian."

I next called the number for Canine Volunteer Rescue of Person County, and I left a voice mail requesting that Annie Turner return my call. That's when Dr. Milne came back inside the exam room.

"So this puppy was never actually diagnosed with ringworm through an actual culture at a veterinarian's office?" Dr. Milne asked.

"I'm not sure," I said, "but all of the veterinarians listed in this paperwork told me they never did any ringworm tests."

Dr. Milne sighed and made a face that I hadn't seen since about 1978, when my father had caught me hurling Star Wars action figures from the bathtub into the toilet.

"All right, then, here's what we're going to do," Dr. Milne said. "We don't actually know that this dog had ringworm. Since you and your other dog have already been exposed, as long as Blue stays in your house and yard, he can't infect anybody else. Notify everybody who's touched him, and have them watch for any signs of abnormalities, especially on that baby. We'll do the ringworm culture today and keep him in quarantine with you for the next two weeks, just to be safe. When you hear back from this woman Annie Turner, call my office and give me all the details you can get. In the meantime, we'll give you a bottle of medicinal shampoo that should kill any fungus that Blue might still have, plus a tube of cream that will help to heal his scabs."

I scooped up Blue and paid my bill, which listed the cost of the shampoo and cream at a combined total of $38.75.

All of this drama over something that costs less than forty bucks to correct? I thought. *I paid $400 for this dog. Why on earth would people charging that kind of money not have just given Blue these things before putting him up for adoption?*

Back at home, I got in touch with the folks from Lulu's Rescue. They were horrified to learn of my experience. They said it was the first time they had ever had a problem with a dog from this particular rescue group in North Carolina, and they'd been given no indication that Blue was anything other than a happy, healthy puppy. The photograph of him hadn't shown any signs of a skin problem, and nobody had ever said the word *ringworm* in their discussions about him. They promised to do further research and let me know if they could find any additional information about Blue's past, and they thanked me for all I was doing to make sure he was healthy. Some people, they told me, would have skipped the shampoo and instead just sent him back, rejected as defective.

It took me a good while to get that repugnant idea out of my mind. I shook my head at the very thought of it, and I spent the rest of the afternoon following Dr. Milne's instructions. Blue seemed oblivious to all the concern and drama, what with his nap at the vet's office having recharged his puppy batteries. He scampered and played with Stella until I picked him up in one hand with the bottle of shampoo in the other.

Not long after I'd finished Blue's first medicinal bath in the kitchen sink, my telephone rang. The woman on the line said she was Annie Turner, returning my call.

At least I thought "Annie Turner" was the name the woman had said. She sounded about as different from me as a platypus from a mountain lion. I was born and raised in New Jersey. Unless I make a serious mental effort, I talk as fast as a freight train and sound just as silly as Snooki or Tony Soprano thanks to my "Joisey Gurl" accent. This woman Annie Turner had a Southern drawl and talked slower than a push mower on a hot summer's day. At first, we couldn't understand a thing that the other was saying. I asked her to repeat a couple of things a couple of times, until I could discern her pattern of speech. I slowed my own sentences and tried to enunciate the way I do when I'm on assignment as a travel writer in foreign countries.

Turner said she had fostered Blue at the farm where she lived after he was found at the local animal-control center in Person County. "They gas puppies like him to death," she said. "They kill 92 percent of all the dogs that go in there."

I paused for a moment, trying to digest what she'd just told me.

"I'm sorry," I said, shocked into responding even more slowly. "Would ... you ... please ... say that again?"

"Ninety-two percent," she said. "They kill almost all of them. We pulled him out at the last minute. He was headed for the gas chamber."

Blue, at that moment, was on my backyard deck. He'd gone outside to dry off, and I'd given him a bone for being such a good boy about the bath. I could see him through the kitchen window. He had fallen asleep while chewing the bone, which lay next to him, half eaten. His little puppy potbelly rose and fell with every breath as his wet fur dried in the afternoon sun.

Gas chamber? I thought. The words echoed in my brain with a muffled dullness, like the way ears ring in the immediate aftermath of an explosion. *Who on earth would throw a puppy like Blue into a gas chamber? Is that even legal?*

I had Dr. Milne's scrap paper in hand, and I needed her four specific questions answered. Turner was at first open and forthcoming with lots of information, which it turns out included all of the first-known details about Blue's life.

Blue, after her group rescued him from the animal-control center, had gone to live on what she described as a farm where she was fostering about twenty dogs. Most of them are Chihuahuas, which she said hold a special place in her heart, but something about Blue's face made her feel that he was exceptional, too. She said that Blue had loved playing with all of her other foster dogs, and that he practically sang with delight when she rocked him in her arms. He had been learning to sleep and eat in a crate at her urging and without any complaint, and he'd grown especially fond of a big Labrador mix who lived on the farm as well. The two of them had become inseparable, Turner said.

I thanked her for having saved him, and for all of the work her group had done to bring him to my attention. I assured her that he was loved and well cared for, and that he had, in fact, just returned from a checkup at the veterinarian's office.

Then I slowly but determinedly turned the conversation back to its original purpose. I needed to know the cause of Blue's scabs, and why and how he was treated for ringworm.

"Oh, he never had a test for ringworm," she said, about as casually as a mother of five whose youngest child is screaming bloody murder over nothing but a little ol' scraped knee. "The vet who neutered him said his rash looked like it could have been ringworm, so that's why the paper says that."

"Great," I said, checking off one of Dr. Milne's questions from the list. "So where it says 'treated for ringworm,' what does that mean?"

"Well," she replied, measuring her words, "it means that I treated him for ringworm."

I couldn't tell whether she thought I was some variation of an obnoxious soccer mom, or if she was just uncomfortable about me asking questions in general, but her tone was definitely changing. She was becoming defensive.

"I'm sorry if I sound pushy," I pressed, "but my veterinarian asked me to find out exactly how Blue was treated for ringworm. We are trying to make sure he has the best possible care now. Any information you can give me about how he was treated would be really helpful."

A few seconds went by, and Turner said nothing. It seemed to me that she was hesitant to answer the question at all.

I let the silence hang in the air, and after a few more seconds, she filled it.

"I treated him the way I was told to treat him," she said. "With bleach and Monistat."

Again, I found myself pausing, trying to digest what she'd just told me.

"Did you say ... bleach?" I asked.

"That's what I was told to do," she said. "The veterinarian from spay/neuter said I could treat with bleach and Monistat."

Monistat, I thought. *Mon-i-stat*. I racked my brain until I remembered where I'd seen it: on the drugstore shelf, in the section for vaginal anti-yeast cream.

"It definitely worked," Turner continued as I tried to calm my own racing thoughts. "None of my other dogs got the same rash, and some of them are as little as three pounds apiece. He was playing with all of them. They would've had it by now if it was contagious."

Still, I remained silent. I looked at the thirty-eight dollars' worth of shampoo and skin cream on my kitchen counter. *On a puppy's skin? On anybody's skin? Bleach?* I couldn't get the word out of my mind.

"You know, he also had toxidia when I found him," she said.

"Toxidia?" I replied, snapping my attention back to our conversation. "What the heck is toxidia?"

"Not toxidia," she corrected me, sounding less like a crazy person and more like someone with lots of animal-care experience. "Coccidia. It's serious diarrhea. Puppies can get dehydrated from it and die. He lost three pounds in a single week. I got him healthy and put the weight back on him."

Turner was now talking with great pride, but I was reeling like an elephant stunned by a dart filled with brain tranquilizers. I again looked out the window at Blue, who was as content as could be sleeping under the sun. Aside from his tiny scabs, he seemed as happy and healthy as any puppy I'd ever known. It was challenging, if not impossible, to imagine that just a couple of weeks earlier he had been in line to be tossed into a gas chamber, was so sick with diarrhea that he couldn't keep weight on, and was covered in some kind of a rash that left people coating his skin with bleach and vaginal anti-yeast cream.

Turner was kind enough to say that I could call her back at any time if I needed additional information. From her end, I surmised, everything she'd said was routine. A job well done.

I thanked her, hung up the telephone, and walked outside to the deck. Blue's ears perked up and then his eyes opened, and he lifted his head out of what looked like a deep slumber. I sat down and crossed my legs, and he crawled into my lap. He curled himself into a ball, rested his head on my thigh, and went peacefully back to sleep.

So began our two-week quarantine for what, mercifully, ended up not being ringworm. I'll never know for sure what actually caused Blue's rash because all of his tests came back negative and his scabs continued to heal. Baby Avery never had any problems, and I—despite a few paranoid moments of feeling phantom itches all over my body for absolutely no reason whatsoever—got to enjoy two whole weeks of paying extra-special attention to Blue. Since I work from home as a writer and have the benefit of making my own hours, there was lots of time spent with just the two of us practicing basic commands, learning how to walk on a leash, and playing on the backyard grass. And it was in the backyard that I started to realize Blue not only had an exceptional emotional effect on a good number of people, but also on other dogs.

At just twenty pounds during those first weeks at home, Blue was literally a third of Stella's size. She's as solid as dogs come, with a strong proud chest, a big square forehead, and muscles so carved and pronounced that you'd think she was hitting the weight room for a few deltoid reps in between her walks at the park. Between her looks and her personality, I used to joke that Stella was an all-star linebacker living in a world filled with powder-puff cheerleaders. She didn't approach other dogs and ask them politely if they wanted to play. She ran up to other dogs and gave them the canine version of a smack across the head as if to insist, "Let's wrestle!"

Blue, on the other hand, was a typical awkward puppy, so eager to run that he sometimes forgot which feet he was supposed to move next. He had all the requisite loose skin on his back and baby fat around his waistline, and his natural instinct was to be cautious and protect himself around other dogs, just as he did with people. He also had what I came to appreciate as a pretty sharp brain inside his little noggin, using it at first to outsmart Stella and then to win her respect.

My backyard is surrounded by a four-foot-tall, split-rail fence. Inside is about fifteen hundred square feet of nothing but freshly mowed grass. Around the fence is the rest of my property, a few wooded acres with tall, old-growth trees. Deer tend to wander by, and though the yard is plenty big for Stella to run at a full sprint, she decided early on that she wanted to follow the deer into the woods instead. She quickly figured out how to leap clear over the fence, pretty much in a single bound. Soon after, I installed an invisible, electrical fence around the regular one, as well as a shock collar around Stella's neck to keep her safely inside the yard.

Blue had no need for a shock collar; it took him a few days to even bark at the deer, let alone try to chase them. But once he took a liking to getting his nose right up into the fence to bark at the deer, he began to realize that Stella always stayed a few feet behind. He would actually look back over his shoulder at her, like an army cadet puzzled by his sergeant's reluctance to engage in the heart of the action. Stella's safety border, Blue was figuring out, was about three feet from the fence edge. Any closer, and she got a warning buzz from her collar.

Blue took about two days to turn Stella's safety zone into his own. He couldn't run as fast as she could, but he was quick enough that he could get about halfway across the yard before she caught up to him in a game of chase. He'd prod her and coax her into playing, and then he would run and run his little heart out, and she'd chase after him like a cheetah. When he heard her steps beating down upon him, he'd dart into the three-foot safety zone and run as close as he could to the fence line. Stella continued to chase him back and forth, but always from a distance where she couldn't actually reach him. They would do this for hours a day, always with the same pattern and result. Blue had figured out how to outsmart the bigger, stronger playmate simply by using the rules of the field to his advantage.

I watched this scene unfold for a few days, thought about making T-shirts that read "Mommy's Little Genius," and in general forgot that we were in fact quarantined instead of just plain having a good time. Then, after five or six days, I noticed the strategies of their game beginning to change. Instead of Blue nipping at Stella until she chased him, and then him dashing as fast as he could to beat her to the safety zone, I watched in awe as Stella intentionally—dare I say gracefully—let Blue walk right past her to get to the fence and start the game from there.

Now, grace has never been part of Stella's personality. Assertive? Yes. Aggressive? Never with people, but sometimes with other dogs. Polite? About as often as an Ultimate Fighter going for the title at a pay-per-view main event. And yet she had not only decided to accept this puppy, but also to accommodate him. He appeared to have earned her respect. He had softened her edges just the same way he'd eased the worst of my grief about Floyd's death. Blue was somehow Zen-like, a calming presence in and of himself.

The more and more I got to know Blue, the more and more I began to obsess about the things that Annie Turner had told me on the telephone. Such disconcerting information didn't match up against the winning personality that this dog was showing me. Not even a little bit. I didn't think about the things she'd said once in a while. I became preoccupied, and even a little bit haunted, by what seemed to be a few more bread crumbs on a trail that begged to be followed into Blue's past.

I did some research and learned that bleach and Monistat are a common, inexpensive home remedy for ringworm. The medicine my veterinarian had prescribed cost just less than forty dollars. I didn't think much of that expense in the context of bringing a new puppy home, but a drugstore website told me that a three-day supply of Monistat plus bleach cost about half as much. Multiply that extra twenty bucks by, say, two hundred dogs with rashes, and the remedy would save four thousand dollars. By my math, from the day I met Blue at the RV, the money saved was enough to transport at least another forty puppies just like him to safety.

That Turner had felt so desperate to save that money, that she had felt the need to use bleach that can burn instead of shampoo that soothes, that she is the head of a countywide rescue group and she made that decision—all of it seemed beyond strange. I talked about it with my husband in the context of our new puppy, and it gave us both pause.

A great deal of pause, actually, and an insatiable desire to learn more.

A Journey Awaits

~

Michele Armstrong looks nothing like the image that I had of her in my mind. On the day that Blue and I met her in Bucks County, Pennsylvania, for breakfast at a dog-friendly restaurant with outdoor tables, I was expecting a cherub-faced, later-in-life woman who had maybe raised a few kids and was now applying the full bore of her maternal instincts to saving dogs. I'm not sure how I conjured this mental picture, given that Armstrong's cofounder at Lulu's Rescue, Jane Zeolla, had looked youthful and polished when she'd come to inspect my home. I guess it was something about the name Lulu's Rescue, plus the fact that the group is based in a town called Point Pleasant. The names just sound so gosh darn quaint that I'd formed a mental impression of Armstrong as being, shall we say, a hair shy of cosmopolitan.

Instead, Blue and I were greeted by a woman who is about my age (forty is the new twenty, right?) and who looked nearly as fit and focused as any member of the U.S. Olympic swimming team. Armstrong wore no makeup, had her blonde locks effortlessly pulled back from her face, and was clad in faded jeans and a T-shirt that appeared custom-made to fit her like a runway model. To see her walking down the street in farm country along the Delaware River, I'd never have guessed that she'd lived a previous, professional life in New York City. And unless I'd talked with her, I'd have missed out on her absolute aura of intelligence. I've only experienced it before with journalists working to expose truths from war zones, and in volunteers working to save lives in the aftermath of natural disasters. Armstrong is the kind of person who needs precious little primping or adornment. Her honesty and beauty seem to emanate directly from her soul, brightened even more by the obvious smarts and sincerity that accompany her every word about the dogs whose lives she is trying to save.

She and Zeolla, who together have more than thirty years of experience saving dogs, started Lulu's Rescue in January 2010. That was just a few months before I applied to the group through Petfinder to adopt Blue, making him one of their first successful adoptions during their initial year of operation. The mission at Lulu's Rescue is to get great dogs like Blue out of high-kill shelters and into permanent homes. Like many rescues, Lulu's doesn't have a brick-and-mortar facility, but instead uses a network of foster homes to keep each dog safe until a permanent home can be found.

Armstrong and I casually grabbed an outdoor table at a restaurant whose owner is a Lulu's Rescue supporter. We each ordered an omelet as Blue rested at our feet, happily chewing on a bone and enjoying a morning out of the house. It was the first day that Armstrong was meeting Blue, even though she'd been instrumental in saving his life. At Lulu's, Armstrong focuses on tasks like vetting potential adopters, organizing major fundraisers, and helping shelters win grants that ultimately bring down their kill rates. Zeolla, meanwhile, has the unenviable job of sifting through the countless descriptions of dogs in need. It's Zeolla who first spots the dogs who will be lucky enough to get a spot in the Lulu's Rescue program. She is the one who saw Blue's face in the photograph that Annie Turner's group had put online, and she is the one who chose to promote him through the Lulu's page that I saw on Petfinder.com.

"He's just so beautiful here in person," Armstrong told me as the waitress brought our orders to the table. Armstrong sounded happy and hopeful, but her exuberance lasted only for a moment. "You know, I've tried to look at all of the photos of dogs like him on the computer, and I just can't do it. I get physically sick. To see all those dogs and know that so many of them aren't going to make it . . ."

Her voice trailed off. She pushed her omelet around the plate with her fork. With her other hand, she reached down and gently rubbed Blue behind his ears.

Our breakfast was supposed to be a casual conversation that I thought might help me learn more about Blue's past, but I was brimming with so many questions that I feared they were going to blast out of my mouth like machine-gun ammo. I didn't want to seem like a CIA interrogator, but I also wanted desperately to know how Blue had ended up in his predicament down South.

"I'm having a hard time understanding how a dog like Blue finds himself headed for a gas chamber," I told Armstrong, with my own omelet now getting cold, too. "I mean, look at him just sitting there politely, not even begging for a bite of food. If somebody had told me where he'd come from, I would have thought something was wrong with him. But this is a great puppy. This is not a problem dog. It's keeping me awake at night. I've never even heard of anything like this, and I've loved dogs all my life."

Armstrong reacted like a Gold Glove catcher, anticipating my pitch before I'd even finished my windup.

"It's because it's not legal up here," she said, the words from my last sentence still dangling between us in the air. She'd obviously answered questions like mine a thousand times. "We don't have dogs being thrown in gas chambers in the Northeast, so people don't know it's happening. People can't even imagine that it could even possibly be happening, it sounds so crazy. But down in the South, those gas chambers are still used in a lot of places. The dogs are killed on a regular schedule, at 8:00 A.M. and 4:30 P.M. We get a list every morning of the dogs who are scheduled to die that day, we get lots and lots of pictures, and we get as many of them out as we can."

She paused a moment and sighed, thinking about the puppies and dogs she's had to leave behind.

"It destroys us knowing that the ones we can't get out are just as great as Blue," she said. "They almost always aren't going to make it."

I nodded my head as if I understood, but she could see in my eyes that I didn't. It's kind of like being told there's a mass murder taking place in Africa as a single, dominant tribe gains control of the freshwater supply. Cognitively, I could comprehend the words that I was hearing. Intellectually, I could understand it was a situation worthy of the world's rapt attention. But emotionally, it was tough to relate. The last time I'd heard about gas chambers was a couple of decades ago in a high-school history textbook, in the chapter about Adolf Hitler. Gas chambers seemed about as contemporary to what I knew of modern American society as, well, bobby socks and zoot suits.

"Would you like to see exactly what I'm talking about?" Armstrong asked.

It was evident to me that she continually agonizes over whatever it is that she has seen, so I took a few moments to consider the question. I looked down at what was left of my omelet, broke off a small piece to give to Blue, and swallowed hard before answering, "Yes, I think I would."

Now, I'm not what most people would describe as a bleeding heart. I vote for Republicans as often as Democrats, and I care as much about budget deficits and tax burdens as I do about the environment and helping the mentally ill. Nor do I fit the description of an animal activist. I'm an everyday person who loves dogs and is willing to consider other animal-welfare causes when they're brought to my attention. For instance, I am a lover of all foods who hosts summer barbecues full of slow-roasted short ribs and pulled-pork sliders, but every recipe that I make features meat that I have purchased only after seeing the animals themselves being treated humanely on the farm where they were raised. After reading a few books[1] about the nature of the U.S. meat supply, I wasn't ready to go vegetarian, but I was ready to vote with my pocketbook to put factory farms and their particular brand of animal cruelty out of business. I thus drive about an hour once each year to the small, family-owned Plaid Piper Farm in Sussex County, New Jersey, where I purchase all of my beef, pork, and chicken from a farmer who treats his animals with respect instead of like commodities. I keep my farm-produced steaks, chops, and cutlets in a large freezer in my garage, eliminating the need to purchase meat anywhere else. I haven't given a single nickel to any fast-food hamburger chains in about ten years, and when I order meat at restaurants, I know enough to look for "grass-finished beef" and "antibiotic-free chicken." Having been educated about the issue, I now avoid supporting operations that treat animals with unnecessary cruelty by cramming them into tiny cages and then stuffing them full of corn and drugs to fatten them for slaughter.

In other words, I'm not a die-hard-vegan-do-gooder when it comes to animals, but I'm also not completely ignorant about the bigger picture when it comes to their treatment. Perhaps that's why I felt I was relatively prepared later that same afternoon, when I used Armstrong's password to log on to the Lulu's Rescue page on Facebook. I figured I had at least a basic handle on animal-welfare issues in America. I'd seen pictures of

---

[1] I highly recommend *The Omnivore's Dilemma* by Michael Pollan, as well as *Fast Food Nation* by Eric Schlosser. They changed the way I buy, cook, and eat meat every day. If you'd rather watch than read, then you can check out their appearances in the excellent documentary film *Food, Inc.*

crippled cows heading for slaughterhouses. How much worse could the situation with dogs be?

The fact that Lulu's does so much communicating via Facebook, too, gave me a false sense of security. My own Facebook page, like many people's, contains smiling photographs of family, smack talk from friends whose scores outrank mine on the game Bejeweled Blitz, and the occasionally idiotic comment from somebody I haven't seen in person since the seventh grade. The Lulu's Rescue page on Facebook, though, struck me from first glance as downright somber. It felt sad, if not ominous, like it should have its own theme song to warn viewers to steel themselves against what they're about to see. After a few minutes of scrolling through the posts, I felt like a person clinging to a palm tree as a tsunami washed over me. Soon enough, I felt like that same wave could wipe away everything I knew to be good about the world.

The stream of photographs was endless. Dog after dog after dog after dog after dog. They had been posted at all hours, like a twenty-four-hour-a-day Animal Planet channel full of death instead of life. When I clicked on one photograph, I was immediately taken to dozens upon dozens more. "Going to be killed at 9 P.M.," one headline read, followed by photographs of about two dozen dogs. "Death row dogs need out by tomorrow," another stated, again with pictures of the helpless dogs' faces.

I zoomed in to get a closer look at some of the photographs, wondering if there was something I was missing. But to my eye, these dogs didn't look sick. There was no indication that they were vicious. Some of them looked nervous and scared, but I think I would be, too, if I were in a cage a couple dozen feet away from a gas chamber while somebody with a camera flashed a bright light directly into my eyeballs and told me to smile. I saw highly desirable breeds such as Terriers, Hounds, and Labradors, with faces so cute that I couldn't believe nobody wanted them. Some of the dogs were puppies who, I surmised, hadn't even had a chance to learn basic commands.

After reading the descriptions of about a hundred dogs whose information flowed through the Lulu's Rescue page on just that one day, I stopped counting and turned off the computer. I didn't feel physically ill the way Armstrong says that she does, but I did feel absolutely sick, in the sense of spiritual debilitation. Pressing the power button and watching my monitor fade to black felt at once like a personal relief and a moral abandonment. It was difficult to comprehend just how many of these dogs and puppies there were. I couldn't help but note the hour and realize that a lot of the ones I'd just seen would not be breathing at this time tomorrow.

Later that night in my kitchen, I thought again about my telephone call with Annie Turner. I had a new appreciation for why she got so defensive when I started peppering her with questions about the way she had treated Blue's rash. No wonder she chose to save those forty dollars on highfalutin dog shampoo. No wonder she'd thought the remnants of a noncontagious rash were not even worth mentioning in the bigger picture of saving Blue's life. If just looking at the photographs of these dogs online had left me feeling so shell-shocked, imagine how she must feel when she has to walk into the shelter, see the actual dogs in the cages, and decide which ones to leave behind. Imagine how many of their faces she sees when she closes her eyes each night and tries to go to sleep.

Armstrong had told me during breakfast that in order for Blue to come to the attention of Lulu's Rescue, he must have been perilously close to the gas chamber—probably on the list for asphyxiation that same afternoon, a dead puppy walking. His was, just a few weeks ago, one of the dozens upon dozens of helpless faces in these photographs.

It's a strange thing, trying to discern a special quality in any dog based only on a photograph—especially one taken when the dog is at his most vulnerable, locked in a cage on the brink of being killed. With Blue, sure, I thought his picture was cute, but I couldn't intuit anything substantial about his actual personality. That would have to wait for things like our daily walks at the park, like the day when we met a woman playing by the riverside with her three nieces. One of the little blonde girls, maybe three years old, took to Blue immediately. I had Stella's leash in one hand and Blue's in the other, and I was focused on Stella, who is so strong that she could have accidently crushed the little girls simply by jumping on them. The older girls started to play with her, and I was keeping an eye on them when I heard the three-year-old squeal with delight. I turned to see that she had inserted both of her hands into Blue's mouth, jamming her fingers right up between his teeth and his flabby lips. All of his loose puppy skin was flapping down over her tiny little palms, and she could not have been more excited, as if she had immersed her entire body into a pile of warm Play-Doh. I immediately extricated her digits from Blue's mouth, explaining that he's just a puppy and we don't want to teach him to bite people, but Blue himself was happy as could be, wagging his tail and darn near smiling from the attention.

Now that's an impressive temperament, and it's certainly not something anybody could intuit from a photograph taken through the bars of a cage inside of a shelter. There is far more to any dog's personality than can be captured in that single digital shot, just as there is, apparently, far more going on behind online puppy adoption websites than I'd ever conceived could actually be possible.

Now, while Blue loves kids, he is absolutely, positively not a fan of books. Whenever he sees me take out my digital e-book reader and flip open the red faux leather cover, he lets out a sigh that could rival any hot-air balloon's belch after a mile-high ride. If I lie on the sofa to start a new book, he crawls onto my lap and plops his head right into the middle of my stomach, forcing me to lift up the reader and pet him instead. In those moments, I call him by his well-deserved nickname—Jealous—and I swear that he actually grins at me like the Cheshire Cat.

It's when I start reading aloud to him that I begin to think we've both cartwheeled down the rabbit hole for good. I'm not sure why the act seems so strange; one recent survey funded by Purina shows that more than half the people who have dogs talk to them, and that a full third of women say their dogs are better listeners than their human companions. Blue is one of those cool dogs who actually seems to be listening, too. He twists his head from side to side and perks up his ears as high as he can, as if he's trying to understand every word that I say to him. What does it matter if, instead of asking "Want to go to the park?" I'm instead quoting to him from a best seller on *The New York Times* list?

On Armstrong's advice, I purchased a few books to help me understand the bigger picture that surrounds Blue's story—and I found myself shouting out quotes to him well into the wee hours, whether he was even awake or not. By reading *The Bond: Our Kinship with Animals, Our Call to Defend Them* by Wayne Pacelle, who is president of the Humane Society of the United States, I learned that America is spending more than a billion dollars a year to operate animal shelters. Some of these facilities are functioning like actual shelters, meaning sanctuaries and places of safety, while others are killing more than 80 percent of the dogs and cats entrusted to their care. That's four out of five dogs, all but dead on arrival at the doors of shelters like the one where Blue was found. Fully three-quarters of those dogs are healthy and adoptable as opposed to sickly and vicious, but only one of four dogs who end up living in our homes come from shelters in any given year. Most people get their dogs from breeders or from pet stores while perfectly wonderful puppies and dogs are left to die in shelters every single day.

Those statistics were bad enough, but the one that got me in the gut is this: If just two in four people, instead of one in four people, went to shelters instead of breeders or pet stores to get their next dog, then the entire problem of killing dogs like Blue would be statistically eliminated across the country. Geographic challenges would remain in terms of supply and demand, but according to this book, there would be more adopters than there are dogs in the shelters. If just two in four people who get a dog chose to adopt, then there would be enough homes for all of the dogs like Blue. None would have to be killed as long as the dogs and adopters could connect geographically.

True shelters that euthanize only the dogs who are vicious or incurably ill tend to have four characteristics in common, I learned from various books and articles written by leading authorities. These best-practice shelters offer low-cost spay and neuter programs, which help their communities reduce the number of unwanted dogs in the first place. They offer dogs for adoption in multiple locations instead of just at the shelter itself, so people can meet adoptable dogs in places like parks and pet-supply stores. They help families with behavioral training so that "troublesome" dogs like my Stella can stay in their homes instead of being surrendered back into the shelter system. And they work with a community-wide network of rescue groups that in turn utilize sites like Petfinder to connect dogs like Blue with adopters like me, when there aren't enough adopters coming forward locally.

"These are the basics of the formula that is making such a difference in the Northeast, where euthanasia rates have declined rapidly," Pacelle wrote, echoing exactly what Jane Zeolla told me at my own kitchen table on the day she came to inspect my home. "Some shelters are actually importing shelter dogs from elsewhere to meet local demand—not only finding homes for those dogs, but at the same time creating space for strays in those other regions."

That is, of course, precisely what happened with Blue, and it's not just Lulu's Rescue saving lives by stepping in to fill the need. On Petfinder alone, more than thirteen thousand rescue groups are trying to do exactly the same thing that Lulu's did for Blue. That's an average of two hundred sixty rescue groups per state. To put that into context, the Red Cross has about seven hundred local chapters in all of America. That's an average of just fourteen local Red Cross chapters per state, eighteen times *fewer* than there are rescue groups now working to save healthy dogs from shelters nationwide.

The scope of the dog-rescue effort is just plain staggering— and not all activists are willing to be politically correct in describing it. Some are so fed up with the status quo that their contempt drips from the pages of their books like wet ink. Nathan J. Winograd, in *Redemption: The Myth of Pet Overpopulation and the No Kill Revolution in America,* argues that some of America's publicly funded shelters have quite simply become places where quick "mercy killing" is now standard operating procedure. He claims that killing dogs like Blue is nothing more than an excuse used by shelter workers who are too underfunded, too exhausted, or too plain lazy to even try to find homes for the majority of dogs left in their care.

While Winograd's tone is less measured than that in some of his colleagues' books, I couldn't help but notice that his underlying facts appeared to be the same—and I gave him some extra attention because Michele Armstrong at Lulu's Rescue had told me that he is one of her heroes. Winograd doesn't stop at the statistics the way other activists do, saying that if only more people would adopt, the problem could be solved. While he does say that the public should make a greater effort to spay and neuter their dogs, he doesn't draw the larger curtain of blame down over the general public itself. He instead points a wagging finger at every shelter director whose salary is paid by taxpayers, whose facility is funded by tax dollars, and who continues to kill more healthy, adoptable dogs than are saved. He talks about professional animal-control workers who insist they simply cannot do what the rescue groups like Lulu's are able to do as volunteers, that they're not equipped or staffed for it, and that it is instead the rescue groups—not the shelters themselves—failing to do enough to save dogs like Blue.

"Imagine hypothetically a Department of Social Services director attacking a private soup kitchen or homeless shelter for not having enough beds or serving enough meals, meaning the department itself has to feed or house the remainder," Winograd writes. "As a private agency, the soup kitchen or homeless shelter does what it can. The mandate to care for homeless people, by contrast, belongs with the city department."

"The mandate to care" is a noteworthy phrase. While I understand that every issue has its many sides, along with its institutionalized personalities and intricate politics, I also began to realize that every book and article I was reading contained shared points that seemed to underpin everything I knew so far about Blue's life story. He was a perfectly wonderful, adoptable dog about to be killed for no discernable reason other than space. To the best of my knowledge, nobody from taxpayer-funded Person County Animal Control so much as took his picture and uploaded it to an adoption website before scheduling his death. It was volunteers in North Carolina working together with volunteers all the way up in Pennsylvania who kept Blue safe, provided basic veterinary care, and made an effort to get him into the home of a willing adopter like me.

I couldn't help but wonder why the tax dollars being spent at the Person County facility didn't simply pay for that handful of things in the first place. We're talking about curing a common rash, giving a puppy food and a clean place to sleep, and publishing his digital photograph online. None of this sounded particularly colossal in scope to me, and not nearly so vigorous that a cross-country network of volunteers should have to exist to get it accomplished. The more I read, the more puzzled I felt.

And the bigger question, I pondered, is how many of the billion dollars doled out to American shelters each year are being spent on gas chambers instead of digital photographs? How many shelters are there in the United States with operations like the one that nearly claimed Blue's life? How widespread is this problem of gas chambers, in a nation where more than half the pet owners surveyed say they call themselves Mommy and Daddy?

The complete answers, unfortunately, were not available to me in any book, on any website, or from any of the leading animal-welfare groups in the United States. I'd have to collect the data on my own, state by state and county budget by county budget— a task that would take me as many months of research as Blue had spent on the planet.

In the meantime, something that Armstrong told me at breakfast continued to weigh on my mind. She'd said it toward the end of our chat, only after she'd pegged me as a kindred spirit to whom she felt safe unburdening just the smallest, most splinter-like, but still-painful piece of her soul.

"You can't imagine the feeling of being at one of these shelters, one of the high-kill operations that use these gas chambers every day," she said. The sparkle had left her eyes, which at first had been filled with hope, but that, the more we talked, came to look as hollow as the gaze of a terrorism survivor. "Walking into these places is bad enough, but having to walk back out, leaving innocent dogs behind, that's something that doesn't leave a person. You cannot see something like that and just go about your daily business. You cannot see something like that and not want to stand up and do more."

What I see every day is a loving puppy who wants only to romp, play, and be forever by my side. On the first day that I left Blue out of his crate and alone in the house—for about 90 seconds while I walked up the driveway to get the mail—he chomped his way clear through one of the painted white wooden window grilles that he saw not as a colonial window adornment, but instead as a barrier to the two of us being together. Had I not walked back inside quickly enough, he no doubt would have begun bashing his teeth against the window glass itself. I'd been away from him for less than two minutes, and he'd been able to see me the entire time, but even still, he marked my glorious return from the mailbox with kisses and whimpers and the kind of bounding leap into my arms that *Life* magazine used to capture among returning sailors and their pregnant wives in the aftermath of World War II. The moment was, at least in Blue's mind, a genuine homecoming. It was a parade-worthy cause for celebration.

Now that Blue has grown a bit older and more comfortable in his own home, he understands that my walking up the driveway to get the mail does not constitute his abandonment. He also has made his peace with my taking out the garbage and doing the laundry (though he remains wary of the vacuum and continues his multifaceted campaign to bark it into submission). And even though I know that the day with the window grille was just a puppy reacting to his new mom doing something he hadn't expected, the thought of how he tried so desperately to stay by my side left me wondering how he must have felt at the moment another human being plopped him into a cage at the North Carolina shelter. The metal door closed in upon him, and then the person walked away with his back as well as his heart turned on Blue—forever.

Though I'd never stepped foot in a place like that, or inside any animal shelter, for that matter, my everyday encounters with Blue had already left me plagued by the same sense of moral imperative that Armstrong talked about at breakfast. I've never been the kind of person who quits after starting a race. When my sister talked me into attempting a triathlon, the organizers literally had to follow me in a pickup truck, removing orange cones from the street as I unceremoniously became the very last competitor to bicycle past them—but I eventually made it, red-faced and gasping, all the way to the finish line. When it came to learning more and more about Blue, I figured that if I already, albeit inadvertently, had become a person who played even a minor role in this national grassroots effort to save dogs like him, then I'd better make every possible attempt to fully understand the problem.

The underlying questions about this world that Blue so deeply embodied were nagging at me, plain and simple. They were rattling around in my brain like the chains of a restless ghost.

According to my map, Person County, North Carolina, is exactly 482 miles from my house in New Jersey. This, to most people, may seem like a ridiculous distance to travel in search of answers about a new puppy. To my husband and me, though, this was who I am and what I do. Most of my work as a journalist takes me thousands of miles around the world an average of once a month. I earn a living writing primarily about boats and travel, so it's not unusual for a magazine editor to call and say, "Grab your notebook and camera. We need you to fly to Thailand for a few days." I'm in the wrong time zone just as often as regular people are in the right lane on the highway. I get sent to the Indian Ocean and the Mediterranean the way other business travelers book flights to Indiana or Michigan. In the context of my life, eight hours of driving, a few dollars' worth of turnpike tolls, and less than two tanks of gas seemed like a small price to pay for finding some more answers about our new puppy. Blue was now a member of our family. I wanted to know who he really was. I was his mother, after all. Something had made him sick and afraid.

My letter to Person County Manager Heidi York and Animal Control Director Ron Shaw landed on their desks in midsummer 2011. I wanted a sit-down conversation and a tour of the building where Blue was once facing a death sentence.

After exchanging a few e-mails with the Person County attorney, I found myself driving up to the facility on Chub Lake Road in Roxboro. The city is a financial flip side of the part of New Jersey where I live, with Census data alone implying a picture of contrast so stark that it would have to be painted solely in black and white. In my community, the median household income is about $98,000 and only 2 percent of people live below the poverty line. In Roxboro, the median household income is $31,500 and nearly 17 percent of the population lives below the poverty line. I marveled at the differences between where Blue had come from and where he had ended up. Not only were these communities separated by hundreds of miles and several state lines, they were also separated by deep socioeconomic differences.

Shaw had told me, via e-mail, that his shelter was small and working with limited funds because of the recession, so I had tried to mentally prepare for a scene that would be tough on my soul. But as I drove closer, it was hard to think about anything other than the fact that, once I stepped inside the building, I would be meeting the man who had once been mere hours away from killing Blue.

My first order of business, actually, would be to introduce myself, reach out, and politely shake his hand.

The Reality of a
Childhood Dream

~

It was hard for me to imagine tobacco fields as far as the eye can see as I drove southbound along Route 49 toward Roxboro. Back in the first half of the 1900s, tobacco is what kept the economy in Person County afloat. Big-type headlines in the newspaper couldn't always fit the word "tobacco," so editors used the shorter word "leaf." Everybody knew what it meant, even if the elders couldn't read, especially when the news was "School Opening Postponed due to Late Leaf Crop."

There's still some tobacco growing today in the fields among Person County's four hundred or so square miles, but as Americans become more health conscious, soybeans are supplanting The Leaf as a more economically viable choice. The county does have two industrial parks, but the nearest center of big business is at least an hour beyond in the Raleigh-Durham region, where Research Triangle is home to a number of high-tech companies and university research facilities. I felt like I was a planet away from anything resembling a corporate skyscraper as I drove around the boundaries of Roxboro proper. Between the "Welcome to Person County" sign and the edge of the city, I passed a great deal of open land and some modest homes with trucks in the driveway that were no doubt used for father-son fishing trips on the weekends. Two signs caught my eye along the side of this main highway, one with a real-estate advertisement for a 106-acre parcel and another handwritten by somebody selling a dozen eggs for a dollar. After I got to Roxboro's three-block-long main street, I saw telltale signs of life as it is today in Person County. "For rent" posters hung in more than a half-dozen empty storefronts.

In the span of a single day, I had driven into a part of America that seemed truly foreign to me. Where I live on the edge of commuting distance into New York City, we have cornfields, for sure, and a fair number of farm stands, but we also have a lot of gorgeous stables used by Olympic-level riders. The "for sale" signs usually refer to homes on parcels that have been subdivided down to less than an acre, any extra cars in the driveways are usually fuel-efficient foreign models, and people selling eggs at $4 a dozen always include the word "organic" on their handmade signs. My town, too, has been hit hard by the recession, but we have new businesses where the old ones used to be, as opposed to rows of vacancies.

As a travel writer, I'm used to seeing a lot of unique communities. I've spent time everywhere from ancient Greek harbors where donkeys are still the primary mode of transportation to Jamaican coffee farms where women live in half-built cinderblock homes to Fijian islands where thatched huts are still the primary form of shelter. Driving into Person County made me feel like I was going not only into yet another new place, but also into a contrasting culture.

I couldn't help but wonder if that culture had anything to do with the fact that so many dogs like Blue seemed to be in trouble here, and whether the way of life where I live had anything to do with the fact that so many of them were finding homes there.

The current animal shelter, as best as anybody can remember in Person County, was originally built sometime during the 1950s. It's a couple of miles outside of town, down a gravel driveway that it shares with the Public Works Maintenance Building. The shelter is prominently advertised along the road by a white sign with bright blue letters and an image of the county seal that has faded from more than a few too many days beneath North Carolina's 100-degree summer sun. But the building itself where dogs like Blue are kept is back behind the maintenance office, and behind the Dumpster, surrounded by a chain-link fence topped with angled barbed wire to keep people out after hours.

According to *The Times-Courier*, the problem with dogs as recently as the 1960s was strays running wild. The edition printed on Monday, February 15, 1960, carries a front-page story stating that the county dog warden picked up 86 stray dogs the previous month and found new homes for all but 7 dogs. The edition printed on Thursday, March 3, 1960, states that in February of that year, 117 stray dogs were picked up in the county. About half of them found new homes. Sixty-one were "disposed of" and another 16 were shot.

I had looked, while driving into town, for dogs running loose or in packs along the side of the road. I'd paid especially close attention to garbage cans behind the local eateries. When people talk about a rural community and an overcrowded animal shelter, the common assumption is that the problem is strays. But I hadn't seen a single one, and apparently, it wasn't for lack of looking. One of the first things that Animal Control Director Ron Shaw told me is that the county no longer has a feral dog problem. There are still strays, yes, but the far bigger problem is people who fail to spay and neuter their dogs. Those people bring box after box of puppies to the shelter, either unaware or unconcerned that the dogs have little chance of making it out of the building alive.

We began our talk in Shaw's office, which is just a few steps from the shelter's main entrance. The shelter's front door boasts a weather-worn Petfinder.com bumper sticker whose top right corner is bent inward in dog-ear style. Inside the shelter's entryway is the dispatcher's desk, where calls are received about vicious animals, strays, or other problems. Behind the dispatcher's desk is an office for the town's three animal-control officers who respond to those calls. That office connects to the smaller office where Shaw works. Most of these spaces are institutional looking with few windows, limited natural light, and neutral yellowish paint. Everything was as clean as a grandmother's favorite serving dish on the day that I visited, but the vibe was a far cry from warm or soothing. I had the same sense that I get when I walk into the police department in my own hometown, minus the bulletproof partition at the reception desk. This place, it seemed to me, was designed to create an aura of authority.

Next to Shaw's office is by far the largest one, used by the facility's kennel attendant/adoption agent. That room has a more welcoming feel, with dog toys and supplies that people can purchase, a vending machine filled with cold sodas, a fish tank, a long table with chairs for groups that visit, and a fuzzy orange orangutan hanging above a desk to lighten the mood. On the day that I stood at this room's entrance, a Golden Retriever mix named Buddy was lounging comfortably on the blue sofa. He might as well have been in my own den at home, he looked so content.

Across the hallway from these offices are a couple of smaller, almost closet-size rooms, including the ones used for grooming and killing by lethal injection. Those two rooms are remarkably close to each other, actually. No dogs were in either of them on the morning that I visited. I actually couldn't even hear a single dog barking as I walked from there into Shaw's office.

Shaw is not a particularly large or imposing man, though he projected an air of serious command and control as he offered me a chair and sat down behind his desk. He wore his official uniform as a county animal-control officer, with solid colors of tan and brown—shades that could have been pulled right out of an Operation Desert Storm camouflage jacket. The official seal of the Person County Animal Control department was embroidered onto his shirt like a soldier's name or the American flag might be. The backdrop behind his desk was a wall filled with official-looking certificates from various training courses. They filled my line of vision like a subliminal show of clout whenever I looked him directly in the eye.

His face is round and kind, though topped by a buzz cut that no doubt served him well during his time as a detention sergeant with the county's human prisoners back in the early 1990s. Given his resumé and the salt-and-pepper flecks in his mustache, I'd guess that Shaw is in his mid-fifties. He has been Animal Control director for the county since 1997, and he is proud to say that he was the first person ever to hold that professional title instead of being called, simply, dogcatcher. Shaw is an ex-military man, and I got the feeling from him that the title distinction was important. The title defines the job. It defines the person's place in the pecking order of the system. It also defines how the person is expected to carry himself. His tone when explaining his title reminded me of people in war zones who are hired as independent contractors to assist troops in combat, and who get offended if anyone dares to call them a mercenary for hire.

One of the first things Shaw did after we sat down across from one another was attempt to size me up. He wanted to know whether I really was the unlikely person I had claimed to be—a journalist from New Jersey who had somehow ended up adopting a dog who was once on death row in this building, and then drove hundreds of miles because I wanted to have a conversation. My entire existence seemed far-fetched to him, like a cover story begging to be blown apart. And I couldn't blame him, seeing as how some rescue advocates try to infiltrate shelters and catch the bosses saying something that will ultimately get them fired. I also didn't mind him poking at me a bit with a few questions, since he was just as respectful as I planned to be with him when I started asking questions of my own.

"I'd like to know, before we get started, what your view is of no-kill shelters," Shaw said. "Everybody who comes in here to talk to me, I always want to know the answer to that question."

I took a moment to think before I spoke, assuming that others with zero experience had sat here plenty of times telling the fourteen-year veteran of animal control precisely how they thought he should be doing his job differently.

"I'm no expert," I said. "I'm just an everyday dog owner. But if you mean shelters where they say 'no-kill' as if it's a good thing but then keep the dogs locked in cages all their lives, well, I'd have to say I think that's cruel to the dogs. On the other hand, if you mean 'no-kill' as in people working hard to save as many dogs as possible and get them good homes, then I'm for it one hundred percent."

Shaw nodded and said, as if checking a box in his mind, "So then we're in agreement on that."

He kept looking directly at me, holding my gaze as if it were tangible evidence, really, as he relaxed ever so slightly in his chair. He didn't sit back the way somebody does when he believes he's completely safe, but his arms and fingers loosened just a few fractions of an inch, as if to say he trusted me—but just a little.

And then he started to talk about life inside this facility as he has lived it, beginning back in the days when things were much worse than they are now.

For about the first two years that he held the job, Shaw told me, he was required to kill every dog who came in unless somebody could prove the pup had been vaccinated against rabies. Plenty of raccoons, foxes, bats, and skunks in Person County are rabies carriers, and far too many dog owners fail to vaccinate their pooches against the disease. The county's rules meant that if a family's dog got loose, and the family could not produce a rabies vaccination certificate, the dog would die at animal control even if the parents and children came looking for him. Period.

Shaw says this was too much for him to bear, so he went to the county Board of Health and asked if he could at least seek new homes for dogs found in areas where no rabid animals had been recently found. "After some controversy," he recalls, "they said yes. And immediately, we were allowed to work with rescue groups and do adoptions. We thought it was great. We started 'Pet of the Week' in the local paper."

At that time, the building filled with offices where we were now sitting comprised the entirety of Person County Animal Control. It wasn't just office space. It held all the cages and animals, too—and precious few people knew or cared that it existed. Shaw describes those days as almost a full decade's worth of years before rescue groups became prominent or vocal, and before people beyond his officers paid any attention whatsoever to what went on inside the shelter. He and his small staff were awfully isolated as he learned firsthand what it felt like to be the human being in charge of enforcing county and state rules regarding unwanted animals. He hardened himself to a job that required him to show up on time, kill healthy puppies, and then get up the next morning and do so again. He tried to do the job and follow the rules in as professional a way as he could, even though the work itself sometimes strained at the best parts of human nature.

Then, in the mid-2000s he learned that the state was going to begin inspecting county shelters and requiring training for the three legal ways to kill a dog in North Carolina: by lethal injection, by gunshot, and by gas chamber. "I didn't have all the rescue groups on my back then," he told me. "I came up with this brainstorm on my own, that we needed a better facility before these inspections started. I came up with a plan and went to the county. There was controversy about that, too—one county commissioner asked me, 'Can't you just have a roof and some cages?'—but they spent about $600,000 to build an addition and make the facility better. And all of a sudden after that, people got interested in us. They realized we existed. And we started hearing from all these rescue groups that put down our employees. Some of them wanted to help us do our jobs, but some said they didn't have to abide by any rules and were going to do whatever they wanted. We had no idea how to work with them."

During the past two or three years, Shaw says, a lot of his time has shifted from doing what he likes best—being out in the community helping people and animals—to defending himself and his employees against animal-welfare activists. The tone that some of the rescue groups take makes Shaw uneasy, to say the least. He felt he had done the right thing by asking the county for the building improvements, as well as for new funding to provide professional euthanasia training within the bounds of state law. He ran a clean operation. Not once, he told me, has his kennel ever been shut down because of parvo or another disease outbreak the way other shelters are because they are dirty and poorly run. He grew so concerned about what felt to him like an onslaught of negativity that he even started reading the fine print when applying for grants that might help the facility improve further.

"I have to make sure the grants aren't attached to a group like PETA," he told me. "They have a history of coming in the back door and taking control. My staff works hard. The job here is hard. Most animal-control officers last two, three, maybe five years. I have a much better retention rate because we give the staff training and send them to conferences. I love animals, but my job is to manage this facility and keep the community safe. Some of these rescue groups, they see a dog on the side of the road suffering and a person on the side of the road suffering, and they ignore the person to save the dog. I put people's safety first. That is part of our job here at animal control. I go by the rules and regulations of the county. I am paid to uphold the law."

Shaw spent a good hour sitting and talking with me, and making sure that I understood how professional his animal-control operation was. But he knew, because of questions I'd submitted in advance, that I also wanted to talk about the gas chamber. It has fast become a lightning-rod topic for him and his fellow animal-control directors throughout the country, as rescue groups call it everything from cruel to barbaric to evil. Shaw made sure to tell me, even before I asked, that the gas chamber is a tool of animal control. It is nothing more, and nothing less. He said that it is not only one of the three legal methods of killing dogs according to the state of North Carolina, but that it is also an approved form of euthanasia by the American Veterinary Medical Association.

I nodded with understanding, and then I asked him whether he was aware that just two months earlier, in June 2011, the AVMA had issued a new proposed set of guidelines. Unlike in so many years past, the group was now specifically stating that gas chambers should *not* be used for routine euthanasia of dogs.

Shaw looked surprised, and then concerned.

And that's when he offered to give me a tour and show me how it worked.

"This is where we're getting to Blue's story," Shaw said as we walked out the back door of the original building and into the area that separates it from the new addition, which is the dog kennel. Local folks call this in-between space a sally port. I've always heard spaces like this referred to as breezeways. No matter the lingo, the construction is the same. We stood on concrete in the open air. On either side of us were floor-to-ceiling chain-link fences with large gates that connect the old building and the new kennel, and that swing open from the middle. This is where cars drive in to drop off puppies and dogs on one side, and where trucks arrive to collect them on the other side after they have been killed.

Blue most likely came in through this drop-off gate, Shaw says. If he was only four or five months old when he arrived in New Jersey, and he had already been neutered and healed from the surgery, then the odds are good that he was no more than two or three months old when he was left here. Since the shelter doesn't name the dogs who come in, there is no way to tell exactly how Blue arrived, but Shaw's best guess based on what he's seen every day for nearly fifteen years in this place is that Blue was part of an unwanted litter of puppies. That means Blue would have been dropped off by a car here in the breezeway, about ten steps away from the gas chamber in plain view.

Now, I'm the first to admit that most pieces of machinery in my own basement are like alien spaceships to me. If I hadn't seen a photograph of the gas chamber beforehand, I would have assumed it was some kind of air handler attached to the original building. It's a large stainless-steel box, about the shape of a palette of bottled water cases being delivered to a convenience store. Its height is about four feet tall and its depth appeared to be a bit longer, making the entire chamber about the size of four bottled water cases stacked atop one another. As people drop off puppies like Blue, the chamber stands off to the right, clear as day. Many people probably don't even notice it, the same way I don't typically look at my own furnace all too carefully. When I asked around town later that day, every local resident I met seemed surprised to learn that they lived in a county that still used a gas chamber at all.

Shaw says that having the gas chamber here is a decision made by the county and the state—not by him. It is a legal tool that he is given in order to perform his job, just like lethal injection.

"Now, in my opinion, it's not a cruel way to euthanize an animal," he says. "There really is no humane way to euthanize a healthy animal. But if I thought it was cruel, it would be lying in a ditch somewhere instead of standing in this building."

He walked over to the chamber and swung its door open so I could look inside. I saw three stalls, much like the ones that separate racehorses at the start of the Kentucky Derby. The separating walls of each stall were see-through thanks to large holes that let the gas flow between them. If Blue had been placed inside, he most likely would have pawed at the separating wall to get to the dog next door, the same way that most puppies paw from inside kennels or crates to get to dogs or people on the other side.

First, Shaw showed me how his staff uses the gas chamber to kill cats. He grabbed a cat carrier from atop a nearby stack and explained how it fits inside the gas-chamber stall.

"Is that size carrier the same as what you would use for a little puppy like Blue?" I asked.

He thought for a moment—and then his eyes grew wide with epiphany.

"If he was really that little, if he was really a puppy, then he wouldn't have gone into this gas chamber at all," Shaw blurted. "Any dog four months or younger is killed by lethal injection, not by the gas chamber. That's the rule. We take 'em inside the euthanasia room. We love 'em and rub 'em for a few minutes. And then we say good-bye."

Shaw next pointed out the carbon-monoxide detector installed just above the chamber door. We were in the open air, so it really wasn't doing much good, but he said the law requires it so his department has it for safety.

I recalled that a carbon-monoxide detector was among the AVMA guidelines for proper gas chamber use. Those guidelines also state that all workers must understand the hazards of the chamber itself. I asked Shaw if his staff had been informed of the reports from the state departments of Health and Labor that showed chambers from the same manufacturer had leaked gas and overexposed workers to fumes in Sampson and Davidson counties.

As with my earlier question about the newly proposed AVMA guidelines, he looked surprised. "I hadn't heard about any of that," he said quietly before continuing our tour.

That's when I started 'doing some mental math. If dogs are required to be separated inside the chamber, and there are only three stalls, and the chamber has to be loaded, filled with gas, and then unloaded to complete a single cycle, then killing dogs in a gas chamber according to the guidelines really isn't all that much faster than killing them by lethal injection, which advocates say is far more humane.

I asked Shaw if he ever puts more than one dog into each of the three chambers, for efficiency. Rescue advocates I spoke with allege that some shelter directors do just that, including gassing litters of puppies in violation of the law. These critics said that since the shelters don't know the actual ages of abandoned dogs anyway, they take the easier route of gassing any puppies they can versus giving them individual, lethal injections.

In fact, a shelter director in Gaston County, North Carolina, did an entire analysis to show how much more cost effective the gas chambers are compared with lethal injection. He determined that killing in the chamber costs $4.66 per animal while killing with injections costs $11.21. "With the [gas chamber] flexibility of euthanizing multiple and not individual animals," the Gaston County director told the local newspaper, "there's certainly less time involved."

Shaw didn't say anything about using the gas chamber in Person County to save time or make the job easier. He once again referred to the way he works within the bounds of the law. "This is a professionally built chamber," he told me. "Before I worked here, it used to be a wooden box that they backed a car up to. Now we have this, and before the state came and said we had to divide it, they'd put five, six, seven dogs in here. But now, it's three.

"I'm not going to say it's only vicious dogs," he continued. "That would not be true. If we have thirteen dogs to go down in one day, we might not have enough [lethal injection] juice to do the job, especially if they're bigger dogs. I have never allowed an animal to be shot inside this facility, so there are times when this chamber is the only legal option."

Our tour ended inside the recent addition, which is the dog kennel. It has two sections of cages. The one closest to the gas chamber contains fourteen cages side by side. The second section, in the far corner, contains ten cages across from one another with five on each side—five for dogs the shelter has decided are preferable for adoption, and five for dogs that rescue groups have offered to take. The dogs in these ten cages are the lucky ones. The dogs who are in the larger row of cages, Shaw told me, don't even get a walk outside before their three legally mandated holding days are up.

"Now, anybody can come and adopt any of these dogs in any of the cages," Shaw said. "It's not like we're saying the ones in these cages have no chance at all. But the dogs in the back have been temperament tested with people and with other dogs, and they're the ones we think have the best chance."

Rescue groups that have attained 501(c) (3) charity status are allowed to enter the kennel and choose any dogs they want to save, except for ones the shelter has deemed rabid or vicious, Shaw told me more than once. He pointed to a cage in the larger row where a dog had been tagged for rescue as an example. I looked down and saw a puppy wagging his tail and trying to jump through the cage to get to me. Next door, in a cage that had not been tagged for rescue, was a tiny little brindle just like Blue. The date on his card was just two days from now. It reminded me of the expiration dates on gallons of milk at the grocery store.

At the time when Blue was here, a volunteer named Rhonda Beach from Canine Volunteer Rescue in Person County would walk through the kennel with Annie Turner and choose the dogs to be saved. While Shaw had no idea which dog Blue might have been, Beach told me that she remembered him distinctly. I spoke to her more than a year after she tagged him for rescue at the shelter, a year when he was one of more than three hundred dogs she helped to save. She could still remember the way he had looked at her, his brown eyes wide and worried, his body cowering with fear.

Blue was in the long row of cages, she told me. He was one of the dogs the shelter did not deem preferable for adoption.

"He was a shy one," she recalls. "He was reserved. He wasn't a bouncy, crazy puppy. He was playful, but he had a very gentle spirit. The other dogs, they all ran up to the front of the cages when I walked near them, but Blue wasn't up front wagging his tail. He is the kind of dog that this shelter always called unadoptable, the kind of dog they would always deny me the right to take out. But I could see it in his eyes that he was just plain scared. A lot of dogs who come out of that shelter are changed. They can smell death in there. They can hear the screams from the other dogs in the gas chamber. Blue was just so gentle and loving after all of that. I remember him like yesterday. There is no other word to describe him but scared."

By county ordinance, Shaw told me, even the dogs in the preferable cages can only be held for fifteen days at most. He does everything he can think to do within his budget, he said, to try to get them homes during that time. His staff puts their photographs on Petfinder.com. They also run "Pet of the Week" advertisements in the twice-weekly *Courier-Times*. He instituted a "Strut a Mutt" program for local residents to come inside the shelter and walk the dogs, to get to know them. He created a gravel trail out behind the kennels, in a wooded, parklike setting, so potential adopters can have some alone time with their favorite pooch and hopefully fall in love.

But few people respond, he said with a sigh. "We only have about thirty thousand people in all of Roxboro," he explained. "In the past five or six years, factories have left. Every year, my budget gets cut by 5 or 6 percent more. There are only so many things that we can do, and unlike these rescue groups from all over the country, we have to try to adopt locally. There just aren't enough people here who want all these dogs."

I asked him what he thought of the multistate transports like the one that brought Blue home to me, matching dogs from places like Person County with locations like mine where there are lots of potential adopters. He didn't know the logistics of how they worked, so I explained that Blue was put into an RV here in North Carolina by the local rescue group, and that I was told to wait for his arrival in New Jersey with the Pennsylvania rescue group by my side.

Shaw thought for a moment about the lack of official oversight. It surely seemed counterintuitive to him, given the way he feels he is asked to operate every day.

"I just hope that these rescue people up North, I hope that they're keeping an eye on these dogs to make sure they're okay," he said. "It sounds like an awful lot of room for error to me."

And it is—for adopters as well as for the dogs. It is a system based entirely upon one rescue trusting the judgment of another about a dog's temperament and where he should end up. A good number of the people involved feel so strongly about saving every dog's life that they will give some dogs a behavioral benefit of the doubt that is unwarranted. Shaw does not have that option. He is required to err on the side of human safety. Not every dog is as sweet and loving as Blue, though just about all are advertised as such. As with any dog acquired from a shelter or anywhere else, there must always be an element of "buyer beware."[2]

---

[2] For tips on bringing home a shelter dog, see "What You Can Do" at the end of this book.

Even so, as Shaw talked about room for error in the rescue system, I couldn't help but notice that we were standing about two feet from the long row of cages where my happy, sweet, and very much alive boy Blue once sat with an orderly, carefully monitored, state-approved death sentence. The rescue system that has emerged in recent years may be haphazard, but it's the only thing that saved Blue's life—and that continues to save the lives of a lot of great dogs just like him.

Shaw must have seen me stumbling to collect my thoughts, because that's when he told me a story that I didn't even ask to hear. He started by acknowledging the notebook in my hand and saying that he wished I wouldn't put what he was about to say into this book. Then he decided to tell me the story, anyway.

"When I was a kid," he said, "I wanted to be two things. One was an animal-control officer. Growing up in Maryland, I used to deliver newspapers, and I'd find all these stray dogs and bring them home. After a while my dad would call me over and say, 'Son, the fence is only so big. You have to take these dogs down to the pound.' So I would call the local animal-control officer, and we'd have a good, long talk, and the next week, when I was delivering my newspapers, I'd see that dog's picture in the paper. I figured that's a pretty good job, being an animal-control officer. It means you get to find homes for stray dogs who need them."

"The other thing I wanted to be when I grew up was a Marine," he continued. "That's what came first for me. I was in Beirut working at a checkpoint, and there were all these stray dogs around. We were ordered absolutely not to feed those dogs or be nice to them, but a few of us, you know, we gave them food and petted them. They were just the nicest dogs. Now, one day, a terrorist drove up to that checkpoint. Those dogs knew it was a terrorist. They started barking. They alerted all of us Marines. And all of those dogs, they died that day in the explosion, but not a single Marine did. All of the Marines lived because the dogs helped to save us."

I looked right into Shaw's eyes as he finished that story, and I realized why he didn't want his fellow soldiers and current colleagues in the Animal Control Department to know it.

He was starting to cry.

Truth in Numbers

～

The microfilm machine at Person County Library was making me blind. Well, maybe not completely blind, but certainly in need of a cold compress across my eyelids. I'd call the machine ancient, but I've seen ruins in Turkey that have held up better over the centuries. And my research efforts weren't being helped by the fact that the ultra-kind, yet ultra-small, library staff had no index of articles. To find anything about the local animal shelter dating back to the first printing of the newspaper in 1881, I literally had to read years' worth of copies, inching the ever-jamming micro-film tape forward, page by poorly scanned page.

It was like finding a gold nugget in a Rocky Mountain stream when I saw the front-page article from Wednesday, January 18, 2006. The headline read: "Larger shelter sparks hope for more animal adoptions." It was written by an intern named Grey Pentecost who has since become a staffer. It included a photograph of construction getting under way for the kennel addition in which Ron Shaw and I had stood that same week, the one with the long row of cages where Blue had once sat.

The paragraph that caught my eye was buried on the story's jump page, almost at the end of the article itself. It stated that thanks to the new addition, "the shelter will be able to hold fifty dogs, twelve more than before."

That sounded awfully good to me, as I'm sure it had to every dog lover in Person County who read it and ponied up the tax dollars to pay for it.

But it also sounded wrong. I flipped the pages in my notebook to the section where Shaw told me about the new kennel as we walked through it together. The new kennel has fourteen cages in one section and ten cages in the other. I later got a map of the facility from a local rescue group, and the map confirmed that I'd taken notes correctly.

Fourteen cages plus ten cages does not equal fifty cages, as was promised to taxpayers in exchange for the money to build the new kennel. It's instead a total of twenty-four cages, which is less than half the number of dogs Shaw implied could be held when talking to the newspaper reporter. With two dogs per cage, yes, the statement would have been accurate, but I did not see two dogs per cage during my tour. In some of the cages, I saw just one dog. In a few of the cages, I saw none.

I next combed through the facility's statistics for dogs, which Shaw gave me after I requested them under North Carolina's public records laws. These are the kinds of documents that give most people a headache, filled with facts and figures so endless that even the best-intentioned public official will go out of his way not to investigate them. I laid them out on a table with a notepad and a calculator, right next to a printout of the newspaper article. I reread the headline: "Larger shelter sparks hope for more animal adoptions." Those last three words were important, I thought—*more animal adoptions.*

But the data show that hasn't happened, either. While the number of dogs being handled by Person County Animal Control has dropped by nearly 30 percent in recent years, and the number of cages has increased with the new kennel, the percentage of dog adoptions has not changed at all. It's been hovering around 5 percent year after year. Without taking into account the work of rescue groups—which I'll get to in a bit—the shelter has an unchanged kill rate of about 95 percent. In 2008, just shy of 5 percent of dogs went to new homes. In 2009, it was also about 5 percent. In 2010, there was a slight uptick to 6 percent. As of my visit in 2011, the shelter's adoption rate was 4.8 percent. Unless a rescue group intervenes, dogs and puppies who are strays or drop-offs, like Blue, have only a one-in-twenty chance of making it out alive.

Next, I took a look at the Animal Control Department's budgets dating back the past five years, which Shaw also gave me under state public records law. He had told me that his department was small to begin with and was doing the best it could while enduring budget cuts of 5 percent to 6 percent each year during the recession. I expected to see an overall funding decrease of 25 or 30 percent in the past five years—but the budgets actually show a decrease of just 6 percent overall. For the year that I visited, the facility's budget had actually been increased. The shelter today has about 94 percent of the budget that it had before the recession even began.

Last, I worked through the *Courier-Times* to get copies of articles dating back to 2005 about the new kennel addition. Shaw had told me the kennel cost the county's taxpayers about $600,000. Yet back in 2005, Shaw told the newspaper the new addition was costing taxpayers "a little over $500,000."

The actual figure, according to Person County's financial records, is $562,954—in the ballpark of what Shaw told me, but an awful lot of money, I thought, to be so cavalierly discussed. Inconsistencies like the ones I was uncovering often lead rescue groups to cast an even harsher glance at operations like Person County Animal Control. They look at the high-kill rate, they scour the numbers, and they assume the shelter director is just plain lying about everything.

I tried hard not to cast so harsh a glance, but the more I researched, the more I felt compelled to keep asking questions. For instance, I wanted to know how much money was spent on the gas chamber during the most recent year, versus the amount of money spent trying to find homes for the dogs like Blue who were on death row. My thinking was that if adopting dogs into new homes was indeed a priority, then it should have been reflected in the current budget.

Yet again, the numbers did not match what I'd been told. While more than $7,600 was being spent on training and supplies related to the gas chamber, only $1,000 was in the budget for advertising. That thousand bucks includes money given to the local newspaper for something other than dog advertise-ments—someone at the shelter had kindly noted for me that the "Pet of the Week" advertisement is free. The person had hand-written that note on my budget printouts after creating a new line that did not exist in the official printout, a budget line titled "marketing for animals." The only three items under it, added in ink from a blue pen, were the free newspaper ad, the free use of Petfinder.com, and the free use of the social networking site Facebook[3]. So, not only were adoptions not a financial priority, but they only became a written afterthought when a journalist like me asked to see them on paper.

Taken together, all of this information made me a lot more inclined to listen carefully to the rescue advocates who had been crying foul from the day I first called to learn more about Blue's background. Sometimes, I will admit, they sounded a little hys-terical. On more than one occasion, the rescue advocates I in-terviewed from all across America ended up screaming at me through the telephone, they wanted so emphatically to make their voices heard. Even though I was listening, even though I was not arguing, a good many of them still felt the need to shout.

Just maybe, I was starting to think, that's because they had been so frustrated for so long by the reality that they say they encounter day to day—a reality that is far more in keeping with the numbers I'd crunched and far less rosy than the prearranged picture that had been presented during my tour.

---

[3] I went on Facebook to check out the Person County Animal Control page about two weeks after I visited the shelter. It had just twenty-three fans, no contact information, and not a single photograph of any dog who was currently available. It appeared that nobody had posted anything on the page, ever.

Incoming Fire

~~

So far, the only human being I'd met face-to-face in Person County was Animal Control Director Ron Shaw. But I'd also gotten an earful of information about what happens to dogs like Blue in this place by way of telephone. I'd called Annie Turner several times to get more details, since she was president of a local rescue group. I'd also spent some time chatting with Rhonda Beach, the society volunteer who had first met Blue at the shelter. My plan was to meet both Turner and Beach later that week, after trying to reconcile what they'd told me with everything that I had seen for myself. Just as I'd done with the animal-control director, I wanted to try to verify that what I'd been hearing out of their mouths was actually the truth.

Blue, I'd been told, was the last dog Turner and Beach worked together to rescue. The women had a falling out around the time that I adopted him, and Beach went on to create her own rescue organization. Blue was apparently one of several reasons for their split. They'd been at odds about the way that a rescue should be run, and when I called asking questions about Blue's rash and background, the finger-pointing about who had done what to him became something of a last straw.

From what they'd told me on the phone, though, they did agree that Beach is the one who first saw Blue in the long row of non-preferred cages at Person County Animal Control. The way Beach remembers it, Blue crawled to her slower than a snail bound for a pot of escargot. He didn't once bear his teeth or do anything else to make her think that he might be aggressive, or that he might bite her out of pure fear. Instead, she recalls him putting his head way, way down so that she could pet it. After a few minutes, Beach decided that Blue was a dog who was just plain terrified. He struck her as the kind of dog who would be all right if he got into a foster home where he'd feel safe and have a chance to act like a puppy instead of a death-row prisoner.

Beach tagged Blue as a dog to be rescued, and the shelter put a note on his cage that kept him alive for the next few days. Then Beach and Turner went to the shelter together to collect Blue along with a few other dogs. Turner offered to take Blue home as a foster dog, something she had done many, many times before. Beach had never been to Turner's home, but as a fellow member of Canine Volunteer Rescue, she assumed that everything would be fine there.

Blue, from what Turner and a friend of hers told me, continued to hang his head low at her house. It was as if he were constantly ducking in anticipation of incoming fire or shrapnel. While rescuers don't always know the history of dogs like Blue, Turner and her friend came to believe that Blue had been abused. If anybody raised their hand above his head, even if just to pet him without warning, Blue would try to bury himself in the floor and hide.

That characteristic alone is something that can get a dog like Blue tagged for death, both Turner and Beach told me. Beach said she has met many, many dogs like Blue inside county-run shelters, and that she has had to overcome resistance to rescuing them from Person County Animal Control specifically.

"I would go to the shelter again and again," she told me, "and they kept telling me that most of the dogs were unavailable. They'd tell me they had maybe two or three dogs available, that only two or three dogs in that whole building had okay behavior and attitudes. It was just insane."

It sounds counterintuitive, that a shelter would want to keep any rescue group out when so many dogs are being killed, but the blocking of rescue volunteers is so common that several states have actually passed laws that require animal-control directors to work with them. In California, for instance, a law had to be passed to force shelter directors to work with rescue groups that were willing and able to find homes for death-row dogs. And that California law was, at the time it passed in 1998, regarded as groundbreaking. The same type of law did not pass in Delaware until July 2010, with the signing of the Delaware Companion Animal Protection Act. It's widely regarded as the most progressive of its kind in the country today. It legally prohibits shelters from killing an animal if a rescue group is willing to take him, and it requires shelters to post photos of stray dogs online so they can be recognized and claimed by their owners instead of simply being held in a cage until they're killed at the end of the state's mandated waiting period.

Beach told me that when she first approached Person County Animal Control about saving dogs who were destined for its gas chamber in North Carolina, she was unceremoniously turned away, just like the advocates in California and Delaware were for so many years before her.

"All shelters operate differently," Beach told me, "and this is one that tried to stop me from pulling out dogs that they called unadoptable. They do not want change. I had to fight for two years to get the right to go in and save a lot of dogs who were very adoptable."

The effect of rescue advocates getting inside is undeniable, even by the shelter's own statistics. In 2008, according to the documents Shaw gave me, 74 dogs were saved by rescue groups in Person County. That's about the same number that the shelter itself adopted out. In 2009, though, the number saved by rescue groups nearly doubled while the shelter's own number of adoptions stayed virtually static. In 2010, the rescue group number climbed to 292 (including Blue), again with the county's own efforts showing little movement. During the first eight months of 2011, rescue groups had already saved several hundred dogs—more than in the entire previous year. The shelter itself, at that point in the year, had a record of adopting out just 38.

So rescue groups in Person County that tapped into the cross-country network of transports and distant adopters like me had achieved a four-fold increase in success in less than four years. And that's on zero budget beyond donated time, money, and supplies, compared with more than a quarter-million taxpayer dollars that the shelter itself receives annually.

Again, these kinds of statistics raised my eyebrow. I remembered that Shaw told me his job duties were clearly outlined by the county—and how he'd specifically mentioned that the state has no law requiring him to run an actual shelter. Yet when I read his job description, which was most recently updated by Person County in 2008, the first sentence beneath "essential duties and tasks" requires the animal-control director to plan and supervise the "care, feeding, medical attention, adoption, and euthanasia of animals." It seemed to me, looking at the statistics from recent years, that the volunteer rescue groups were the ones doing most of the care, feeding, medical attention, and adoption that was supposed to be happening inside the shelter's walls.

And even with such recent progress and momentum, rescuers in Person County still cry out that the shelter is getting in their way as they try to save even more dogs like Blue. Beach and Turner both told me that they have tagged dogs to be saved only to learn that the staff had gone ahead and killed them, anyway.

"I'd go to get 'em out of there, and he'd say, 'They're gone,'" Turner told me. She didn't mention whether she'd been on time to get the dogs, or whether she'd asked Shaw for an extension of a few days. I could imagine her swinging her head low and shaking it with disgust. "He killed them," she said. "Just like that."

I'll never know exactly what goes on during killing days at Person County Animal Control. I did not see a dog killed during my tour, and I have never seen a gas chamber in use. The precise fate that seems to have once awaited Blue will forever be a mystery to me.

But it's not a mystery to everybody. Plenty of rescue workers have seen the gas chambers in action at shelters nationwide—and some of those advocates were carrying video cameras.

Behind Closed Doors

~~

If you type "animal shelter gas chamber" into the search engine on YouTube, you can see for yourself how they work. Supporting information from the American Humane Association documents what I saw in a gas-chamber video, lest anyone believe it was doctored to make a point. To me, it certainly sounded like the dogs were suffering as the gas overcame them. If Blue made a noise like that, I'd go running to find out what was wrong. What I heard in the video of a gas chamber being used can only be described as desperate screams.

The video opens with a view of shelter workers wearing thick canvas gloves. They are moving dogs and puppies, one by one, into a metal box that sits on the ground. The box doesn't look much different from the one that I saw in Person County, except that it does not contain individual stalls to separate one dog from the next. The workers filling this chamber are methodical, almost rhythmical, like convenience-store employees stocking the auto section with jugs of wiper fluid. Their faces show no expression, and they don't utter a single word.

The gas chamber has an open lid, high enough off the ground that dogs placed inside can't easily get out. Some of the dogs are dropped inside willingly, as if they have just been lifted into a playpen. Their faces bear the same expression that Blue's did on the day that I met him and plopped him into my old wine box lined with a sheet, because I didn't have a crate for our car ride home. The look in the eyes of these dogs is quizzical, even curious. Some of them, no doubt, are simply relieved to be free from their cages.

Others go less willingly and must be moved by a restraint pole, which captures the dog by his neck and lets the worker carry him without touching him. Perhaps these dogs are skittish by nature, perhaps they are vicious and biting, or maybe they recall the sounds of the dogs they watched being put into the box the day before. It's impossible to say, of course, but for whatever reason, they resist.

Once there are six or eight dogs in the box, the lid is secured. A hose is attached, and carbon-monoxide gas is turned on. The shelter worker holds the knob on the gas line open, and the dogs hear the hiss of the gas as it pushes inside. Dogs squeal and scratch at the box's walls, their untrimmed nails no match for its metal. The screams grow louder at first, perhaps from disorientation and dizziness, perhaps from pain, or perhaps from terror at the sight of the first dogs dropping dead inside the dark chamber. Unlike with lethal injections, which are designed to knock a dog unconscious before his vital organs shut down, gas chambers stop a dog's organ function before the animal loses consciousness. Frightened dogs sometimes fight with other, impaired dogs. And in some cases, chambers can take a half hour to be fully effective. Only then do the wails end. The strongest dog's final whimper comes last, and then, in the end, there is silence.

The worker in the video turns off the gas, opens the lid, and begins moving the next batch of dogs and puppies into the metal box. He places them atop the limp bodies of the dogs who have just been killed, where the new arrivals struggle to find their footing until the lid is closed atop them, too.

Once this gas-chamber session is complete, a garbage truck arrives to lift the box, just as it would any other can of refuse. The truck's mechanical arms swing the box up past the headlights and cab, and then backward over a large holding container. The driver presses a button that tips the box sideways, and the dogs fall into the container atop the local trash. They are then taken to the dump, where they are left to rot alongside everyday household garbage.

The lives of these puppies and dogs are treated with less meaning than a piece of kindling thrown into a fireplace. Their fur is not used to make clothing. Their rumps and ribs are not used as food. They are not being killed for a purpose of any kind, except to make room for the next batch of dogs like them. In this respect, they are of a lower value in our society than cows, deer, and squirrels. Nobody speaks a kind word. Nobody even knows their names, if ever they had names at all.

And sometimes, nobody checks to make sure they are actually dead. In April 2005, Jeff and Susan Armsworthy of Mocksville, North Carolina, were at the local dump depositing their trash. They told reporter Mike Gunning of the *Davie County Enterprise Record* that they heard a squeaking noise coming from the Dumpster. At first, they thought it was a discarded toy. When the squeaking continued, they realized it was a live animal. Jeff Armsworthy said he jumped into the Dumpster and found two large, plastic bags. Both contained dead dogs, including three puppies—"but one was still wiggling. It was all matted and nasty, but it was alive." The pups had been brought to the dump from Davie County Animal Shelter, where they had been left in the custody of taxpayer-funded animal control a week earlier. A session that morning in the shelter's gas chamber had knocked this particular puppy unconscious, but he had awoken inside the trash bag at the dump.

And that Davie County puppy is not alone in having survived an actual gas-chamber session. Rescue worker Randy Grim wrote the book *Miracle Dog* about a pooch who shocked shelter workers in St. Louis by standing there, staring back at them from atop a pile of dead dogs, when workers opened the chamber door after turning off the gas. A rescue advocate in North Carolina told me that shelter workers don't even check to see whether limp, unconscious dogs are actually dead, either. "One guy who works at a landfill told me that he has seen dogs digging themselves up out of piles of trash," she told me. "Another guy who drives a dump truck from a shelter told us that he sometimes sees dogs still twitching."

I'd like to think that Blue would have been one of those so-called fortunate ones, with the spirit and strength and, let's face it, luck to survive the assault. But in my heart, I know that Blue is too gentle and sweet to achieve this kind of a miracle moment. Blue is the dog who lets toddlers take toys right out of his mouth, then waits politely until they give them back so he can play some more. Blue is the dog who runs eagerly into the living room of my neighbors and their hundred-pound Rottweiler, Rocky, thinking that maybe, just maybe, this one time Rocky won't sit on his little head while they romp. Blue is the dog who races across the house when I holler that I have a treat for him, realizing only after a few chews, when it's already too late, that what I really want is for him to take a bath or let me clip his nails or do something else that feels like doggy scutwork. Blue is the dog who falls for it every time. He is childlike and trusting in the best senses of those words. He would have gone into that gas chamber filled with tender innocence, probably licking the shelter worker's cheek if given the chance. He would have been unsuspecting and unassuming and then, suddenly, unable to breathe.

Blue would have been, in other words, like the majority of dogs who find themselves in the Person County Animal Control system, and in the many shelters just like it that still use gas chambers across America today.

"It's bad enough that we can't find homes for these dogs, that any of them have to be killed at all," says Jane Zeolla of Lulu's Rescue. "But these gas chambers, they just add pain and suffering. They must be made to stop."

The only thing that makes Blue different from all of the dogs he once sat caged alongside is that he was among the handful in a hundred who had the good fortune to get pulled out of the shelter before he was killed. He happened to catch the eye of Rhonda Beach on the day that she happened to walk through this particular internment camp offering a chance at salvation, the way a game-show host might bestow a million-dollar prize on one lucky member of a studio audience. If you're the guy sitting next to that big winner, the guy who just gets stuck with the hand that fate dealt him, then the whole show sure can feel fixed against you. I wonder if the dogs who sat in the cages next to Blue's even knew what a big prize, what a literal chance of a lifetime, they had just missed.

At this point, I had visited the shelter in Person County, talked with both Annie Turner and Rhonda Beach, and gotten a sense of what usually happens in gas-chamber shelters. I now understood the initial fate from which Blue had been saved. Yet I still had questions about how he had come to be coated in bleach, not to mention about how he'd apparently been neutered in the back of a van. Turner had told me that she had used bleach on Blue's rash because she'd been told to do so by the veterinarian in that van.

Thus, I decided that the next thing I needed to do was take a drive and go knock on the door of Dr. Wendy Royce. I found her converted RV in the side parking lot of Orange County Animal Shelter in Chapel Hill. In the past, Chapel Hill had always made me think of expensive college tuition and fanatical basketball fans. This was, though, a different world within the

North Carolina town. This was the reality that dogs like Blue know, not the reality that sports broadcasters see. The shelter looked pretty big and nice, but the RV where Royce awaited me was on the hot asphalt close to the Dumpsters. I expected the smell to be worse, given the summer heat.

The RV was hidden from the main parking lot by a couple of trees, and if I hadn't known to look for it, I probably wouldn't have even noticed it. I walked right up with my notebook once again in hand, rapped a few times on the door, and waited for it to open.

And then for about an hour after that, I stood in the very spot atop four wheels where Blue had been intubated for surgery. I watched how Royce and her staff treated the dogs in their care, and I double-checked Turner's claim against what I saw.

The more I learned that day, the more I realized there was likely something more that I hadn't yet been told.

As Many, and as
Fast as They Can

~~

Dr. Wendy Royce is even softer spoken than a church mouse. She's more like a church librarian's hamster, even cuter and tinier and just trying to stay out of trouble while she runs and runs and runs on her wheel.

Royce became medical director and surgeon for Pet Overpopulation Patrol of North Carolina in 2005, following a stint as a veterinarian for the SPCA shelter in Wake County. There, she had to decide which dogs would die on any given day. In her POP-NC mobile clinic, which she drives from county to county for the sole purpose of performing spay/neuter operations, Royce gets to help limit the number of dogs who arrive at shelters in the first place. Blue is among the 20,000 dogs and cats Royce has personally sterilized in the past six years of running the mobile clinic, and he is one of more than 30,000 she has spayed or neutered throughout her career. She showed me the calluses on her thumb and finger, which are both deeply scarred from holding the same type of needle all day, almost every day. Heavy-machinery operators have nothing on this tough working woman. She looks just as tired, and just as weary, albeit in hospital scrubs from the petites section as opposed to a pair of forty-long coveralls.

Person County is one of the lowest-income areas that POP-NC serves. In 2006, the county began working with the non-profit agency AnimalKind out of Raleigh to create "the $20 fix," a program that lets low-income residents get a dog or cat spayed or neutered for just twenty bucks. Royce's POP-NC is the only veterinary agency that accepts the $20 vouchers inside Person County's borders, she says. Her company is then reimbursed by AnimalKind for the rest of her expenses. For rescue groups like the one that saved Blue, the price per surgery is in keeping with the rates at local veterinarians' offices, but comes with a 15-percent discount. In a good year, Royce says, she breaks even, but she gets to do the right thing.

"I started this when I was very young," she told me with a chuckle. "I didn't realize I needed money back then. I just felt that I could make more of a difference if I kept the animals out of the shelters in the first place, because in my job at the shelter, I saw that once they got in, they had very little chance of getting out the front door."

Her clinic is an RV that has been converted into a veterinarian's office. I expected to step inside and see something resembling a homemade bomb shelter, but instead, I found a facility that looked much like my own veterinarian's office back home, albeit more compact. At the front of the RV, just behind the steering wheel and seats, was a station with a counter where two veterinarian assistants handled paperwork and prepared dogs and cats for surgery. Syringes were neatly organized in plastic bags, and operating instruments were cleaned in a sink before being placed in a sterilizing machine. Along both walls of the RV were about twenty cages filled with dogs and cats in various stages of loopiness thanks to sedation and pain medication, with another twenty or so cat carriers stacked up nearby. In the back of the RV, where a bedroom might otherwise be, stood Royce's operating suite beneath the same swing-mounted, halogen lamps that doctors and dentists use to perform operations on humans. There were two operating tables side by side, one where she was performing a surgery, and the other being prepped for the next surgery to begin at the next possible moment.

The idea is for her to be operating almost constantly, with the dogs and cats being prepped and brought to her in assembly-line fashion.

"I'm aware of the stigma, that we're doing operations in the back of a van," she told me, as if burrowing into my own brain and the prejudices I had assumed when I first heard about where Blue was neutered. "But it's really like walking into a vet's office on wheels. Our RV must pass inspection by the state's veterinary board every two years, just like regular offices. We also answer to OSHA [the federal Occupational Safety and Health Administration]. The way we're different from other, full-service vets is that while they may do three or four spay/neuters in a day along with everything else they have going on, we average thirty. It's the only thing that we do."

Person County is a good location for the POP-NC spay/neuter business model because the people who live there often cannot get their dogs spayed or neutered any other way. Meredith Barthelemy, the program director for POP-NC, told me that driving to within easy distance of the clients makes it more likely that they will participate. With high gas prices on top of the economic recession, many dog owners in Person County cannot afford the fill-up to get to a veterinarian on the outskirts of town, even if the surgery itself is only going to cost $20. Heck, even if it were free.

Plus, POP-NC accepts dogs before 8:00 A.M. and is willing to hold them until well after working hours for owner pickups. Most full-service veterinarians only allow drop-off after 8:30 or 9:00 A.M., with post-operation pickups before 5:00 P.M. sharp. For anyone who works a twelve-hour shift, as POP-NC says many of its clients do, getting a dog spayed or neutered could mean walking off a job that might not be there the next day.

"Person County has our nicest clients," Barthelemy says. "Absolutely the nicest people. They care about their animals. There is just a lack of education and finances. A lot of our clients in Person County don't have a television. They don't have the Internet. Their grandmother had dogs that had puppies. Their mother had dogs that had puppies. So now they have dogs that have puppies. It's what they do. It's what's always been done."

Royce knows that she, alone, cannot spay and neuter dogs fast enough to make a documentable impact on the intake numbers at Person County Animal Control, but she also knows that she is making at least something of a difference. Her two visits each month work out to about sixty dogs in Person County who will not breed additional puppies. Blue's mother may not have been spayed, but at least one part of his family chain of unwanted pups being dumped inside the metal gate will stop with him. The line was drawn with a scalpel on Royce's operating table in the back of her RV.

Actually, Blue's new destiny with me began at the POP-NC mobile clinic, too. Rhonda Beach told me that Annie Turner had brought Blue there for his surgery at a time when something had been preventing a good photograph of Blue from getting uploaded onto adoption websites. Beach said she had been asking and asking Turner for Blue's picture, always to no avail. So, while Turner held Blue and waited outside the RV to hand him over to the POP-NC veterinarian assistants, Beach snapped the photograph that I saw on Petfinder.com. It's the photo that made me fall in love with him. Blue actually looks like he is smiling in this photograph, almost as if he understands the bigger picture of which he is becoming a part.

This story about the photo being taken, of course, reminded me about how Turner said the spay/neuter veterinarian had told her that Blue had ringworm, and that she should treat it with bleach and Monistat. Having spent a fair bit of time getting to know Royce and the way she conducts her business, I wasn't quite sure I believed that story anymore. Then I repeated the story to both Royce and Barthelemy—and they both physically recoiled at the thought. They actually went completely silent for what felt to me like a few awfully heavy moments.

Royce shifted her body forward before saying anything in response, like a teacher leaning in to make sure a student hears her point clearly. She shook her head no, incredulously, as if I'd just told her that her assistants had recommended bathing a dog in antifreeze. And then she explained, in as definitive a way as she could: Not only is bleaching not a recommended treatment for ringworm, but she does not give medical advice of any kind to clients who visit POP-NC to receive her very specific services.

She couldn't. She'd be out of business, and fast.

"We try not to irritate the local vets by doing anything other than spay/neuter," she said. "We don't want them to think that we are trying to steal away their business. We may have described a lesion that we saw as part of our routine exam, but we do not diagnose, and we do not recommend treatment. We recommend follow-up and testing at a regular, full-service veterinarian. Doing business that way lets us get our job done, focusing on spay/ neuter, while keeping the local vets happy and even sending them new clients."

Barthelemy told me that sometimes, especially in places like Person County—where, according to the 2010 Census, only about fourteen percent of people hold a bachelor's degree— follow-up instructions after medical procedures can get unintentionally lost in translation. Health literacy is different than general literacy, and it is something that many people find challenging. According to the nonprofit Institute of Medicine, some 90 million Americans have problems with health literacy. The National Network Libraries of Medicine says some of the most vulnerable people can include those with high school diplomas who actually read at a seventh- or eighth-grade level. POP-NC sometimes sees these difficulties in follow-up care. As an example, the team recently learned that some of its clients were squirting oral medications onto the scars left from spay/neuter surgeries because they couldn't understand the instructions to give the medicine by mouth. In the same vein, Barthelemy said, somebody from POP-NC may have told Turner to bleach her sheets if Blue had been on them and was later diagnosed with ringworm, but nobody would have told her that's what he had just by looking at his skin. And certainly, nobody would have told her to put bleach on Blue himself.

But they've heard stranger things, she said. Once, a dog arrived at POP-NC for sterilization while covered in third-degree burns. The owner had believed that coating the dog in oil would keep away fleas and ticks. A cigarette butt then went astray, lighting the family pet ablaze.

Hearing Royce and Barthelemy say these things left me believing that they most likely were telling the truth. Later, when I watched the POP-NC team in action, I felt zero doubt.

The veterinarian assistants on duty the day of my visit were Christina Tozeo and Tamara Matheson, both exceptionally well-spoken and professional brunettes in their twenties. Tozeo wants to be a veterinarian herself and was in the process of applying to school. The two of them moved dogs and cats to Royce with the practiced precision of a NASCAR pit crew. Their roles were well defined, and they clearly knew what they were doing, right down to administering the rabies and distemper vaccines that are given for free along with the $20 fix.

Several of the dogs getting surgery that day in the POP-NC mobile clinic were from a rescue group near Chapel Hill whose volunteer was waiting outside to collect the dogs as I left. I watched one dog go into his transport crate willingly and another put up enough of a snarling fight that Tozeo used a restraint pole—firmly, but not cruelly, with the dog's feet remaining wholly on the ground—to get him inside without anyone getting bitten. Then I watched her go over the discharge papers with the rescue volunteer, just as she or one of her colleagues would have done with Turner when she came to collect Blue.

Tozeo ran down the day's surgery notes just as my own veterinarian does, explaining that there were no complications and pointing out anything else that Royce noted during the pre-operation exam. She mentioned one or two things, such as a dog whose tooth was cracked so deeply that the root was exposed. "If he's not eating, then it's probably because he's in pain," she told the volunteer. "The owner should take him to the local veterinarian to get the proper treatment for that problem."

It was exactly what Royce and Barthelemy had told me would happen, and it was happening right before my eyes.

Which could mean only one thing: There was more to the story about Blue's life as a foster dog at Turner's farm. That rash, those scabs—a puzzle not yet solved. I had to go and see where Blue had lived, if only to figure out whatever it was that I was still not being told, despite all the questions I'd already asked.

I was yet again about to be reminded that while all of the so-called bad guys in any story are not always completely bad, neither are the so-called good guys in any story always completely good.

Something Eerie
in the Dark

~~

I arranged to meet Annie Turner for dinner at her choice of restaurant in Roxboro, and she selected a place called Clarksville Station. It's a converted railroad building connected to an old railroad car that I got a lot of time to look around, since Turner was well more than a half hour late. I chatted up one of the owners and talked to the waiters about a recent experience they'd had with a spirit guide. They all believed the railroad car was haunted by the ghosts of dead soldiers whose bodies had been transported in it from a Civil War battlefield. Apparently, these apparitions occasionally show up while the staff is doing prep work and washing dishes in the kitchen.

There didn't seem to be any spirits around at that moment, though, and neither was there any sign of Turner. I'd called her en route to say I was on time and an hour away, and she'd told me she could be there in five minutes and would see me soon. Now it was long past that hour plus about forty minutes' worth of ghost stories later, and I was getting worried that she'd been in some kind of an accident. The waitress kept coming over and refilling my glass of sweet tea, so finally I asked her if she happened to know who Turner was.

"Oh, is that who you're waitin' on?" the waitress said. "I know her. That's just Annie. You could be waiting here for hours."

When Turner finally arrived, I warmly accepted her big, bear hug. She didn't even say hello. She just walked right up to me with outstretched arms and a broad smile, as if I were her long-lost friend. She is an attractive woman, perhaps my age or a few years older, who looks like she might have been a popular cheerleader back in the day. We sat down and ordered from the dinner menu, and I took out my notebook. While we noshed on appetizers, I asked Turner to tell me a little about herself and about how she'd become involved in rescuing dogs like Blue.

Turner was born and raised in Person County. Once upon a time, she said, she worked in a job that let her take care of people who needed all kinds of help. She told me that she liked the job well enough and figured she'd do it forever, but then one day, when she was twenty-five years old, her then-husband hit her square in the face. His punch broke her nose, which was shoved so far back into her head that it created a blood clot in her brain.

She told me that she was blind for a while and lost her depth perception, but her normal vision returned enough that she can

once again drive. She still can't walk along the railroad tracks—
she gets dizzy and falls off the ties—but all in all, she figures it
could have been worse. She is remarried now and lives off her
disability payments, which gives her plenty of time to do rescue
work with dogs. While I found her speech and thought patterns
a bit jumpy as we moved from topic to topic, her heart remains
big and generous, especially to pooches in distress. From the
time she was a child, she says, she was always one to get yelled at
for bringing home too many strays.

Two or three times during our conversation, when I asked her
about her dealings with Ron Shaw and Person County Animal
Control, she avoided details but said Shaw has learned not to
mess with her over the years. Several times when I asked her for
specifics, she referred to the fact that she's much shorter than he
is and said, simply, "Dynamite comes in small packages."

She told me that she thinks Canine Volunteer Rescue was
founded around 1975 because she's seen a banner celebrating
a former president, and that date is written next to the lady's
name. Turner has been with the group since about 1990, which
is at least seven years before Shaw took over as director. She
says the facility has had problems for as long as she can recall, and that she remembers having to go at one point to the
county's Board of Commissioners to even be let inside to see
the dogs.

It all seemed logical enough to me, based on everything I'd
learned so far, but something about Turner's demeanor left me
feeling as though I might not be asking all of the right questions. I couldn't tell what it was for sure, but after years of in-

terviewing people for stories of all kinds, I had a feeling that something was missing.

After we finished dinner, I did what I'd planned to do all along—asked Turner to walk with me to the parking lot and surprised her with a forty-four-pound bag of dog food. It was the biggest one I'd been able to find back home. I figured Blue couldn't possibly have eaten that much during his short stay with her as a puppy. I wanted to repay her, and then some, for providing him a safe place of refuge.

I then asked Turner if I could visit her home, something I knew was forward but that I felt I had to ask. I wanted to learn more about where Blue had lived. It's a truly bold request, I know, asking a woman you've just met to take you back to her house for a look around. I would have understood if she'd said no, but she could tell by the look in my eyes that I really wanted her to say yes.

Turner hesitated and thought it over before agreeing, and then she told me I could follow her home. She next pointed to her vehicle across the parking lot, and I guess the look of surprise on my face made her feel like she had to provide an explanation. She said she'd recently inherited the luxury truck. It was an interesting sight as the $70,000 vehicle worked its way along the streets of town.

I followed diligently behind, driving right past the animal shelter on Chub Lake Road and then beyond along the beautiful country roads that make this part of North Carolina a place where people want to stay long after they're old enough to leave. After turning down a few side streets and passing a charming white general store, I was parked in Turner's driveway. She vanished for a moment and then reemerged in a golf cart, where she asked me to sit beside her so she could drive me down to the house next door.

That's where she was living when she brought Blue home, and she said that she still owns the property today. It was not at all the farm that I had imagined when I'd heard that word over the telephone, with open fields and crops growing and maybe some hay bales stacked in a barn. Instead, it's a regular house—the kind that can be found in plenty of neighborhoods all across America. A good-sized yard is around back and off to the right, surrounded by a chain-link fence. "That's where Blue used to play, with a clear view of the pond," she told me as a pair of dogs ran barking toward us. She told me they were her dogs, even though she now lived one house over, up the hill. They seemed desperate to get to her for attention, the way Blue does when I come home after being away for even a half hour, but Turner barely even acknowledged them. Nor did she stop the golf cart to get out and go say hello to them. About the same time, I heard barking out behind the vacant house near the pond and asked if those were her dogs as well. "Oh yes," she said. "There's some more babies out there, too."

We continued our golf cart tour by riding around to the left side of the house, which abuts an overgrown field. This, she said, is where she used to take Blue for walks. She must have once again noticed my quizzical look, because without my even asking she felt the need to explain how Blue might have walked through what I was seeing—a stretch of land overgrown with grass nearly as high as my belly and weeds as far as the eye could see. "I kept this all mowed when I lived here," she told me. "He never did like to pee in that field, though. He liked to go over to the fence on the other side of the house and pee on that while the other dogs were still inside. You know, like he was saying, 'Ha ha, I'm special. I got out.'"

I turned my head to look back at the fence, and instead saw what looked like a swap meet at best, and a junkyard at worst. A covered area toward the back of the house was littered with old four-wheelers, tools, and various other parts and machines. My first thought was that if this was an area where Blue had ever stepped foot, then he probably needed a tetanus shot. And again, my expression gave me away. Before I even asked about the rusted and wrecked machinery, Turner said, "My son can fix anything. He can take any of those things apart and turn them into something else."

Next, she drove me in the golf cart around the back of the property and the pond, heading up the hill to the house next door, where she now lives. We stopped to pick a few grapes from her bush—they were so tasty and sweet that I felt like I got an ice cream headache—and as we sat there in the golf cart discussing the merits of fresh fruit, I saw two dogs run up the road in the distance, right into the vacant house's yard.

"Yeah, they're my neighbor's dogs," she told me. "He has fifteen acres, and he says he doesn't believe in fences. Or neutering. Those dogs have knocked up the Cocker Spaniel up the road about four times now. I got the lady with the Cocker Spaniel the vouchers for the twenty-dollar fix, but she keeps telling me that she forgot to go cash them in at the mobile vet. Whatever."

Our tour continued up over the hill behind Turner's current house, where I heard more barking than I'd heard inside the Person County Animal Control kennel. The golf cart struggled to make it up and over the crest on the dirt path, and once we were there, we got out to walk. I saw at least three large kennels plus a fully fenced-in area, with at least a dozen more dogs yipping and yapping to get our attention. I had never seen so many dogs in one place, except in the kennel I had visited earlier that week. It seemed like an awful lot of dogs for one person to take care of, even with help from a friend or two. Some of the dogs were puppies who had been outside in these pens for at least the hour or two since she'd left to meet me at the restaurant—and Turner didn't even open the gates to go inside or acknowledge most of them. They yipped and barked and clawed at the fencing, trying desperately to break through.

My first instinct was to go to the dogs and play with them, but Turner quickly dissuaded me of that notion. Some, she said, I could pet. Others, she told me, would bite. One dog, who had white fur with the potential to be gorgeous, had so much brown gunk running down from her eyes that I wanted to get a tissue and clean her up myself.

"Now, Blue would never have been out here," Turner told me. She noticed the way I was looking at the white dog, and then she rubbed at the dog's eyes with her own thumb before continuing. "He was way too little and sick. He had the ringworm—oh, did he have the ringworm somethin' fierce—so I had to keep him away from the other dogs. He stayed crated in the house. I have some dogs inside in crates now. I can show you in the house how it would have been."

As we made our way back up the driveway toward her home, I felt incredibly uneasy. This was not at all what I'd imagined when she told me by telephone that Blue had lived on a farm. This is not what I'd had in mind when she said he played with lots of other dogs, so much so that at least one really missed him. Those claims, to me, suddenly sounded the way the packaging does on "free-range" chicken that comes from places where the birds aren't technically in cages, but never actually see the light of day.

I thought carefully how to ask my next question. I wasn't sure how she would react, and I didn't want to be rude.

"Is there a point," I said slowly and deliberately, "at which the county or the state says you have too many dogs to take care of by yourself? Might they, for instance, want to qualify you as a kennel? Or maybe, I guess, are there laws about hoarding?"

She didn't look at me, and she didn't seem upset, but she answered in a snap. "Oh I looked into that," she said. "I made a call. You aren't a hoarder unless they can find sixty dogs. Believe me, honey, I'm under the limit.

"Now," she continued as we stepped out of the golf cart and onto her front porch, "housekeeping is not my specialty." I nodded and smiled politely, thinking that it's not exactly my specialty, either. I figured I'd see dust on the tables, an unmade bed, and maybe some dishes that needed washing in the sink as I followed her inside the house to learn more about how Blue had lived.

I'd barely made it three feet inside when I stopped to get my bearings. As with all of the dogs outside in the pens, I was now seeing something inside that I'd never before encountered. This wasn't a messy house the way I understand that phrase. This was a house where a path had been cleared across the floor to get to the various rooms and then back outside.

We entered through the front door and were immediately in what appeared to be the living room—which I say because I saw parts of two black sofas. They were covered in so much debris that there was barely anyplace to sit. To my left, where some people might have placed a coatrack, huge bags of dog food were stacked about waist high. Junk seemed to be littering most of the floor on the right side of the room, as well. I couldn't make out exactly what was in the short and tall piles all around, but I'm pretty sure I saw various combinations of old newspapers, boxes, clothes, and the like. The table between the sofas was covered with what looked like bits of packing Styrofoam peanuts, which someone had strangely organized into color-coded piles of pink and green.

We walked into what I took for a spare bedroom, and Turner flipped on the lights. I counted seven crates. Only one was empty. The dogs barked crazily, like the ones who don't get walked down at the shelter. As with the dogs outside, Turner left all but one in the crates and didn't even acknowledge their presence. One of them was a big, brown boy who could barely stand up straight, his crate was so small. The crates looked clean to me, but I noticed the floor peeling up in sections beneath them.

"Are all of these dogs currently available for adoption?" I asked.

"Well, most of them are," she said. "Some of them are mine. Some of them aren't ready yet. The ones that can't find homes, now, this is going to sound terrible, but they have to live with me forever."

She smiled as she said it, like she was telling a joke.

Then she flipped off the lights, led me back past the crates of barking dogs, and shut the door unceremoniously behind us.

Next came the kitchen, where I heard more barking than in the spare bedroom. The door to the kitchen had a glass pane in the center that was covered long-ways by a beach towel so that nobody could see inside. "Let me just go through there, and you can see them from outside," Turner said, leaving me alone in the living room. She walked into the kitchen and closed the door behind her, as if there were something inside that she needed to rearrange before I could see it. I waited a few seconds and then pulled the towel over with one finger to sneak a peek. I counted at least a half dozen small dogs, maybe more. A lot of them appeared to be Chihuahuas. Then I quickly let the towel snap back, feeling guilty to have looked at all.

Once we were both back outside, she let me look through a glass door not only into the kitchen, but also at the adjoining room's windows, which had been painted black. They looked like the windows at strip clubs, completely slathered in darkness to ensure that nobody sees what's happening inside. She told me that was her post-op room and that more dogs were inside, healing from whatever ailed them. The phrase "post-op" startled me. I immediately wondered who, precisely, was doing what kind of operating.

I also wondered, as I stood there, how many of the dogs hidden behind those blackened windows had been "treated" with bleach just like Blue. I wondered what else was being done to them. I wondered how many of them would eventually get to leave, if ever.

Unsure of what else to say or do, I thanked Turner again for having helped to get Blue out of the shelter. I told her that I appreciated all she had done to help save his life. I got into my car and turned the key. I prepared to head from Turner's house back down the road that leads to the local shelter, and then to my hotel.

I drove in stunned silence, wondering how my boy had ever made it out of Person County alive.

A Cool Breeze
in Hell

~~~

The next morning, after a night of precious little and entirely disturbed sleep, I got an early start and drove about three hours south of Person County. My destination was Robeson County, whose animal-control facility has received a lot more publicity in recent years than the one where Blue was found. While Person County Animal Control has quietly plodded along in something of a public-awareness vacuum, Robeson County Animal Shelter has been like a murder suspect sitting in a police station with bright lights shined directly into his eyes. Advocates told me that things there had been even worse than the situation that Blue faced, and that somehow, under the glare of harsh public outcry, the shelter had found a way to turn things around.

I wanted to know what Robeson County had done to bring change, since it certainly didn't involve throwing money at the problem. The median household income is $28,202. Nearly 30 percent of the residents live below the poverty line. Robeson holds the unfortunate distinction of being the absolute poorest county in the entire state of North Carolina.

I drove into the town of St. Pauls by way of NC-20, a two-lane road that seems at least one lane too big for anything that might even remotely be considered rush-hour traffic. Mine was one of the only cars in motion along the flat, paved stretch, which cut through swaths of tall, proud trees climbing from beneath blankets of healthy, green grass. The scenery that nature had created here looked as soft and welcoming as any state park under a crisp blue sky. Where it had been cleared for structures built by man, though, things looked hard gained and worse kept, even in the morning's best and brightest light.

The names of the side streets are a lot like the people I would soon meet in Robeson County: They tell it like it is, in plain language that everybody can understand. Two of the streets I passed were called Grassy Road and Bumpy Road. A bit farther up the main road, a little ways beyond the vacant storefronts and across from Bo's Food Store, was the only place I saw with a full parking lot and any kind of hustle. A good number of people walked through the front door, right under the white banner with big red letters announcing that a "Summer Sale" was on at the Family Dollar.

Somewhere in this vicinity is where the county's animal shelter used to be, according to Timothy Mason, who has been with the program for the past eighteen years. As recently as about 2000, he told me, the shelter was housed in the old office of a veterinarian. I heard him debate with a coworker whether the old office had a dirt floor, or a floor so dirty that it could no longer be cleaned, but either way, the place was scary nasty. It's where he used to go to work every day.

Today, Mason walks with the kind of wise elder's gait that tells you there's no reason to be in a hurry, because in life, change isn't coming anytime soon, anyway. As he told me the story of his job as it used to be, he shifted uneasily on both of his feet. He moved around the room a little, too, as if his own words made him feel uncomfortable in whatever space he chose to stand.

"They'd bring the dogs in," he recalls. "There were always so many dogs, but we only had ten pens. We couldn't tell what was what, there were so many dogs in each cage. Once a week, the city would send a dump truck. Now, this wasn't a pickup truck. This was a big, tall dump truck. We'd get each dog with a catch pole and give it a heart stick[4] to kill it. I didn't want to do it that way, but they were going to take my job away if I didn't."

He stopped for a moment and rubbed his right shoulder with his left hand.

"Now my shoulder is bad because after we did the heart sticks, we'd have to hurl the dogs up into that dump truck. We'd just throw the dead dogs up in there, and everybody in town would

---

[4] A heart stick is just what it sounds like, an injection directly into a dog's heart. National veterinary standards require sedation before it is used, as well as worker training to ensure that the injection actually goes into the dog's heart. Without sedation or proper staff training, I was told by rescue advocates as well as by Person County Animal Control Director Ron Shaw, a heart stick is a painful and cruel way for a dog to die.

see, because we were right there on the main road. We all felt so ashamed. And it wasn't very long ago."

As he finished his story, everyone in the room went silent. It was the first time he'd ever shared that memory with the current staff.

I cleared my throat and asked, in an almost reverent tone, "What happened that finally brought change?"

The answer I received from a new employee, while just three words, might as well have been louder than a bomb.

"Faith Walker happened."

Actually, as Faith Walker herself later told me by telephone, the changes in Robeson County started with a dog named Fannie Mae. Walker had just moved back to be near her family in North Carolina after living out West, where her husband was a professor at the University of Southern California. She learned about the deplorable conditions at the old Robeson County shelter, and she went over to adopt a dog. She figured she could save at least one.

Walker thought Fannie Mae was just beautiful, with a mostly black coat and a black streak on her tongue, maybe a Chow Chow mixed with a Cocker Spaniel. Walker wanted to give her a good home, so she asked the shelter director to let Fannie Mae out of her cage.

"The shelter director told me that I couldn't adopt her because she was scheduled to be put down in fifteen minutes," Walker recalls. "I said that I wanted her, and he said, 'You heard me, that dog is going down in fifteen minutes. You can't have her.' Well, I threw my purse down on the ground, right then and there. I'm five foot one and I weigh ninety-seven pounds. I put up my fists and said to that man, 'You try to take me if you can, because you're going to have to take me first.'"

That was in 1997. Fannie Mae has been dutifully by Walker's side ever since, through more than a decade's worth of time that Walker has spent lobbying tirelessly for change. At first, she says, she used proper channels and made requests to the county officials in charge of the shelter. When she realized she was getting nowhere, she enlisted People for the Ethical Treatment of Animals, some lawyers, and a television news station's hidden camera. Walker quickly earned a reputation among county officials and shelter workers alike as an out-and-out gadfly with intentions of neither shutting up nor backing down. She's the kind of person people on the inside of any system tend to describe while rolling their eyes, just as people on the outside of that system are clapping wildly in applause.

By 2001, Walker had grown so frustrated that she sued Robeson County on allegations of animal cruelty. Evidence in the case included a videotape that reporters from WRAL in Raleigh shot with a hidden camera that PETA provided. It showed animals in the shelter being slapped, kicked, and held by their necks in midair on restraint poles, Walker says. WRAL reporters interviewed a veterinarian who had no connection to the case and asked him to explain what the tape showed in terms of the heart sticks. He told them, "It's terrible. There's no attempt to look for the heart. They are just sticking at the chest. They'll die eventually because it will go into the lungs and from the lungs it will filter back to the heart. It is not a quick and humane death. Watching this, I don't have the sense that they care to do it properly. It's just an assembly line."

Walker's lawsuit was ultimately dismissed, but the surge of publicity that came with it got the county's attention. Staff were certified and trained in the legal ways to work with and euthanize animals, and the current incarnation of the animal shelter that I'd driven to visit was built.

But still, complaints persisted. They piled up along with the bodies of dead dogs for a half dozen more years. According to *The Robesonian* newspaper, the worst of the public outcry spiked less than a year before I arrived in Robeson County. In December 2010, a puppy was found among newly killed animals en route to the county landfill. The puppy had been sedated, but not actually given a lethal injection. That brought a state fine of several thousand dollars and a temporary ban on all killing at the shelter, until officials could figure out what was still going wrong. "What happened was they finally built the new shelter, but they didn't change the people in charge," Walker says. "I begged them to hire a new director who was experienced in animal control, but they didn't, so we ended up with the same problems in the new facility, only now on a bigger scale."

Given this decade-long drama about the conditions inside Robeson County Animal Shelter, it's no wonder the new facility was built in a place that nobody would ever find unless they made an effort to go looking. When I made the turn down Landfill Road, the first sign that I saw warned, all too presciently, "Dead End." Next, I saw the row of Dumpsters where local residents sometimes leave unwanted puppies because they can't be bothered to drive any farther. Beyond that stood the county landfill, an actual mountain of trash. And then, once I passed that, I found the Robeson County Animal Shelter, good and hidden away from civilization and any possible comforts that it might offer.

The people in charge at the new building today are not the same ones who were in charge when it was built. They hadn't even been there a full year on the day that I walked through the front door. They, as well as Walker, told me that one previous director was a man, and one was a woman. Both of them drew so much community outrage that the county's leaders got bombarded by animal activists demanding more change. The male director, I was told, was even receiving death threats.

"The woman director who followed him, she was killing willy-nilly," says Sara Hatchell, who works as adoptions and volunteer coordinator. "I heard she'd tell the people who came in to ask about dogs, 'I'd love to stand here and talk to you all day, but I'm down on my killing.' The rumor is that she once killed eighty dogs in a single day. Nobody even used to answer the phone by saying, 'Hello, animal shelter.' They'd just pick up the receiver and say, 'Yeah, this is the pound.'"

Hatchell came to work for Robeson County Animal Shelter in November 2010, just one month after the current director, Lori Baxter. They arrived to find an annual budget of $382,474 for all animal control and more than 3,100 dogs entering the shelter each year. That's three times the number of dogs entering the Person County facility where Blue was found, and only one-third more dollars to deal with them. Robeson County is also more than twice the size of Person County, at about 950 square miles. On any given day, the animal-control officers in Robeson County have to cover a heck of a lot more ground.

Baxter hails from Ohio, and Hatchell from Napa Valley, California. Baxter arrived with previous animal-control jobs on her resumé, including having been director in Cumberland County, North Carolina, while Hatchell spent thirty-five years as a groomer and obedience instructor. Hatchell had zero experience working with rescues and adoptions before she got the job of coordinating both for Robeson County.

They were not hailed as saviors, by any means. Baxter was an unknown person to many of the local rescue advocates, who immediately began researching her history. "One of them," Baxter remembers, "called my boss and gave him every address where I'd ever lived and every last name I've ever had. She told him, 'Don't you think it's weird that she's moved around so much and been married so many times?'" The shelter's own telephone continued to ring constantly, too. Walker kept calling and calling, demanding faster and faster change, once aggravating the staff to the point that Baxter said she was resigning before she'd barely had a chance to get started.

Baxter and Hatchell didn't immediately trust one another, either. While Baxter reports to the county's health director, Hatchell's position was created so that she could report directly to the county manager. Everybody in power wanted somebody on the inside in case of another negative publicity explosion. "The rescue people," Baxter says, "wanted somebody who reported directly to the county manager so they could keep an eye on all of us who work for the health director. It's lucky that we get along so well and that we have learned to share the same philosophy, but at first, I thought she was nothing more than a spy."

Both women told me that what they faced inside the shelter wasn't any less a blasting fire hose of constant pressure, either. They inherited a system of record keeping that looked an awful lot like an obstinate teenager's bedroom. Papers and files were strewn around the office without the basic rhyme or reason of a Dr. Seuss book. The adoption process consisted of workers saying, "Give me five bucks and you can take a dog." They lack confidence in the statistics that previous directors provided, but Hatchell says they are certain the kill rate was at least 90 percent, and probably higher. There was never a gas chamber in this facility, but even after the heart sticks stopped, Walker continued to call every single day about all the dogs being killed. "That woman was riding the county officials to town and back to get changes made," Hatchell says. "Just in the past four or five months, she's stopped calling. I guess she liked the changes that she sees us making."

Hatchell presumes that there's a written job description for her somewhere in the county bureaucracy, but in practical terms, from the day she started she knew only two things: There was a huge public outcry about so many dogs being killed, and she was hired to find homes for as many dogs as she could.

"I didn't know how to get started," she says, "because I'd never worked on rescue before, but I figured as good a place as any was to take their pictures and give them names. I just started giving every dog that came in here a name, which to me means they matter in the world."

Now, Robeson County Animal Shelter is a kill facility, just like the shelter where Blue was found. Make no mistake about that. Not every dog will be saved. Some are rabid, some are vicious, and some are too sick with mange or heartworm or other treatable illnesses to be cured within the facility's budget. Others who are perfectly wonderful, like Blue, will get killed for space when adopters cannot be found in time. Hatchell and Baxter were clear about those things when they spoke with me, but they said them in a way that made me think they meant them differently than the director I'd met in Person County.

Then Hatchell showed me around the kennel, and I could see that while the language may be similar, the attitude here was different.

In Person County, the larger section of cages where Blue was found is reserved for dogs considered non-preferable for adoption. In Robeson County, the opposite is true—by a multiplying factor of five. There are fewer than twenty cages separated off to the back for what Robeson's staff calls "the biters and the diseased," while a full hundred cages are for dogs the staff believes are deserving of, and likely to thrive in, good homes. Those cages are up front, not in the back like in Person County, and they start within steps of where potential adopters walk through the door. The first thing folks find are dogs deemed "good" instead of having to get to those dogs after walking past the ones who are considered less preferable. The kennel is much bigger and therefore better able to handle larger intake numbers than the one where Blue was found, and it has been organized in a way that gives far more of the dogs like him a chance of getting out.

Robeson County Animal Shelter had a Facebook page when Hatchell started, but like the one in Person County, it rarely got used by the three animal-control officers or the three kennel attendants. Hatchell started regularly posting the photos she took of the dogs. She also found computer software called PetPoint that logs a dog's photograph and information into a kennel's back-end system while simultaneously uploading it to websites including Petango.com, which is similar to Petfinder.com, only smaller. The more Hatchell realized that rescue groups from well beyond Robeson County's borders were responding to those websites, the more she tried to figure out how to use them to get the dogs inside the Robeson shelter noticed.

"For one thing, I started taking the dogs' pictures outside," she says. "Nobody had ever taken them out of the cages to take their pictures. I thought that taking their pictures out in the grass was a lot better than showing them behind bars. It makes them look so much more adoptable."

She did this for all the dogs who arrived at Robeson County Animal Shelter, not just for the ones destined for the preferable adoption cages.

"The thing is, and I know this from years as an obedience trainer, dogs can go from bad to worse in this atmosphere, or they can go from rotten to great," she says. "If we have the time and the space, then we work with the dogs that aren't naturally easy to adopt out. If we don't have the time and the space, then we have to make choices that are hard, but everybody who works here now is down with the program. They know that the goal is to get every possible dog out and into a home."

That attitude, of trying to get every possible dog a home, is one shared by millions of Americans who have made the Internet the fastest-growing tool in dog rescue. Hatchell was realizing the same thing I had learned back home when I'd logged on to the Lulu's Rescue Facebook page: that the stream of homeless dog photos is endless, and for a very good reason. Advocates are learning that the more dogs they display online, the more people like me will find them and adopt them. Geography is irrelevant. A good story and a great picture will get a dog a home plenty of times.

Some people have so embraced this attitude that they've co-alesced into a new force within the rescue movement. They're known as cross-posters, people who spend their entire days sitting at computers and republishing information about homeless dogs to gain as wide an audience for each dog as possible. Some cross-posters receive messages from shelter workers like Hatchell and then republish as many as two hundred of them a day, each featuring a different homeless dog. Some of these cross-posters have more than one Facebook page because they hit the five-thousand-friend limit on their first page or two.

Every dog's photo that a cross-poster publishes is akin to a chain letter or telephone tree being set in motion. Rescuers then communicate about each dog by posting a series of comments. A typical series starts with something like this: "I have space for this dog in my program, but no way to transport him to the foster home." Another rescuer then comments: "I can transport him tomorrow, but I can't get him from the shelter in time. Can somebody pull him from the shelter tonight and keep him safe until morning?" And then another rescuer states: "I can get him out tonight and meet you tomorrow morning. What group is reposting him on Petfinder to find his forever home?"

And so on, and so forth, until a group of people who were formerly strangers have formed a chain of rescue—one that can span hundreds or thousands of miles from the shelter where the dog actually sits on death row, just as Blue did about five hundred miles from me. Hatchell told me that Robeson County has adopted dogs to people in the North this way, including not far from where I live in New Jersey. The Internet, she said, has been Robeson County's main tool for creating change.

It didn't happen overnight, she said, but about eight months after she started posting the photos of Robeson County dogs online, the shelter's Facebook page got the attention of a large rescue group called Pet Pardons. Just as with cross-posters, Pet Pardons has a large number of followers who share information among rescue groups. In just three days, Pet Pardons converted more than nine hundred of its Facebook members into fans of Robeson County Animal Shelter. All of those people could then see the photos that Hatchell had been so diligently uploading.

The adoption and foster requests, Hatchell told me, flooded across her desk like the first truly cool breeze ever to blow through the gates of hell. And about a week after that, Robeson County Animal Shelter celebrated its first-ever back-to-back days when not a single dog had to be killed for space. The staff were positively cheering—including Timothy Mason, even with his bad shoulder.

Hatchell was telling me about those two glorious days as she pulled out a clipboard to make a notation about one of the dogs who had just been requested by an online adopter. I asked if I could see what she was writing, and she handed me the paper without hesitation. It showed the shelter's adoption statistics so far for that month. In that period of less than three weeks, the staff at Robeson County Animal Shelter had gotten twelve dogs adopted locally. They had gotten seven more adopted within North Carolina, beyond the Robeson County borders. They had found homes for another fifty-six out of state. And they had transferred another twenty-seven to rescue groups.

That's 102 dogs with new homes in less than three weeks, with three-quarters of the heavy lifting done by the shelter itself as opposed to the rescue groups.[5]

"A lot of our dogs end up in Pennsylvania, New York, and New Jersey, just like Blue," Hatchell told me. "Ideally, the dog is kept either here or in foster for about ten days. He's monitored for behavior. He's neutered. He's vaccinated. And then he's moved in a way that is comfortable and safe, not packed in like sardines. To me, if that's what happens, I'm all for it. Those transports are helping us get more and more dogs out of this county where they really have much less of a chance of being adopted at all."

Baxter is also thankful for the transports that take dogs like Blue to safety, but she knows they are not a panacea for the greater problem that the Robeson shelter continues to face— the same problem that is happening in so many counties like the one where Blue was found.

---

[5] By the end of that month, Robeson County had found homes for a total of 185 dogs.

"What I'm worried about now is that, while we're definitely doing more adoptions than this shelter ever did before, there's no longer this big emergency because people think all the animals are being tortured and have to be gotten out by any means," she says. "I want to see local people coming in to adopt these dogs. I want to see local people getting their dogs spayed and neutered. The truth is, as much as I love these rescue groups, it's just a Band-Aid. Eventually, New Jersey isn't going to need any more dogs."

As I drove away from Robeson County and thought about my home state, I stopped to grab a sandwich and call my parents, who were graciously dog-sitting for Blue. In our family, dogs are treated far differently from all the ones I'd seen in North Carolina. They don't stay in kennels, ever. They are treated like children, given room and board at a relative's house, and spoiled rotten by whichever grandma or aunt is in charge of their care. When I travel for work during times of the year when my husband is also working long hours at his job, Blue always stays with my retired parents and their Doberman pinscher, Quincy, who is one of Blue's best friends. My parents love Blue like a grandchild, and he plays every day with Quincy in their big, fenced backyard until he passes out in exhaustion on my mom's lap.

Quincy is a great dog, but, unlike Blue, he is a hand-chosen purebred who holds many American Kennel Club ribbons and the distinction of being a champion. He has been pranced around countless rings by the same handlers who appear every year on television during the famous Westminster Kennel Club dog show in New York City. While Blue was once considered worthless and, ultimately, deemed worthy of a $400 adoption fee, Quincy cost four figures at the outset and has had thousands more invested in establishing the awesomeness of his pedigree.

I always find this to be an interesting disparity when the two of them are wrestling or cuddling or chewing bones side by side, behaving in exactly the same way. I like to say snarky things to my dad like, "Money doesn't grow on trees," recalling the days when I was a teenager who absolutely, positively had to have the name-brand designer jeans that he thought were a waste of hard-earned cash. Marketing, I argue today, is a powerful force. Somebody has convinced them that one of these two wonderful dogs is far more valuable than the other, only because he comes with a well-known label.

My mom always argues that purebreds are indeed special because responsible breeders like the one who created Quincy are attempting to perfect the standard of each breed. She says that not everybody is breeding dogs purely for profit and dumping the runts of the litter off at shelters to be killed in gas chambers. "Our breeder has people lined up to buy puppies before she even breeds them," Mom always says. "That's responsible. She is making sure those dogs have homes."

I used to see the logic in that reasoning, especially because I love Quincy so much, just as I've loved all the purebred dogs my parents have brought into our family over the years. But after I visited Person and Robeson counties, after I walked through the kennels and saw cage after cage of beautiful, healthy puppies like Blue who were lined up to be killed, after I realized that people were buying purebreds as everyday pets for a thousand dollars or more instead of saving these dogs for a couple hundred bucks—something inside of me changed. It was hard for me to think about what was happening to these dogs like Blue as anything other than immoral. I had spent the past few days looking at the faces of some of the estimated 14,000 companion animals a day who die inside America's shelters. These puppies had licked my hand. Their tiny little eyes had looked with wonder into mine. And they would all be dead before I got back to New Jersey, for a simple lack of homes, while more and more puppies continue to get bred and sold at higher prices.

I could no longer see the intentional breeding of more puppies for sale as pets as acceptable in any way, at least not until the killing in the shelters has stopped.

This was not a topic I was comfortable discussing with my parents, whom I respect a great deal. I know they love their dogs just as much as I love mine. They plan to breed Quincy someday, which is why they refuse to have him neutered. My mom, especially, looks forward to giving one of his puppies a home in exchange for collecting any stud fees of any kind. To her, breeding Quincy isn't about making money. She just thinks he's a great dog, and that more great dogs should come from his genetic line.

I'm never going to change my parents' minds, or the minds of people who share their opinions, but I did decide during my time in North Carolina that maybe I could help to change others. I realized that I could do more than simply having adopted Blue, and I set about helping even more dogs like him.

I started with just two.

More Lucky Pups

~

I had mentally prepared, before I even arrived in North Carolina, to see dogs and puppies who were going to die, dogs and puppies I could not save, dogs and puppies for whom nobody but the Grim Reaper would come. All throughout my journey to trace Blue's past, I'd tried to do what journalists all around the world do every day when they encounter things that are traumatizing. I sucked up my feelings of disgust the way an alcoholic's liver sponges liquid poison. I lay in bed at night trying to think about pretty beaches and smiling faces that are far less likely to induce nightmares. I reminded myself again and again and again that getting to the truth of the hardest chapters is often the only thing that can change the bigger story for the better.

Ultimately, though, there was only so much I'd been able to anticipate or brace myself against. I knew I was going to hate the things I saw inside the high-kill facilities, but it hadn't occurred to me to prepare mentally for the same feeling of powerlessness to hit me after going to Blue's foster home. Some of the things I'd seen at Annie Turner's house, instead of calming my worst fears, had only made the pit in my stomach swell. I kept seeing the desperate eyes of that big brown dog looking up at me from inside the really small crate in Turner's spare bedroom. The dog's face got stuck in my mind like a splinter. It was big enough to crack an entire psyche.

I'd thought more than once during my travels that I should turn the car around and go back for a few of the dogs whose faces had become a looping slide show in my brain. But then I kept telling myself, even out loud sometimes, *Just stick with the plan.*

Jane Zeolla at Lulu's Rescue had educated me in advance about why it was a lousy idea to scoop up whichever dogs I wanted and make a run for the border. She explained that dogs in this area, even if they're in the care of a shelter, are likely to have kennel cough, the parvo virus, heartworm, and other medical issues. The shelters don't typically treat for those conditions. Often, only the rescue groups do. Newly saved shelter dogs require quarantine and care that is expensive up North. They need vaccines and neutering, too, which can be done far cheaper in Person County than it can be done where I live on the outskirts of New York City. I didn't want to get myself into a situation I could not handle, and I most definitely didn't want to expose Blue to any dogs who might have contagious diseases.

"Your best bet," Zeolla had told me, "is to take a few dogs that Rhonda Beach has already pulled from the Person County shelter and gotten ready for adoption. Bring them home to save the cost of transport and serve as a foster home for them while we market them to find permanent homes. That way, Blue won't be exposed to any illnesses, you won't go broke, and you'll be opening up a few spots in the pipeline for new dogs to be pulled from the shelter who can also be prepared for transport and adoption."

And so I did exactly that. I tried to put out of my mind all of the dogs at Turner's house, all of the dogs at the shelters, and all of the dogs who'd barked at me as if begging for a chance. I realized that I couldn't be a hero and save every single one. I accepted the fact that the best I could do was my part, which meant joining the existing pipeline that so many other people had so diligently laid before me.

I made room in my car, and in my life, for two little black dogs named Izzy and Summer. Beach had pulled them from Person County Animal Control, and they'd been living in foster homes in North Carolina while they got spayed and vaccinated. Beach agreed to let me drive them up to New Jersey and take care of them while Lulu's Rescue marketed them for adoption. Their spaces in the North Carolina foster homes would thus become vacant, and two more dogs could be saved from Person County Animal Control.

It's no small thing, accepting two dogs into your life when you've never before met them—especially having learned through Blue's rash and the situation at Turner's home that things are not always what they seem in the world of dog rescue. But during my travels and interviews across North Carolina, I'd learned to trust Beach the same way that legitimate Northern rescues are continually learning to trust legitimate

Southern rescues, and vice versa. Everything Beach had told me had panned out when I'd double-checked it, even when the facts didn't make her look perfect. As with so many things in life, good and smart people seem to find one another and figure out how to best make a difference. Lots of people may have good intentions, but the people actually doing the most good, I'd learned, are the ones like Beach who actually walk into the Southern shelters, get dogs like Blue out, and follow up to make sure they receive appropriate care. That's who I wanted to associate myself with, along with the team from Lulu's Rescue up North. I was happy to help people who had proved to me that they were doing things the way that seemed reasonable and right.

Beach arranged for me to collect Izzy and Summer from her early on a Friday morning at the Carolina's Finest diner in Roxboro. I met her in the front parking lot, and I was pleased to see a woman who fit the mental description I'd conjured. She had long, dark hair and a distinctly businesslike air about her. She shook my hand as if we were meeting in a conference room, and I noticed that she had files for Izzy and Summer ready to hand over along with the dogs themselves.

The first thing we did was take the dogs for a walk on the grass out back. They'd been in separate foster homes and had only just met each other that day, and now they were meeting me for the first time and, unbeknownst to them, about to begin an eight-hour drive north. Beach and I both thought it was a good idea to give them some exercise, some hugs, and some time to simply adjust to their new crowd.

Beach and I chatted a bit while we walked, and I told her what I'd seen and learned during my week in North Carolina. I hemmed and hawed a little when describing what I'd seen at Turner's house, since I didn't want to seem accusatory or out of line. After a few minutes, though, I got the sense that Beach has standards similar to my own when it comes to dog care. I finally asked her flat out if she knew anything about Blue's life at Turner's house a year ago.

"I didn't want to say anything about it because I didn't know you when you first called me," she said, almost apologetically. "But right before I stopped working with her and the Canine Volunteer Rescue and started my own rescue, I saw inside that house. I saw the same thing that you did, and I didn't want to be a part of that at all. It's not what rescue is supposed to be. Now, I may have more dogs than most people at any given time, but I don't have dozens of them. And I keep my house clean. The dogs who are with me get proper medical care, too."

I followed her lead when she mentioned medical care, and I asked her if she knew anything about the bleach that had been applied on Blue's rash.

"Bleach!" she cried, almost gasping to get the word out.

Her eyes bulged from her head like deviled eggs laced with hot sauce. She shook her head, and she sighed.

"Did I ever tell you the story of Blue's transport day?" she asked. "You had offered to adopt him, so we had to get him on the RV. Annie and I were supposed to meet at the Country Kitchen just up the road here. She was going to bring Blue from her house, and I was going to take him with these two other

Labrador puppies to meet the transport in Raleigh at 3:30. She was supposed to be there at two o'clock, but I just sat there, waiting and waiting. Now, Raleigh is a solid hour's drive away, so it got to be 2:25, and I'd called her and everybody else I knew at the Canine Volunteer Rescue, and finally, I decided to leave without Blue. He just wasn't going to make it on time.

"Then out of the corner of my eye, I saw another rescue volunteer come racing into the parking lot with Blue at the last minute," she continued. "That dog was dirty. He hadn't even gotten a bath. I knew his skin looked funny, and I called Annie to say that we could get in real trouble for transporting a sick dog across state lines. She told me he was fine, even though I knew he hadn't looked like that at the shelter when I tagged him for rescue. I trusted her and called the transport people and asked them to wait for me in Raleigh. Luckily, they were running twenty minutes late that day, too, or Blue wouldn't have ever gotten to you at all."

I took a moment to put all the snippets of information together that I'd collected from everyone involved in Blue's early life. He most likely started out being mistreated or abused, which scared him so badly that he cowered in fear when people tried to pet him. Then he was dropped off within steps of the Person County Animal Control gas chamber, placed in one of the cages for non-preferred dogs, and given three days to live without so much as a walk. Beach tagged him for rescue because he somehow, in that horrible situation, found the courage and grace to inch toward her and let her pet him. Turner brought him as a foster to her house, where he likely spent most of his time in a crate when he wasn't having bleach applied to a rash on his tender, puppy skin. At some point he visited the POP-NC mobile clinic and was neutered by Dr. Royce, who recommended follow-up treatment that he failed to receive. Then he nearly missed his RV transport north and ended up arriving in Raleigh sometime around four o'clock in the afternoon, having been neither bathed nor brushed. He got placed in a cage on the RV, whose driver told me that Blue shared the confined space with a dog he didn't know, and that one of them got sick somewhere along the ride. After sitting in that cage with vomit for at least some part of the sixteen and a half hours that it took the RV to drive to New Jersey, Blue found himself being cleaned up by the woman in the RV. Seconds after that, he'd been handed to me.

It is astonishing that Blue was friendly and good-natured at that moment when he first met me. Of course he was a little skittish and fearful. He deserved to be as downright enraged as I was.

I didn't know the life stories of Izzy and Summer as I helped them begin their journeys north, except to say that they were both old enough and big enough, at about twenty-five pounds apiece, that they likely would have ended up in the gas chamber if Beach hadn't pulled them from Person County Animal Control. When I met them at the local diner, they both still had most of the hair missing on their bellies—a telltale sign of a close shave at the POP-NC mobile clinic. Beach took my picture as we loaded them into the travel crates that I'd bought and arranged in my backseat, each one lined with fresh towels and a brand-new chew toy. Then she handed me everything she had for them, including their files, and she prepared to drive away with tears of joy in her eyes. The last thing she said was that she felt confident I would keep Izzy and Summer safe until Lulu's Rescue could help me find them homes up North, just as they had with Blue.

Transporting dogs is a big responsibility—one that not all people involved in rescue take as seriously as they should. I had asked for advice in preparing to bring Izzy and Summer home, and I had heard horror stories about good-intentioned people having horrible accidents because they failed to transport dogs safely. I learned about people who had dogs fight in the backseats of cars, people who accidentally injured dogs by placing too many of them inside cars at once, even one woman who had a loose dog urinate all over the car's steering wheel while she was trying to drive. I'd always let my dogs sit freely in my cars because that's how they seemed the most comfortable, but for Izzy and Summer, I bought the plastic travel crates. I positioned them carefully in the backseat to make sure they were secure—in a way that I thought the dogs would feel better because they could see me and listen to my voice throughout the journey.

Blue didn't have that luxury during his transport in the back of the RV, nor do most dogs who are moved from the South to the North.

I learned a lot about the real conditions that dogs in transport endure from Kyle and Pam Peterson, and Pam's sister, Karen York. I called them to find out how they began moving dogs from the South to the North in 2004, and to ask about everything that they've learned since. They've certainly had enough practice in their company, which is now known as Peterson Express Transport Services. They delivered rescued dog No. 35,000 to a loving home sometime before New Year's Day in 2012.

They started quite a bit like I was starting, by trying to do a good deed for just a couple of dogs. Pam worked for the Tennessee District Attorney's Office in the early 1990s, and her job meant that she was always driving clear across the Volunteer State. She would constantly see stray dogs on the side of the road. She'd bring them to her house and try to find them homes.

When the Internet became popular, she started connecting with other dog lovers, and she realized there was a larger need for transports. She got to talking with Margo McHann of Good Dog Rescue in Memphis, who said she could find the dogs homes in the Northeast if Pam was willing to transport them. Pam and a girlfriend made the first three-day drive up North in about five days because they got so lost. Soon after, McHann called and said she had more dogs with adopters up North, if Pam was willing to go again. She and Kyle made that second trip in his pickup truck. "It was pretty redneck," he told me. "The camper top didn't match the truck, and we had eight dogs inside going up to Boston. But that started the snowball rolling."

Demand grew, so the Petersons rented a van that let them take twenty dogs at a time. This was a major idea, as there were no companies doing transports of rescue dogs on a large, multistate scale. Eventually they bought a bigger truck with a camper top. (That one was swanky—it matched.) Then they bought a small horse trailer that held about forty dogs. Demand rose again. They got a second horse trailer that could hold sixty dogs. Then they got another one of those to double their capacity. Their operation grew into what it is today: able to move nearly two hundred dogs in a single day.

The Petersons quickly realized that while the idea of moving rescued dogs was good, the way it was being done was sometimes bad. They were hearing all of those stories that I'd also heard when researching how best to transport Izzy and Summer—only they were hearing terrible versions that involved people trying to move far more than a couple of dogs at a time.

"When we first started out," Kyle recalls, "I called the U.S. Department of Agriculture to get licensed. It took them a month to figure out how to even classify us. We realized right away that you could follow all of the rules out there, and you still would not be working in the best interest of the dogs. There was nothing that said the dogs even had to be walked or given constant access to water or be in a climate-controlled space. So we not only became the first rescue transport to get certified by the USDA, but we also became the first to impose our own rules on the rescuers who wanted the dogs moved. We tried to pioneer the industry while we were flying by the seat of our pants."

One of the unsettling things the Petersons noticed was that a lot of dogs were being transported straight from the shelters in the South to the foster homes or adopters like me up North, taken straight from the cages without getting the kinds of basic shots and sterilizations that Blue, Izzy, and Summer had all received. The Petersons quickly realized that was a health problem—not just with dogs like Blue suspected of having communicable rashes like ringworm, but also with everything from the parvo virus to mange. They now refuse to transport any dog who has not been out of a shelter and with a rescue for at least two weeks. They find that's enough time for the dogs to get all their vaccines, as well as for the dogs to have settled down from the shelter experience so that they're not stressed out when they go into the transport, which can be stressful enough to make even a healthy dog sick.

"We also don't transport any dog unless it's spayed or neutered," Kyle told me. "That's another one of our own rules. We don't want to be in the business of transporting the dog overpopulation problem. We want to be in the business of helping to end the dog overpopulation problem."

While it never occurred to me that driving Izzy and Summer across multiple state lines might put me in violation of any laws, the Petersons are now spending a fair amount of time worrying about that very issue. They are beginning to see some lawmakers creating barriers that make it harder to transport rescue dogs. Lawmakers in the North are trying to make sense of the sea change that is occurring with shelter dogs, and they have some serious concerns, including the transport of disease.

Behind those legitimate concerns that lawmakers have, though, are substantial lobbying dollars for breeders and pet stores.

"There are a lot of people doing it wrong," Kyle told me. "They'll move dogs in a van without health certificates, park in a Walmart parking lot, and just start selling dogs out of the van without any rabies shots, spay/neuter surgeries, nothing. The ones they can't sell, they dump in the local shelters. So you're spreading problems and disease, and the Northern states are right to try to stop that. But we also are now seeing something else in states like Connecticut, which just passed a law that was sponsored and written by a breeders' association. They feel they are not selling as many purebred dogs because people in the North are starting to adopt more mutts. The pet stores and the breeders feel the rescue groups are eclipsing them in, well, sales. So they are taking their lobbyists and money into the government to get these laws passed that have only to do with rescues. The one that just passed in Connecticut has a pet-store exemption. It's that blatant."

I looked up Connecticut House Bill 5368, and Kyle's description was surprisingly accurate. The law clearly outlines how anyone who transports a dog into the state must register with the state Department of Agriculture, have each dog examined by a state-licensed veterinarian, and notify local zoning officials before offering the dog for sale, adoption, or transfer—unless the dog is being delivered to a pet shop to be sold.

That seemed like a ridiculous exemption to me, plus an awful lot of requirements for somebody like me, who wanted to take two dogs named Izzy and Summer to my own home while a rescue group found them permanent adopters. It seemed incredible to me, the lengths to which special interests will go to ensure that dogs like Blue remain mired in places where they have a 5-percent chance of survival, to protect the ability to make money off the lives of other dogs and animals.

"What is sad about laws like these is that it will do nothing more than stop some rescue groups from using proper transports," Kyle says. "They'll just sneak the dogs in to the families that are willing to save them. They want to save these dogs, so they load them up and drive them wherever."

That's exactly what I did with Izzy and Summer. I didn't think for a moment that I might be doing something wrong. I just thought they were really nice dogs who didn't deserve to be asphyxiated in a gas chamber, and I wanted to help them the same way that other people had so generously helped to save Blue.

Izzy, I learned by reading her paperwork, was about six months old. I could immediately tell that she was as playful as any puppy I'd ever known. She was listed as a flat-coated retriever mix, and she had adorably fuzzy hairs sticking up all around her face, as if she'd just rolled around on a carpet and jumped up fluttering with static cling. She looked healthy and had a super-shiny coat, and she came right to me with her tail wagging. Her foster mom in North Carolina had loved her so much that she sent a bag full of treats and toys and food, as well as a long note that instructed me to contact her if the northbound transport didn't work out. The only reason she'd given Izzy up is that the dog needed a big fenced yard for running, and while she didn't have one, I did. Under no circumstances did she want sweet Izzy ending up back in a shelter. She would drive the hundreds of miles herself to come and collect Izzy if necessary, she promised.

Summer, on the other hand, arrived in my care with as little paperwork and history as Blue. She was listed for adoption as a petite black Labrador, which I suppose is rescue-speak for "cute little black dog we have no idea what else to call." She was probably at least a year or two old and was sadly skinny, so much so that I thought she may have recently been left tied to a tree and starved. Later, I'd learn that she was more likely a stray, one who had arrived at the shelter with a litter of four puppies. They had all been adopted after suckling her weight right out of her, and she'd been left to die. Summer was confused about eating food out of a bowl at first, but she would sit beautifully on command and gulp treats from my hand like a well-practiced beggar. She mostly just wanted to sit in a way where she was constantly touching me, which seemed to make her feel safe.

I put Izzy in the crate behind my driver's seat and Summer in the crate behind the passenger seat. As I drove north toward Interstate 95, I had a box of dog treats up front with me. Every twenty minutes or so, I would slip one treat apiece through each of the crate bars, to make the dogs feel safer during the first part of the drive. I kept the volume on the radio low. I made a point of talking to Izzy and Summer in a calm, soothing voice.

Izzy seemed just fine and lay down in her crate to take a nap, but I soon smelled that something was amiss in Summer's crate. At first I thought it was nervous gas, but then the stench got so bad that I had to roll down all of the windows. I pulled off the highway at the first possible chance so that I could stop the car and see what was wrong.

In the gas-station parking lot, I opened Summer's crate. She had gotten so scared that she urinated and defecated everywhere. She hadn't just soiled the towels on the bottom; the crate looked like a filthy monkey cage at the zoo. There was poop all over the crate walls, somehow on the crate ceiling, and even on Summer herself.

It was at that moment that I realized I'd thought ahead to bring dog treats, bottled water, and a few extra clean towels, but not to bring any cleaning supplies or dog shampoo. I had

thought that one of the dogs might vomit, but I hadn't anticipated having to wipe poop off the plastic crate's walls or give
either of the dogs a bath on the side of the road.

Since I was alone in the gas-station parking lot with Izzy and
Summer, now both out of the crates and on their leashes, I had
to rely on the goodwill of a stranger to help. I explained my situation to a woman who was walking inside the station's convenience store to buy a soda, handed her a twenty-dollar bill, and
asked her to please bring back any cleaning supplies she could
find. She could have easily pocketed the money and snuck out of
town without me noticing, but she kindly returned with paper
towels and spray cleaner—and she brought a few extra people in
tow. All of the people petted Summer and Izzy while I cleaned
out the cage, and two of them asked me where they could look
online for adoption information about dogs like Summer and
Izzy in their own areas.

"You're doing such a great thing," the woman said as she
handed me my change and the cashier's receipt. "These seem
like terrific dogs. I'd take one myself if I didn't already have my
own at home."

The crate came clean easily with the spray and paper towels,
and Summer, well, she also ended up smelling lemony fresh. I
had to wipe the poop off her fur with the paper towels after
giving them a small squirt of the stuff, since I didn't have dog
shampoo or a bathtub in the backseat. I took both dogs for a
walk on the grass next to the gas station before returning them
to the crates, and I sat down for a minute to collect my thoughts
before beginning the rest of the drive home.

That's when I realized that Summer was shaking. She was like Blue had been, submissive and terrified. She struck me as the kind of dog who, like him, would have cowered in the back of her cage at the shelter. She, too, was most likely from the long row of cages, the ones for the non-preferable dogs. She could have just as similarly ended up being transported in the back of a dark RV where nobody talked to her or took her out for a walk. She could have easily been forced to ride the whole way covered in her own filth, just as Blue had been forced to ride next to a pile of vomit.

Instead, she was now sitting in my lap on the grass next to the rest stop, burying her eyes and nose in my armpit. I stroked her black fur and told her everything was going to be all right. I wished somebody had done the same for Blue when he'd been so afraid.

Dogs like Summer and Blue who seem to be further traumatized by transport are the reason some rescuers now forgo long-distance ground transports altogether. Instead, they work with groups like Pilots N Paws, a charity that provides private planes for rescue dogs. This is the organization I'd first heard about at my kitchen table as a possibility for moving Blue up to New Jersey. At the time, I'd thought the woman telling me about it was insane. Now I understood exactly why such a service is invaluable.

When I spoke with Debi Boies, who cofounded Pilots N Paws, she told me that the idea stemmed from the death of her twelve-year-old Doberman. She looked into dogs needing rescue, just as I had, and decided to adopt a Dobie from Florida into her South Carolina home. She asked everyone she knew for help driving the dog north, and a friend named Jon Wehrenberg offered to go her one better. He's a pilot from Knoxville, Tennessee, and he said he would skip the driving altogether and pick up the dog in his plane.

The experience left Wehrenberg wondering whether dogs needed long-range transports on a regular basis. He and Boies conceived Pilots N Paws that same day. They started small, with Wehrenberg's sixteen-year-old son building their first website. Soon after that, *USA Today* took notice. Two days before Thanksgiving in 2008, the newspaper published an article about what Pilots N Paws was trying to do. And then, Boies said, every news organization in America called. The carmaker Subaru offered to become a financial sponsor. The company Petmate offered to donate supplies. Today, about 2,000 registered pilots are among the 9,500 people who regularly use the Pilots N Paws online forum to arrange transports of dogs just like Blue, Izzy, and Summer.

"Contrary to what some people believe, these pilots are not always wealthy people," Boies told me. "Most of our pilots are hard-working people with daily jobs that run the gamut from airport workers to heads of corporations. They own small planes, and they love to fly as a hobby. Since they do this out of their own pockets, Jon and I pursued 501(c)(3) charity status, which means they can now be eligible for some tax benefits as humanitarians. But I'll tell you, they'd do it even without that. These pilots are so committed. We had one pilot who couldn't fly because of weather, so he rented an RV and drove the dogs himself. We have another pilot, one single pilot who has been with us for less than a year, and he alone is already approaching his thousandth dog moved. He had 'Pilots N Paws' painted on the side of his plane, and a big picture of a beagle painted on its tail. I have no clue how many dogs we've moved overall, but I would not be surprised if it's in the tens of thousands by now."

I'm sure that Summer would have preferred the two-hour flight in the back of a private plane to the eight-hour drive in the back of my car, just as Blue's stomach would have been better off without the sixteen-and-a-half-hour drive in an RV. Heck, if Blue had been flown to New Jersey in just a few short hours instead of spending so much time in that RV, he might have avoided feeling scared in the car for all of his young life. He'd vomited a few times after first coming home, during random drives we took together, and I'd chalked the incidents up to his still-settling nerves or the fact that he didn't yet understand what cars were. But Blue's carsickness was becoming more commonplace the longer he was with me. He seemed to have some kind of a deeper fear. I couldn't help but wonder if it had something to do with that long, bumpy drive in the RV.

I thought about how much better Izzy and Summer had things as I drove them up Interstate 95, along the same route that had carried Blue. It was just the three of us. They heard my voice talking to them the whole time. If the bang of a loud truck or the hum of being inside a tunnel pierced our calm, I let them know that everything was all right.

Indeed, I told them, everything was finally going to be all right for the rest of their lives.

And I hoped it was true, since nobody had actually applied to adopt them yet.

Loving, and Letting Go

～

My niece Kate Deurr is one of the people who helped to convince me that I could handle the responsibility of fostering two dogs. She and my nephew live in a modest home in Wall Township, New Jersey, where, from morning till night, she looks over two energy-packed pre-teen daughters, an autistic son, and, for the past few months, two foster babies. In her spare time, which she somehow finds tucked away in the deep recesses of her ever-giving soul, Kate opens her home to dogs who are being rescued by Canines in Need of Ocean Township. It's a group like the one that saved Blue—a team of volunteers who work with people in the South to move dogs up North and put them into foster care until permanent homes can be found.

On the day I called her to tell her what I was preparing to do, I expected to hear kids screaming and babies crying and dogs barking in the background—the kind of mutinous cacophony that most people only need imagine once before deciding that fostering a homeless dog is simply too much of a hassle. Instead, though, we enjoyed a quiet half hour conversation. She told me the foster dogs were no problem at all. They are, to her mind, just one more blessing in her day-to-day life. Like Blue, most of them arrive from North Carolina.

She has lost count of how many dogs she has fostered, but she thinks it's in the neighborhood of fifty or sixty during the past five years. Most of the dogs come through her home like transient borders, just needing a warm bed for a few days or a couple of weeks, but a few have left lasting impressions on her entire family. There was Wyatt the Labradoodle, for one. "He was such a beautiful boy," she says. "I got e-mails from as far away as Canada from people willing to drive to New Jersey to take him." There was also Willie the Terrier. "He was a pee-er," she told me. "He couldn't hold it and wait to go out. I had him right around Easter, and my whole house smelled like pee." With her encouragement, Willie was adopted by a family whose house had a doggy door that he could use at any time. He not only stopped wrecking the carpets, but he also went on to become a therapy dog and remains a beloved family member today.

Kate seemed to know her own foster dogs the way I was getting to know Izzy and Summer after spending just a few hours with them in my car—not just as numbers moving through a system, but as individuals with distinct personalities and needs.

This is key to the adoption process. The better the fosters get to know the dogs, the better the rescuers can match them with homes where they are likely to fit in and remain happy forever.

I decided to learn as much as possible about Izzy and Summer so that I could give Lulu's Rescue some great nuggets to include in their online profiles. I figured if my niece Kate could do it with all of her other obligations, I could sure as heck do it without any kids or other responsibilities of my own besides my work. I really had no excuse except to try. I frankly felt a little guilty for never having tried before.

My biggest worry at first was making sure that both Izzy and Summer got along with Blue. Adding two dogs to any household with another dog can be a challenge, and if Stella had still been living with me at the time, too, I don't think I'd have even attempted it. She had a history of showing aggression toward female dogs in particular, and Izzy and Summer both likely would have ended up in a dogfight with her at one point or another.

But Stella, my wonderful alpha menace, was no longer a part of our lives by the time I returned from North Carolina.

A few months before I drove down South to trace Blue's history, I caught my husband in what turned out to be an affair that can only be described as calculated, sinister, and cruel. Everything about our lives had seemed wonderful, from our home and careers to our beautiful dogs, right until the moment I saw the text messages on his BlackBerry. About an hour earlier, he'd been telling me how much he loved and appreciated me. And then, suddenly, I was horrified to be looking at similar words having been sent to somebody else. He admitted that he was in love with two women, and that the other one, he'd met before he and I even began dating nearly thirteen years earlier. I'd soon learn that she is a married mother of four. They'd been sleeping together since before he and I were married. Her phone number traced to a location about twenty minutes from his dream job that had brought us to New Jersey in the first place.

I threw him out that night, and he left without argument—as if he'd been waiting for years for the very moment to come. I still remember the way Blue and Stella looked, huddled together on the sofa well after midnight, staring at me with wide eyes as I screamed and cried and dragged the garbage bags full of his clothes across the house and into the garage. I never saw him again except for the day just ten weeks later that we went before the judge to get divorced. While he did send me a single, apologetic e-mail of precisely eight sentences, he never once uttered the words "I'm sorry" or even attempted to reconcile. He fled from our life like a con artist, literally reaching for his coat before I could even ask what had happened. With the exception of his car, he didn't ask to keep a single possession we had collected during more than a decade together. Blue, who had loved him the way any puppy loves his new daddy, who had snuggled with him on the sofa and played with him in the yard, wasn't any more of a consideration in my husband's mind than I was as I lay weeping in our bed, cursing the tainted sheets.

Stella, though, for some reason was different. Not only did he want her, but everyone offering me emotional support reminded me that she had always shared a more special bond with him than she had allowed with me. She had spent far more time with me, since I work from home and walked her just about every day, but she'd always listened better to him. Blue was clearly my dog, just as Floyd had been. But Stella, if I was being honest, was his.

I last saw Stella on a sunny winter's day when I left her in the care of our veterinary surgeon. She recognized Stella immediately; hers were the talented hands that had saved Stella's life during the great Gorilla Glue-eating incident of 2006, which coated Stella's stomach and intestines in the nasty, sticky stuff. This time, Stella had torn her knee ligament by making an Evel Knievel-esque leap off the back deck's stairs. She needed expensive reconstructive surgery just a week after I discovered my husband's secret other life and paid a large retainer to a lawyer. I'd gotten the X-rays and the bad news late at night while sitting by Stella's side and petting her on the cold floor of the emergency clinic where we'd put Floyd to sleep earlier in the year. It was the same room where I'd held him in my arms as he took his last breath.

Between Floyd's recent death, the shocking discovery of my husband's affair, Blue's erratic sleep schedule as a puppy, and my own new battles with the symptoms of depression, my psyche quickly became the equivalent of a mass-murder scene. I thought about how difficult it was going to be to keep Stella calm and contained while her knee healed. I reluctantly accepted that that there is only so much any single human being can bear. I offered to pay four figures toward Stella's knee surgery so that she would be able to have it, I packed up her food and favorite things, and I agreed to let him collect her at the vet's office and take her to his new home to heal, and then to live. I blubbered like a desperate parent in a hospital waiting room as the veterinary technician took Stella away. After the vet tech handed Stella's leash to me, with her no longer attached, I walked outside to my car, placed Blue gently on my lap, and wept uncontrollably into his soft puppy fur.

Bringing Izzy and Summer home as foster dogs obviously could not quench the loss that I felt for Stella and everything else that had vanished so horribly from my life, but the extra puppy love in the house sure helped me to smile at a time when it seemed all but impossible. During the first few months after my divorce, when loyalty and trust seemed like figments of an imaginary life, these foster dogs gave me both, immediately and completely. They did what dogs do best in times of sadness—snuggled by my side, encouraged me to get out into the fresh air for walks at the park, and licked away any tears that streamed down my cheeks. My bond with Blue grew even stronger, too, as I made sure he knew that while Izzy and Summer were our houseguests, he was my number one priority in the whole world. I couldn't help but smile when I saw how much he loved playing with them the way he used to play with Stella all day long. The activity helped the house to feel somehow, blessedly, happy and full.

And as much as I missed my little maniac, as much as I tried to convince myself that giving Stella up had been the right thing when it further cracked the already broken shards of my heart, I soon came to realize that perhaps the universe had a plan when it brought the two of us together for just a few years. Maybe she was always meant to be my husband's dog, and I was destined instead to reap the benefits of the years spent working with her on good behavior—so that I could put everything I'd learned toward helping Izzy, Summer, and lots more foster dogs like them.

Unlike many first-time fosterers, I had every puppy supply that I could possibly need thanks to Stella's early days of nonstop training challenges. Small crates, big crates, squeaky toys, plastic puzzles, regular bones, plastic bones, movable gates, regular leashes, training leashes, flexi-leashes, tennis balls, hard plastic balls—I'm pretty sure I looked like Santa Claus to Izzy and Summer as I took out what remained in my neatly packed doggy toy bin and dumped it across the floor to let them pick through the goods and figure out what they liked. Once I got a sense of their preferences (Izzy likes things that squeak, while Summer likes puzzles filled with treats), I started putting their favorite toys into large, open crates. Neither of them had been crate trained, and Izzy's foster mom from North Carolina had actually written to me that Izzy hated confined spaces. But I knew that to get them good homes, adopters would want to see some crate training. Their favorite toys became lures, along with bones filled with peanut butter, and by the end of day two, both Izzy and Summer were going happily into their crates to play with their favorite toys and take naps. After an hour or two, when they woke up, I'd let them out into the yard with Blue and the play routine would begin anew. By the third day, Izzy and Summer would go into their open crates to hang out and relax, without my even asking.

Blue, Izzy, and Summer formed a happy pack inside of about three days. They didn't so much walk into the yard as they galloped across the deck and then hurled themselves gleefully onto the grass, as if they were swimmers launching from diving boards into the deep end of a pool. Then the racing would begin, with one of them running along the fence line and the other two trying to give chase. In this game, Blue didn't have the added bonus of the other dogs wearing electric-fence collars, but he also didn't need it. Izzy and Summer are pretty fast, but Blue knows the home turf, and he can corner like he's on rails.

The threesome would do this at least five times a day, in between the times they spent playing with toys in my den. The tennis balls and chew toys were high on their Top Five lists, but the braided ropes usually ended up being the ultimate fan favorite. Blue grabbed the rope in the middle, Izzy grabbed one end of it, and Summer grabbed the other end. The three of them jerked all over the house in hilarious unison, like a bunch of kids trying to navigate the three-legged race at an elementary school's field day.

Izzy had precisely two accidents in my house, both of them on the first day when she followed me upstairs and couldn't figure out how to get back down before I realized she needed to go out. Summer had zero accidents the entire time she lived with me. By their third morning in my house, they were letting themselves out the doggy door just like Blue. Feeding time, too, brought far less drama than I'd envisioned. It took me a few tries to get Summer to eat from a bowl, but once I figured out that she preferred canned dog food to dry, I'd load up her bowl with a can of beef or chicken stew and watch her wag her tail the entire time she chewed. Blue usually finished his food first, followed by Izzy, and then Summer last, as if she were savoring every last bite. After each dog finished eating, I told them to sit in their respective corners of the kitchen. Blue did so beautifully, as did Izzy. They both watched and waited patiently until Summer was done and the three of them were all allowed to go back outside to play.

During their first few days with me, I e-mailed new photos of Izzy and Summer to Lulu's Rescue. These pictures showed the dogs playing happily in my backyard, to replace the ones from North Carolina that showed them in the shelter environment. They looked far happier in the new photos, even healthier, and certainly more adoptable. Lulu's put my photos on their website and on the Petfinder section where I'd originally found Blue, and I put them on my personal blog and Facebook page. The entire effort took me about thirty minutes. I also searched on-line for dog bandanas that say "Adopt Me." I figured that once they came in the mail, I could put them around Izzy's and Summer's necks and take the dogs for walks around our local parks. I started scoping out the local soccer and field hockey practices so I'd be able to give the dogs the most public visibility with the families in town.

By Day Five, before the bandanas even arrived—and less than a month after Izzy and Summer had been pulled from death row at Person County Animal Control—no fewer than four families in New Jersey and Pennsylvania had already come forward with interest in adopting them both. Lulu's Rescue wasn't struggling to find good homes; instead, they were deciding which adopters were the best.

And Summer, who was older and less "perfect" than Izzy because, like Blue, she'd learned to be a bit afraid in life, actually generated the most interest first. At the end of Summer's journey from the long row of cages for non-preferable dogs, she had people standing in line and hoping they would be the lucky ones who got to give her a loving home.

I couldn't contain my excitement, so I picked up the phone to call my sister, Michelle. She had, several years ago, fostered a dog who ended up taking the better part of a year to find a home. Our whole family had assumed I'd be stuck with Izzy and Summer for several months at least.

My, how things have changed, I told her. The Internet really does seem to make the entire process a lot easier nowadays.

"Not just that," my sister told me. "You'll never believe what I saw today when I took Sadie May to the vet. I walked into the waiting room, and there were these cute puppies available for adoption. It turns out my vet is doing the same thing you're doing, taking the dogs from the shelters down South and helping to find them homes up here in the North. I couldn't believe it when she told me. You really need to drive out and see this."

So it was that I found myself going to meet Dr. Corrine Thomas at Aardvark Animal Hospital in Exton, Pennsylvania. I'd heard a lot of things about saving foster dogs during my travels to trace Blue's story, but this was the first time I'd heard of a veterinarian getting involved with the cause. That she happened to be my sister's veterinarian, I must say, made it seem like the cosmos wanted me to go see what she was doing, too.

Persistence and Hope

~~

It all began, Dr. Thomas told me, just a handful of years ago. Although she is currently happy and thriving in her own veterinary practice, she started out in schools and at other practices absolutely hating what she was being told. She had this idea, this fantastic idea, and everyone in a position of authority shot it down. For the life of her, she couldn't understand why. To her, it seemed like an absolute no-brainer.

"I always wanted to have an animal rescue that is run through a veterinary hospital," she told me. "I really didn't see why it would be a problem. They kept telling me that it flies in the face of the business model. They'd go so far as to tell me not to get to know the clients too well, because then you spend too much time talking with each one. The more time with one client, the fewer clients there are to charge. And time rescuing animals? Well, that's just a big drain on everything."

On the day that I walked into her practice, Aardvark Animal Hospital was preparing to celebrate its first full year in business. Her lobby had already evolved into about 15 percent waiting room and 85 percent menagerie—a combination foster space and display area for animals in need of homes. While most other veterinarians think of their entranceways as places where humans and animals await appointments, Thomas, quite fittingly, calls hers a petting zoo. Among the guinea pigs and chinchillas and cats and adult dogs, I saw a large, open pen on the floor where three puppies romped with glee. One was jet black with almond-shaped eyes, perhaps a mix of a Labrador and a pit bull. Another looked like a Beagle mix. The white and tan dog, I couldn't place; he's what my own veterinarian would call a Heinz 57. And he sure did have gorgeous coloring, including a proud brown spot about the size of a silver dollar on his forehead, which was otherwise nearly pure white.

"They're from North Carolina," Thomas told me as her tall, athletic frame towered high above the puppies' heads. "And actually, the black one and the one with the brown spot have already been adopted. The Beagle mix is the only one we're still trying to place."

Thomas began using her office as a foster and rescue location for dogs just two months after she opened for business. She put the word out to local rescue groups in eastern Pennsylvania that she was willing to do discounted spaying and neutering, and that she had a vision of doing more. She became involved with interstate transports when one of her local rescue partners told her about a Labrador who had just given birth to three puppies in Gaston County, North Carolina. The Pennsylvania rescuer was trying to do everything possible to save them from the Gaston County gas chamber. At most, the rescuer told Thomas, this Labrador and her pups had forty-eight hours to live.

With Thomas's blessing, two of her veterinary technicians, Randi Warfel and Paige Lukas, hopped into a car. They began the same day-long journey along Interstate 95 that I'd made to North Carolina. At the same time, a woman working in the Gaston County shelter took the Labradors to her own home, to keep them safe until the help from Pennsylvania could arrive. Warfel and Lukas collected the dogs, turned their car around, and drove through the night back home. The sun was rising when they returned, so they clocked in to start working that same morning.

"That was how we started with the Southern dogs," Thomas says. "The rescues, they're not really set up to take a mom and newborn puppies. The rescues are trying to move as many dogs as they can, as fast as they can, and a mom and newborn puppies need time. They need weeks of time and veterinary care before they can be adopted. We were in a situation where we could give them that time and care."

Since Aardvark Animal Hospital is not licensed as a kennel, Thomas kept the Labradors in her lobby by day—when potential adopters could see them and play with them—and took them to her home at night. All of the dogs, including the mom, found adopters, and Thomas began earning a reputation among local rescues as an ideal foster candidate for newborn puppies and their mothers. She made sure they had all their shots, took them home to give them even more human companionship each night, and spayed or neutered them before adopting them out. Then she repeated the process again and again, whenever space opened up for new dogs in her lobby. She started working with the kinds of ground-transport operations that moved Blue from North Carolina to New Jersey. She pays the transport fee and donates any required medical care, then adopts the dogs out of her lobby at a rate of $300 per puppy and $150 per adult dog. She advertises the pups on an electronic billboard above a local highway, believing that the idea "We Have Puppies Available" is a much stronger marketing hook than "We're a New Veterinary Office in Town."

In her first nine months of following this approach, Thomas found homes for more than one hundred dogs just like Blue from the South—and about 70 percent of the Pennsylvanians who adopted them became clients of her veterinary practice.

"We really do lose money on every dog," Thomas told me, "but we feel passionate about rescuing dogs and doing our part. I think the people who stay with us after adopting through us, they see that what we're doing speaks to our character. We love animals. We love *their* animals. There is a financial strain, yes, especially when we bring up a puppy that's sick and needs a lot of extra time and care. But my feeling is that ultimately, we are doing the right thing morally. And I may lose money on saving these dogs at first, but I'm going to gain a client that I will work to keep forever. We haven't been at this long enough to document the financials, but I believe that in the long run, the money will work out. I think it's a real win-win."

All of this, to me, was just starting to seem way too good to be true. Izzy and Summer had received adoption applications awfully fast. My sister's veterinarian seemed like a poster child for rescue who had dropped out of the clear blue sky.

If fostering and finding homes really is this easy, I thought, *then why isn't everybody doing it?* The question led me to start a search for somebody who had a challenging case—a dog with problems who would seem far less likely than Blue or Izzy or Summer to ever find a home, a dog who could not be advertised as healthy, a dog who had endured serious trauma. I also looked for a dog in the care of a first-time foster parent who might get stuck with far more than he anticipated, for far longer than he wanted.

I found a man named Eric Kleman and a foster dog named Hope.

Kleman's first foster experience was with a dog who, in most animal-control facilities, would never stand a chance. As he told me by telephone, Kleman is a Pennsylvania native who moved to Charlotte, North Carolina, a few years ago, long after he realized that helping shelter dogs was as much a part of him as having toenails and eyelashes. When he was a college student in Lancaster, Pennsylvania, he would spend his weekends at the local humane society making sure the dogs there knew that somebody cared about them. He realized that he wasn't supposed to feed them, but he couldn't help bringing a box of bones along with him during every visit. By the time he left each weekend, the box would be empty and his soul would feel a little fuller.

He'd already bought his first chocolate Labrador from a store by that time, and though he loved her, he quickly learned enough to know that he would never buy another dog from a store again. His next three Labradors were all rescues, and he kept his eye on the Internet for postings about Labradors who had been found by rescue organizations.

On December 7, 2010, he saw a posting from Lulu's Rescue on Facebook. The title was "Hope: A Christmas Miracle." The photo showed a yellow Labrador mix, obviously still very much a puppy, with what looked like a white cast around her front left leg.

Below the photograph, Lulu's had written: "This beautiful, sweet girl was discovered when a good Samaritan called the police to say a trash bag was moving on the side of the road. Hope was double-bagged and thrown out of a moving car, sustaining multiple injuries including a leg broken in two places, a dislocated hip, both jaws broken in three places, and broken teeth. The vet has found that many of her injuries, including one of the jaw breaks, are not recent and this girl has been enduring pain and suffering before she was thrown out of the car. Despite all of this trauma in her short ten months of life, everyone who meets her is astounded by her sweetness and her ability to be open and trusting. Hope's recovery will be extensive and costly: She needs surgery on her jaws to realign them, teeth removed, and bones set. Will you help Lulu's Rescue show this sweet girl that many do care about her, love her, and want to help her on the journey to a new life? We can't think of a better gift than that of a loving forever home and family providing her unconditional love and affection. Do you believe in miracles?"

The Christmas spirit had nothing to do with Kleman's reaction. It might as well have been Memorial Day. He would have felt the same.

"I had an instant belief that I had to help that dog," Kleman told me. "I sent that story to everybody I know, and I donated to the chip-in fund, which raised more than $2,000 in forty-eight hours. Then I wrote to Lulu's and asked how I could do more to help."

Kleman would soon learn that Hope's injuries were even more extensive than the Facebook post indicated. She had burn marks the size and shape of cigarettes on her face and body. X-rays showed further, unmistakable signs of previous abuse, including that her jaw had once been broken completely. For the handful of months that she had been alive, when she weighed no more than twenty or thirty pounds, the puppy had been beaten and tortured mercilessly, and nearly to death.

Given the extent of Hope's injuries, the shelter had deemed her unadoptable and put her on the list to be killed within a few days. This, despite the fact that the puppy, so brutally treated by humans, still showed nothing but love and affection toward the ones she now met.

"The initial vet who treated her said he'd never met another dog like her in his entire career," Kleman told me. "She was obviously in a tremendous amount of pain. Her broken leg was literally hanging off her body. She allowed him to set her leg. She just stared at him and let it happen. He said it was like she knew that he was helping her. Her pain threshold was unbelievable. You would expect a dog who had been through all that to cower in fear, but she never did. Not once. She was really unique."

Kleman lives in a condominium with his fiancée and three-year-old chocolate Labrador, Hudson. After talking it over,

Kleman and his fiancée decided to bring Hope home to recover with Hudson by her side. Like me, they'd never fostered before, but Hudson was like Blue and got along well with other dogs, and something about Hope's story made them feel that they were just plain meant to become a part of it.

"Everybody I knew all said the same thing—we wanted five minutes in a room with whoever had done this to her," Kleman recalls. "But then we got to know Hope, and the anger went away. She had the saddest looking eyes. Her jaw was broken in three places. But on her very first day with us, she started to eat hard food again. She just started eating Hudson's food. The veterinarians decided not to reconstruct her jaw at all because she wasn't experiencing pain, and she was healing fine on her own. She was just amazing."

Hope ended up staying with Kleman for nearly three months—far longer than Izzy and Summer would live with Blue and me. She got stronger and stronger each week, and she refused to deny her own spirited puppy instincts, once even leaping from a bed and snapping her leg splint so badly that Kleman had to get her a new one. Each night, Hope slept in bed between Kleman and his fiancée. She was almost always in the same position, curled tightly into a ball.

By March 2011, Kleman knew that Hope was well enough to be adopted into a permanent home. But by then, he and his fiancée had fallen desperately in love with her.

It's one of the biggest problems that rescue groups face with new foster parents. A lot of them end up wanting to keep the dogs, making fewer foster homes available overall. It happened to me, actually, with Summer. She was so skittish and loving like Blue, I instinctively wanted to protect her myself for the rest of her life instead of trusting her care to somebody else.

Kleman and his fiancée talked about keeping Hope, but they ultimately decided she would be better off with another family. While Hudson likes to exercise by swimming in the lake near Kleman's condominium, Hope seemed to need a backyard. "When she finally got the cast off and we took her to the local parks, we saw that she loves to run," he says. "She is a dog that is born to run."

Kleman wrote what he calls "a novel" about Hope for Lulu's Rescue, which posted her story and photo on its website. In just one day, a family in Bethlehem, Pennsylvania, applied to bring Hope home. They had previously adopted a black Labrador mix through Lulu's, and they and their sons liked that dog so much that they decided to bring home another. Their house, it turns out, is about twenty minutes away from Kleman's parents. He appreciated the fact that they invited him to visit Hope whenever he was up North visiting his own family.

Kleman then found himself bringing Hope to a northbound transport in North Carolina, just like the one that had carried Blue to me.

"It was just me, Hope, and Hudson," he recalls. "My fiancée couldn't go with me, she was so upset. It takes a lot for me to cry, but when we left her with the transport, man, I bawled like a baby. I tried not to cry in front of all the people there, but I just couldn't stop, and then I kept crying half the way home."

Hope's new family met her in Trenton, New Jersey, some six hundred miles later. They had driven an hour and a half from their Pennsylvania home to collect her. When she came off the truck, she was barking, happy, and—much to their surprise—fully house-trained. They thought her slightly crooked jaw was absolutely adorable, and they were impressed that she exhibited no fear of cars, even despite having been thrown out of a moving one and left for dead.

Kleman says he can't imagine a better outcome for a dog who was once called unadoptable and scheduled for immediate death.

"I think Hudson is happy to have us back to himself, but I do think that he misses Hope," Kleman says. "We're definitely going to take in more rescues and foster again. It was an absolutely amazing experience."

I found the same thing to be true while fostering Izzy and Summer. I also realized that as Blue's adopter, the idea of the foster system had made a huge difference to me, too. Fostering solves the problem that so many people who buy puppies from breeders or pet stores believe exists with shelter dogs—that you just don't know what you're getting. When a foster person is honest about what she sees in a dog's behavior, it is easy to tell an adopter exactly what kind of a dog he is getting. A dog living in a foster home is being evaluated in real-life conditions, not in a cage. He's getting a chance to display his true personality so that rescue groups can match him to the best possible adopter.

In foster homes like mine, shelter dogs also receive basic training. I treated Izzy and Summer the same way that I treat Blue, so by the time they were ready to leave, they both knew how to sit on command. They were as housetrained as any puppy can be. They understood that there would be regular feeding times.

They knew that if they asked me to snuggle, they would receive plenty of hugs and love.

I couldn't help but think, as I learned more about fostering and the many ways it is done, that what Blue had experienced at Annie Turner's house really was outside the norm. He didn't arrive at my house looking or acting anything like Izzy and Summer did after staying with me and settling down from their previous experiences. He arrived with scabs from a rash and incomplete medical records and a serious fear of cars, one that seemed to be getting worse instead of better. I'd been dutifully putting him in the car every day and driving him to places like the park and the pet store, hoping he would learn that getting into the car meant going someplace fun where he would get treats. Blue always had a great time wherever we went—he even learned to love arriving at the bank's drive-through window, where my deposit receipt regularly arrived with a treat from the smiling teller inside— but the car rides that got us to these places, Blue didn't like at all. The mere thought of getting into the car seemed to put his stomach into a state of tumult, one that forced me to travel everywhere with a fresh roll of paper towels and disinfectant.

As I learned more about fostering and the way the rescue system works when it's at its best, I became increasingly concerned about the dogs I'd seen at Turner's property in North Carolina. I thought about how she'd put bleach on Blue's rash, and how she'd described it to me repeatedly as if she did it to lots of dogs, all the time. I thought about the big brown dog who seemed to be in a cage far too small for his body, and about the little white dog who had rivers of gunk running from her eyes. I thought about the room that Turner called "post-op" with the blacked-out windows, and I wondered what, precisely, was being done to the dogs I'd heard inside. I wondered why there had been some dogs Turner told me not to pet at her house, because they'd bite. I wondered how dogs who bite people could have anything to do with rescue at all. Everything that before had seemed strange to me now suddenly seemed almost eerie compared with the fostering experiences of Izzy, Summer, the dogs at my sister's veterinarian, and the incredible puppy named Hope.

I kept my concerns to myself while waiting for Izzy and Summer's adoption applications to be processed, and I focused on learning more about the big picture of rescue efforts to save dogs like them. It was hard to understand how little oversight was involved, how people like Turner, Dr. Thomas, and myself for that matter could really do just about anything we felt was right. There were big, national rescue groups like the ASPCA and the Humane Society out there in the world, but they didn't seem to have much to do with smaller rescue outfits like Lulu's or Rhonda Beach, which were actually moving quite a lot of dogs. Individual people involved with rescue seemed to be doing things however they decided was best, without any licensing or seal of approval that a regular dog lover like me could find and check.

In fact, the more I looked into things, the less rescuers seemed like an orchestrated army and the more they appeared to be a loosely banded gang of mercenaries—ones who, I'd next learn, were taking the fight to save dogs like Blue to levels all across America that I could not even imagine.

The War Across America

~

When I wasn't driving hundreds of miles to find answers, helping Izzy and Summer to get adopted, or playing with my sweet
puppy Blue, I spent time during summer 2011 trying to figure
out how many animal-control centers are like the one I'd seen
in Person County. It seemed impossible to me that more than a
handful could exist in modern-day America.

Surely, I thought, *facilities like the ones I'd seen were aberra-
tions from the everyday norm. What was going on in North Carolina
couldn't possibly be going on anywhere else, at least not on the same
scale.*

I started by asking advocacy groups for their information
on a state-by-state basis. I learned that killing shelter dogs in
gas chambers is illegal in twenty-two states: Alabama,[6] Arizona,

---

[6] Beckham's Act in Alabama was scheduled to go into effect in January 2012. The law
is named for a dog who was nearly gassed in a Cullman County shelter, and who now
lives with a family in Maine.

Arkansas, California, Connecticut, Delaware, Florida, Georgia, Illinois, Louisiana,[7] Maine, Maryland, New Jersey, New Mexico, New York, Oregon, Rhode Island, Tennessee, Virginia, Washington, West Virginia, and Wyoming. That doesn't mean that healthy, adoptable dogs and puppies are safe from other forms of killing such as lethal injection. It also doesn't mean that gas chambers are being used in states where no laws are on the books. But it does leave twenty-eight states that still legally allow the asphyxiation of healthy, adoptable dogs like Blue. My search for answers about my own puppy had led me to a specific part of North Carolina, but I soon learned that similar scenes were playing out in taxpayer-funded animal-control facilities in many parts of America.

The American Humane Association launched a campaign in 2009 to try to extend gas-chamber bans across the country. So far, that campaign's success is still a hope, not a certainty. One of the biggest challenges is simply getting information about what is happening inside some taxpayer-funded animal facilities—something I learned in my own research, too. When I asked national and state organizations for statistics about the county shelter where Blue was found, the statistics almost always differed from the ones that I got from the shelter itself. And at least I could verify that a gas chamber was being used there. Sometimes, major advocacy groups can't even get that far.

Tracy Coppola of the American Humane Association explained it to me this way: "In most states, there isn't a government agency that keeps records about which shelters are using gas chambers

---

[7] The Louisiana state Legislature passed a gas chamber ban in 2010. It is scheduled to take effect in January 2013.

and which are not. If there even is any record keeping, it's done at the county level, and a lot of these places are really rural. So it's hard to know what's actually going on. You're sometimes dealing with things like shelters that have gas chambers but that are not using them right now because of public pressure. But the chamber is still there and ready to go. Is that a gas chamber shelter? It's hard to quantify."

I was able to verify, working county-by-county, that more than forty animal-control centers in the United States still have gas chambers. North Carolina, where Blue was found, far and away has the most, with twenty-two. Michigan is next, with seven or eight. Activists believe that Pennsylvania has at least five, and that Ohio, Louisiana, and Alabama each have a handful still in operation.

In some of these states, people who believe in rescue are working to create change at the local level. They're no longer waiting for state lawmakers to enact a ban. One of my favorite examples of this is in Fayette County, Ohio, where Sheriff Vernon Stanforth fought for several years to get control of the county dog pound. He watched with disgust while warden after warden killed far more dogs than were saved, and he agreed with advocacy groups like Ohio's Society for the Prevention of Cruelty to Animals that said conditions at the gas-chamber facility were disgusting. Finally, on October 18, 2010, a day that was about 50 degrees with partly sunny skies, Stanforth took over day-to-day command. He showed up not only with his badge and his gun, but also with a nice-sized backhoe. Its giant yellow arm crashed into the gas chamber as Stanforth told the local paper that from now on, dogs in the pound would be treated the same way that he treats his own. He promised to use lethal injection, and only when absolutely necessary. The pound's new policy would be to work with rescue groups to encourage as many adoptions as possible.

"It's really not all too complicated," he told me a few months later by telephone. "As the saying goes, there is a new sheriff in town. We are now doing things the way that I believe they should be done."

In other states where gas chambers remain legal, and where local advocates don't have the benefit of being a modern-day Wyatt Earp, the fight to ban asphyxiation is waged in the halls of state legislatures. If the directors at the county facilities won't change, advocates figure, then state laws must be passed and imposed on the county directors.

This is what has been going on in North Carolina for a number of years, in a fight that has raged since well before Blue was ever born. The advocates, so far, have been unsuccessful. They have instead learned that the legislature is a battlefield mined with so many other explosive animal-welfare issues that it is hard to even guess where the next bomb might get dropped.

It's a little-reported fact, but many of the states where gas chambers are most prevalent are also the same states where big agribusiness and big pharmaceutical interests reign. The same lobbyists fighting to protect factory farms that keep cows, pigs, and chickens caged for their entire life spans, and the same lobbyists who work for pharmaceutical companies that use animals for medical experiments,[8] are often the same lobbyists who work behind the scenes to defeat legislation that could help save dogs like Blue from gas chambers.

Advocates in North Carolina didn't realize this when they set out to ban the gas chambers statewide in 2009, a year before Blue was born. They heralded the introduction of Davie's Law—nicknamed for the whimpering puppy found in a trash bag at the dump after a failed gas-chamber session at Davie County Animal Shelter. Davie's Law called for the dismantling, destruction, and removal of all gas chambers from animal shelters in the state. It would have required shelter dogs to be killed only by sodium pentobarbital, which is the drug that "puts dogs to sleep" without pain in veterinarian offices across America every day.

I learned about the attempt to pass Davie's Law from the perspective of Michele King, a Board member of the North Carolina Coalition for Humane Euthanasia.

"I didn't realize how many enemies these dogs had until that bill went up in 2009," she told me by telephone. "All of these state agencies opposed it. The Farm Bureau, the state Association of County Commissioners—they all fought against it because they don't want control over animals taken out of their hands. At one of the hearings, I walked in and saw at least two hundred people in this small committee room, all of them wearing Farm Bureau tags. I thought I was in the wrong place. I asked one of them, 'Why are y'all here?' I didn't get the relationship between the Farm Bureau and shelter dogs. At another

---

[8] For insight into how the world of shelters intersects with the world of medical research, check out the book *How Shelter Pets are Brokered for Experimentation: Understanding Pound Seizure* by Allie Phillips.

hearing, one of the House representatives who co-sponsored the bill told me that in order to pass it, the volunteers trying to help shelter dogs would have to neutralize the entire Farm Bureau and the North Carolina Association of County Commissioners, that they were the two biggest blocks. Now how the heck are we supposed to do that? These are huge, powerful groups. It's a completely lopsided fight with these groups that have been around forever and that aren't even thinking about the dogs."

What people like King view as enemies of dogs like Blue are actually the well-funded, well-connected lobby for influential business interests. Well more than half of the beef, pork, and chicken consumed in America comes from factory farms controlled by fewer than a half dozen corporations. North Carolina has more factory farms than most other states—so many, actually, that in 1997, because of pollution and other concerns, a moratorium was placed on any more being built. Lobbyists for the companies that control factory farms don't have any specific interest in the treatment of shelter dogs, since the dogs aren't turned into hamburgers or chicken nuggets after they're killed. However, big agribusiness does have an intense interest in any law that might affect the way animals can be legally confined and killed. The introduction of Davie's Law, which was intended only to eliminate gas chambers like the one in the shelter where Blue was found, created shock waves of fear that lobbyists spread throughout the North Carolina farming community and well beyond. Everyday farmers even heard about Davie's Law in states like Michigan that are hundreds of miles away. Fears were irrationally spread that all animals, not just homeless dogs, would have to be killed by lethal injection.

"In addition to the Farm Bureau, we also came up against a bunch of groups that are friendly with the American Kennel Club," King told me, sounding downright exasperated. "It was just so shocking. All of these hunting and breeding groups, all of them have banded together to lobby against any type of animal welfare ordinance. They see it as a slippery slope, too. Hunters want to be able to breed their hunting dogs, and they don't want to be told what to do with their animals when they're done using them. Breeders don't want to have to pay any kinds of fees or have any laws telling them what to do with their dogs, which they see as property instead of as living creatures. You see the names of these groups, and you think they would be on the side of the dogs, but they were not. The whole situation made my head spin."

Davie's Law died in committee. It was never voted upon by the full general assembly despite the fact that it had forty-five cosponsoring lawmakers, which is more than a quarter of North Carolina's House and Senate combined.

As I heard the behind-the-scenes story about what happened in North Carolina, I realized that it sounded an awful lot like what I'd heard about in Connecticut, where the law was passed making it harder for rescue transports to enter the state—the law with a blatant exemption for pet stores. Forces seemed to be at work in back rooms, where people appeared to be cutting deals for industries that had more pull than rescue advocates. I found something similar happening in Pennsylvania, too. The state's lawmakers also recently considered a law that would have banned gas chambers. It also ended up stalled in committee—by lobbyists for the Pennsylvania Veterinary Medical Association. The PVMA wanted to maintain the legal ability to gas dogs who were violently out of control or difficult to inject, which, to me, seems like an awful lot of leeway for shelter directors who describe scared, submissive pups like Blue as potentially aggressive. I also couldn't help but note that the PVMA wanted exemptions for "normal agricultural operations." It might as well have been language right out of the playbook that outmaneuvered Davie's Law from passing in North Carolina.

Then there is the money. Wherever lawmakers and lobbyists and activists are milling about, there is certainly going to be a trail of cash just waiting to be wallowed in and handed out and ultimately traced in the aftermath of a grand scandal. It's the same trail almost every time. It usually ends with a big pile of tax dollars paying for things that hardworking citizens have no idea they are buying.

The issue of animal shelter gas chambers is no different. Places like the one where Blue was found are funded by taxpayer dollars. Records must be kept on how those dollars are spent. It seemed natural to me, after all I'd learned about the swirling politics, to get copies of the actual financial records from the more than forty counties where I had learned about gas chambers still being used.

I printed out my Freedom of Information Act letters from my home computer during the hours when Blue, Izzy, and Summer took their naps. I addressed all the envelopes at the same desk where I send out my annual Christmas cards. Then I carried my pile of mail in a shoe box over to the local post office. The middle-aged postman behind the counter dutifully scanned each of my letters and saw address after address of various animal shelters. After about the twenty-fifth letter, he looked up and caught my eye.

"Are you trying to find a dog?" he asked.

"No," I answered. "I'm writing a book about my dog. He came from a kill shelter with a gas chamber. These letters are for other shelters that kill dogs in gas chambers, so I can make what they're doing public, too."

He took a moment to make sure he'd heard me correctly, nodded as if to say my cause was admirable, and then quipped, "I wish I could give you a discount on the postage."

It took a few months to receive all of the responses. The final answer came only after I went a few rounds with a lawyer who represented a nonprofit group that a bunch of towns created to deal with homeless dogs in Colbert County, Alabama. Even though the nonprofit was funded by taxpayer dollars, the lawyer insisted that it wasn't legally required to give me its annual budget. I had to send yet more Freedom of Information Act requests to the individual towns that funded the organization. I'm sure the local clerks in Muscle Shoals, Tuscumbia, and Sheffield really appreciated that when my certified letters landed on their desks.

What I found when I added up all of the county budgets is that Americans are spending just shy of $15 million local tax dollars each year to fund animal-control facilities with gas chambers. That's not chump change. It's the kind of money that can boost entire industries. It's what New York State gave farmers after Hurricane Irene washed away crops. It's what a transit company paid to build a thirty-four-acre train terminal in Louisville, Kentucky. And it's money that I have to believe most taxpayers—especially the dog lovers—have no idea is being spent in such a way.

I always thought of my tax dollars going to support local shelters that keep the majority of puppies and dogs safe until homes can be found. I knew that not every dog survived, but it never occurred to me that tax dollars would go to shelters like the one where Blue was found, that have a long record of killing nineteen of every twenty dogs in their care. It is anathema to me that anyone's hard-earned money is financing a facility whose primary contribution to dogs like Blue is killing them as quickly as possible, especially in gas chambers that can cause them pain and fear. Yes, animal-control facilities have a broader mandate that includes public safety and many other things, and I understand that sometimes, finding homes for dogs has to take a backseat to other priorities. But when a facility's kill rate is 95 percent year after year after year, it seems to me that taxpayers have a right to ask when, if ever, the adoption of dogs into homes is being given the attention it deserves.

And while I may have been naïve in my thinking, I most certainly am not alone. All across America, when I asked everyday people what happens to dogs and puppies inside of their local shelters, they told me the workers try to find the dogs good homes. I'm sure that is true in some communities, but in all of the same places where waitresses and gas-station attendants told me they thought their shelter was doing the right thing, rescue advocates told a different story.

"It's not just North Carolina," a marketing executive named Danielle Dunfee told me while I was with her in the Bahamas for a travel-writing assignment. "I work with a Labrador rescue group in South Florida. There is an owner surrender at one of the local shelters in Miami today, and when the owner surrenders the dog, they don't have to wait to euthanize. They can kill it that day. I have to drive over to that shelter and get that dog out. It only has a few hours left, and it sounds like a really great dog."[9]

Other rescue advocates told me that they receive the same responses from the general public in places that they know to be among the worst when it comes to high-kill rates.

"We stood there at Gaston County's shelter one day in North Carolina, and family after family was walking in with crates and crates of puppies and kittens," Jane Zeolla of Lulu's Rescue told me. "One man said, 'Well, we're moving and we can't take them with us.' I asked him and his wife if they understood that when dogs are surrendered by their owners, the shelter doesn't even have to wait. They can kill them immediately. The wife was in tears. She had no idea. She thought the shelter would try to find the puppies a home."

---

[9] Dunfee made it in time to save Tanner, a chocolate Labrador who arrived at her home covered in ticks and fleas, and with dried blood in his ears. "The shelter did absolutely nothing to care for this guy," she says. "I can't believe they couldn't even bathe him." Tanner got adopted less than two months later. He's now among the fifty or so dogs she has helped to save in just four years, including a black Labrador named Shadow who was found on the streets of South Florida and now lives with his family on a motoryacht in the Bahamas.

That's also what a family in Jackson County, Mississippi, thought when they relinquished a six-month-old Bulldog/ Labrador mix named Chloe to the county's animal shelter on a Monday morning. The family had wanted to raise the puppy, but Chloe was spending so much time in a crate that the mother felt guilty. "My main thinking," the mother wrote on a Facebook page that she created for the pup, "was while she was small and cute, she would find herself a home that would love her and take great care of her." The workers who received Chloe at the shelter remarked about how adorable she was. The mother had taken care to bathe Chloe that morning, to make her more appealing to potential adopters who could give her a better life.

The mother reconsidered that night during a tear-filled conversation with her ten-year-old daughter, and by the time the shelter opened at 10 A.M. the next morning, the mother was en route to retrieve Chloe and bring her back home. But the puppy was already dead, killed less than twenty-four hours after arriving. The *Ocean Springs Gazette* reported that the shelter's holding capacity was maxed out, and that all dogs who get surrendered are "guaranteed to be euthanized within a quick period of time." The mother was shocked and asked if she could at least retrieve Chloe's body to give her a proper burial. She claims that the shelter workers handed it to her in a trash bag and told her to have a nice day.

I couldn't help but wonder, as I thought more about the big picture, *How on earth did we get to this point, of the lucky few like Blue and Izzy and Summer being snatched from the brink of death while the masses are killed every day? If so many people are dog*

*lovers like me, how did the system become so warped and dysfunc-
tional in so many places?*

For the answer to that question, I'd have to look not to the
people trying to create change all across America today, but instead to the people who were leading the fight back in the era of
America's Civil War.

From Humble
Beginnings

~~

On February 8, 1866, a fifty-three-year-old man named Henry Bergh walked through the storm-soaked streets of New York City. This son of a wealthy shipbuilder was headed toward Clinton Hall, which stood at the triangle of Astor Place, East Eighth Street, and Lafayette Street, in what today is known as Greenwich Village. Despite the unpleasant weather in the dead of winter, the hall was packed with people, many of them from the well-to-do social circles that Bergh frequented. It was a time when draft horses were regularly beaten in the city streets to make them pull carts at a faster pace, an era when the mere thought of a shop selling organic dog treats would have been met with an incredulous chuckle. And yet, Bergh had managed to create a groundswell of interest for the lecture he intended to give. The place was jammed with people eagerly awaiting his report on "Statistics Related to the Cruelty Practiced on Animals."

Just two months later, Bergh was at the state capitol in Albany with a petition signed by a hundred people. That was enough, along with his "Declaration of the Rights of Animals," to help him win a charter from the New York State Legislature to create the American Society for the Prevention of Cruelty to Animals. On April 19, 1866, just two months after his lecture in Manhattan, the state legislature passed a law that prevented cruelty to animals. It authorized Bergh, through the newly founded ASPCA, to enforce that law.

This was America's first humane society, the first organization of its kind given legal authority to investigate and make arrests for crimes against animals. The ASPCA's large-scale efforts would be followed in 1877 by the creation of the American Humane Association, in 1954 by the launch of the Humane Society of the United States, and in 1980 by the formation of People for the Ethical Treatment of Animals. Each of these organizations today has its favored target efforts, which include eradicating puppy mills, stopping medical experimentation, prosecuting dogfighting, shuttering factory farms, ending the fur trade, and engaging in legislative lobbying. Some of the nationwide groups are regularly criticized for failing to offer enough direct financial support to shelters like the one where Blue was found, as well as for giving aid to shelters that continue to kill more dogs than they save. All of these groups, however, do offer at least some kind of support to shelters or campaigns that are intended to save dogs' lives.

These nationwide organizations, as well as most local and state SPCAs, rescue groups, and private shelters, originally arose because private citizens did not like what they saw happening to animals in their local communities. The folks at Lulu's Rescue today aren't all that different from who Henry Bergh was so many years ago, simply wanting to put some muscle behind the idea that animals should be treated with respect and kindness. Unlike in Bergh's time, though, today's activists aren't always seeking to create an official, state-sanctioned infrastructure. They are instead working to change what they see as an existing infrastructure that has become desperately twisted from its original mandate several generations ago.

Most parts of the United States today have animal-control centers that serve several towns within a county or a single large city. The job of these centers is just what their name states—animal control. The dogcatcher, or animal-control officer, is typically hired to enforce leash and licensing laws, to prevent the spread of diseases like rabies, to protect people from vicious animals, and to eliminate stray dogs from the streets. The job description does not include easing the nerves of frightened puppies like Blue, nor does it always require seeking permanent homes for healthy dogs who are perfectly adoptable. Instead, the animal-control officer is required to keep the dogs for a state-mandated holding period—usually two or three days for strays scheduled to be killed, or five days for dogs who will be sold to federally licensed brokers and used for medical experiments. In the most crowded shelters, as well as those that make no outreach or rescue efforts, these holding periods are the only safeguard a dog's owner has if she wants to reclaim a lost pet. For dogs like Blue, the holding periods are nothing more than a final few days trapped in a cage before death.

The way that the worst animal-control centers are run is counterintuitive to the natural bond that most people instinctively feel toward dogs, and that most dogs instinctively feel toward people. For some dogs, the experience of being inside these centers also alters the natural ease that they feel toward humans in general. Newborn puppies, like most newborn animals, are not innately afraid of people. Puppies are usually absolutely content not only to go to people, but also to be touched and petted and held by them. For some dogs who spend time in the worst animal-control centers, though, it becomes far harder for them to trust. As Blue got older and overcame his initial skittishness, I noticed that his distrust of certain people never fully left him. That same bit of cautiousness I'd seen on Blue's first day home, when he belly-crawled across my neighbor's yard to meet her teenagers, was a seed of caution that, so firmly planted in his soul as a baby, would grow like an unwanted weed later in his life.

One of Blue's favorite things to do is visit our local dog park. It's a fenced-in old baseball field that's now full of agility equipment for dogs to run around, through, and over. Dogs are allowed to romp off leash and play with one another by racing and wrestling to their hearts' content, and there's even a fake fire hydrant available should they feel the need to give it a spray. As with any dog park, there are always at least as many pooches as there are humans on any given day. When we visit, Blue takes a minute or two to get his bearings with all of the dogs, and then he runs around the place like it's a Willy Wonka factory made entirely of liver and rawhide. He is immediately friendly with just about every person he meets at the dog park, men and women alike, and will wag his tail for two hours straight if I let him stay and play that long. He goes to people inside the dog park like a pinball bouncing from one person to the next, and he lets them pet him from ear to toe without so much as a curious cock of the head.

At our other local parks, though—where dogs must be leashed and not everybody has a pooch—Blue is far less trusting. If someone approaches during one of our afternoon walks, and that person is also walking with a dog on a leash, then Blue will go over and say hello with his tail wagging. Sometimes he gets so excited that his entire butt starts to wag. It is as if the very presence of the other dog has given the person at the other end of the leash a canine seal of approval.

On the other hand, if someone approaches us on the trail without a dog, then Blue moves to my side and uses me as a physical barrier between himself and the oncoming person. He hangs back until he gets a sense of whether the person might be a threat to his safety, and he sometimes won't allow himself to be touched unless the person kneels down at his level. The older Blue gets and the more people he meets, the more he's becoming a tougher judge of character. A day at the park with Blue is often like watching a father size up a daughter's first boyfriends, knowing full well that some mean a lot more harm than good.

It's easy to see how Blue's natural instincts could have been honed into this more cautious state by the people he met in North Carolina. The human-animal bond is mercilessly quashed, in dogs and people alike, when shelter policy is to not even give the "less-desirable" dogs a walk. And once the legally mandated holding period ends in animal-control facilities across America, then animal control takes precedence over animal welfare. That can even be true if the local SPCA serves double duty as the region's animal-control center, and it's how a sweetheart of a pup like Blue or Izzy or Summer can end up just a few hours from being killed in a taxpayer-funded facility. The people running these shelters are, according to the letter of the law, quite simply doing their jobs by disposing of the dogs in their care as more and more arrive, day after day.

A rescue worker told me that she once asked a young woman at a North Carolina shelter with a high-kill rate how she could wake up every morning and go to work, knowing that her job would require her to kill healthy, adoptable dogs. "I didn't ask her to be judgmental," she told me. "I really wanted to understand how she can do this every day. Well, she got tears in her eyes and said, 'I give them lethal injections. At least I know they're being killed in a humane way, that they're not being thrown into a gas chamber or starving to death where somebody left them tied to a tree."

A shelter worker having to make that distinction is certainly a far cry from the vision that Henry Bergh had back in the 1800s, when the ASPCA became America's first rescue organization.

And that same distrust that dogs like Blue can learn is not altogether different from the distrust that shelter workers often develop toward the public at large. People like me, who consider dogs to be members of the family, can't conceive of ever handing Blue or any other dog over to be euthanized except in cases of extreme sickness, like when my Beagle mix Floyd got so old and weak that he could no longer even drink water. I'd no sooner relinquish Blue, Izzy, Summer, or any dog in my family to an uncertain future than I would my own mother, father, or sister.

But there are plenty of people in America who drop off their dogs and puppies at the shelter door in much the same way as they toss a bag of tattered clothes into the pile at Goodwill. There are rural shelters in North Carolina, for instance, that have maybe forty cages inside, but that receive upward of seventy dogs on some days. The people on the receiving end, inside the shelters, routinely see dogs left to die because the pups had an accident on a carpet, or because they chewed a favorite shoe, or because the owner grew tired of their company, or because the owner failed at basic training and blames the dog for bad behavior. Shelter workers learn to recognize local dog owners who fail to spay and neuter their dogs, and who then leave puppies by the dozens at the same shelter door during the course of several years.

Shelter workers can quickly, and understandably, learn to resent the public as a whole. They often meet people who aren't just irresponsible with dogs, but who are sometimes downright cruel. The same sense of helplessness that I felt during just a few hours in those shelters overcomes many workers who endure the conditions inside on a daily basis. It's only natural that they come to distrust, and even dislike, the people they feel are creating this never-ending crisis. From the eyes of shelter workers, the public is not seen as a source full of willing adopters for dogs like Blue and eager fosters for dogs like Izzy and Summer. Instead, the public is seen as the callous, heartless source of all the dogs the workers themselves are hired to kill.

By this logic, the gas chambers are an unpleasant but necessary solution to the problem of a thoughtless community at large.

So it continues today in America's worst shelters. Large national organizations collect donations and then give grants to help some of these struggling local facilities, trying to support the ones whose directors are working to overcome the institutionalized problems of the system as a whole. The Petfinder Foundation, for instance, gave hundreds of thousands of dollars for shelter improvements in all fifty states during 2009. In the second quarter of 2010 alone, the ASPCA gave more than $3.3 million in grants and services to help animals across the country. This money is a godsend for shelters that are on the path to reform, of course, but it does nothing to address the problem in shelters whose directors are resistant to change. The worst shelters in America today are as brutal for some dogs as the streets of Manhattan were to horses when Henry Bergh created the ASPCA more than a century ago.

Luckily, as with so many things, history has a way of repeating itself. Animal lovers are just as adamant today as Bergh was in the 1800s that cruelty, in all its forms, be eradicated. They simply see a different solution to the problem in modern times, a path that has evolved in ways that Bergh never could have anticipated, thanks in large part to the creation of the World Wide Web. Instead of building shelters to house dogs like Blue, today's activists are stitching a nationwide net of volunteers who work together across state lines. For the first time in American history, dog-rescue volunteers are beginning to function like a modern-day version of the Underground Railroad.

It's impossible to say when the first volunteer rescue group was formed to work in conjunction with shelters, instead of from within them. It's also impossible to determine the number of rescuers who serve as part of the national network on any given day. They do not originate from a centralized source, but instead rise up independently in similar ways. Like-minded people from the Atlantic Ocean clear across to the Pacific Coast see the same things happening in their communities, and they want to help the dogs and puppies so desperately in need. They are everyday people, just like me. They're like dandelions growing simultaneously across a 2,500-mile-wide piece of the planet, all reaching up and out toward the same flicker of sunshine.

While more than 13,000 self-described rescue groups are listed on the Petfinder website alone, in some cases, volunteers who contribute to the network aren't affiliated with any organization at all. Lulu's Rescue in Pennsylvania, for instance, once received a call for help from a couple in South Carolina who would describe themselves as neither activists nor volunteers, but who contributed to the rescue network nonetheless. They had found a two-year-old Boxer/pit bull mix with golden fur and a white chest. She was a sweetheart of a dog even though she had been tied to a tree, was visibly malnourished, and was being used for target practice by a boy with a shotgun. The couple took in this dog, named her Apple, and tried to figure out what to do with her since they already had two dogs of their own. They'd read about local shelters killing more dogs than were saved, so they reached out to rescue groups nationwide. They offered to drive Apple anywhere from Greenville, South Carolina, as far north as Amherst, Massachusetts, if a rescue group could find her a loving home somewhere in between.

I myself once received a call from a woman who shopped at my favorite pet store and learned from its owner that I was writing this book. The woman had been helping friends in Tuscaloosa, Alabama, who were recovering from the massive tornadoes that struck the region in April 2011. She would never be counted in an official registry of rescue workers, but she certainly was contributing to the nationwide network. "It was bad enough, what happened to the people in the storm, but then I went over to the local dog shelter," the woman told me. "I had no idea the situation was so bad—and that it was bad before the tornado even hit. When I learned about what they have been doing to these dogs, I tried to charter a private jet to get the dogs out. I came back to New Jersey and have been finding homes that are willing to take them. I will do whatever I need to do to get them transported up here to safety."

Sometimes, volunteers who contribute to the network are not even adults. In Burke County, Georgia, after authorities found squatters living in a local house, volunteers from Old Fella Rescue were called to help. The authorities had their hands full with the dozen or so children who were living in the house, and who had never been to a doctor or a schoolroom in their entire lives. Old Fella's volunteers were asked to gather up the countless cats and kittens living in the same house. During the two weeks that it took to collect all the felines, the volunteers kept seeing a single dog on the property who looked ragged, but otherwise seemed healthy. They called him Sarge because he barked and barked, like a sentinel standing guard, and he would not let any of the volunteers touch him. They brought him food for days, tried to calm him down, and were at their wits' end when Sarge took a liking to a rescuer's seven-year-old daughter. Sarge felt protective of her, just as he had of the kids who'd lived in the house. It was the seven-year-old who got Sarge to follow her calmly into a rescue volunteer's truck. That was the beginning of his journey through the cross-country network to a foster home and, eventually, his permanent home on a private cove in Massachusetts, where he lives happily today.

These small-scale beginnings of the rescue mind-set are no less noble than the large-scale effort that Henry Bergh sought to inspire back in the 1860s, but today they are emerging in an entirely grassroots way. They are neither directly sanctioned by, nor are they seeking legal authority from, state legislatures like the one in New York that Bergh petitioned to create the ASPCA. Instead, they are coalescing by finding one another via word of mouth and the Internet, the way Rhonda Beach in North Carolina found Lulu's Rescue in Pennsylvania after pulling Blue out of the shelter to safety. The current heroes to so many dogs like Blue are part of the social media generation. And they have, since about the year 2007, begun to go viral.

If there are just three people like these volunteers working with each rescue group on the Petfinder website alone, then there are nearly forty thousand people supporting this effort across the country. That's more people than are enrolled every year at the University of Southern California, Boston University in Massachusetts, or DePaul University in Chicago, Illinois. And that's only the rescuers listed on a single website. It doesn't count the innumerable people like the South Carolina couple who saved Apple, the woman who was willing to fly dogs to New Jersey from Alabama, the seven-year-old girl who saved Sarge, or even the couple who drove Blue to meet me in their RV full of rescued pups. It also doesn't count everyday people like me who both adopt and then agree to foster—and I'd helped to save three dogs inside of six months.

All of this is a glorious thing to see if you're a fan of grass-roots populism, but the way the rescue network has evolved also comes with inherent perils. The complete lack of government oversight, the ignorance about health and safety regulations, the different laws in every state—all of these things mean that dogs like Blue, Izzy, and Summer are relying on individual human beings to do the right thing, every single time. People have different opinions about the right and wrong ways to treat a dog. People can take shortcuts when they think nobody is watching. They can become lost in the flood of desperate dogs and try to save them in ways that inadvertently cause them additional harm.

As I realized just how much of the rescue network is held together by nothing more than trust, I couldn't help but return to my thoughts about the way that Blue was treated as a foster dog at Annie Turner's house. I was caring for Izzy and Summer just the same way I cared for Blue, ensuring proper veterinary care, giving them plenty of walks and training, and making sure they felt safe and loved. The way that Blue was treated as a foster dog at Annie Turner's house was better than being killed in a gas chamber, of course, but as the director at Person County Animal Control had told me, the system of rescue left an awful lot of room for error. I began to realize that I agreed with him on that point. It seemed to me that where there is no official oversight, only the goodness of everyday people can prevent harm.

I didn't think that Annie Turner had in any way intended to cause Blue harm, but I also didn't think that what he'd received at her home represented my definition of appropriate foster care. The more I learned about the rescue movement in general, and the more time I spent learning about the fostering process with Izzy and Summer, the more I realized there are precious few people in a position to know the full story about any rescued dog. Unless you take the time to verify and scrutinize everything you've been told, it can be tough to know the real truth about anyone and anything happening along the rescue path.

That means there are just a handful of people in a position to seek help when something may be frighteningly amiss, as was about to happen to me next.

A Tough Call
to Make

~

It's an excruciating thing, deciding the actual moment that you want to become a Benedict Arnold. When I'd ventured to North Carolina to learn more about Blue, my primary goal was to learn everything that I could about his story. My secondary goal was to thank the people who had helped him, including Annie Turner. I'd treated her like an old friend even though she was a woman I'd spoken to a few times on the telephone. Because of our shared relationship with Blue, I'd felt like we were kindred spirits. I'd never imagined that I'd walk into her home later that night and see anything that gave me serious concern. She was the president of a local animal protection group, for Pete's sake. It had not dawned on me that what she'd called "fostering Blue" might look more to me like something dangerous. I was neither prepared nor equipped to deal with what I had seen.

My first instinct was to consult with people smarter than I am about rescue, to get their advice. I mentioned what I'd seen to the team at Lulu's Rescue in Pennsylvania, as well as to Rhonda Beach in Person County. Both immediately expressed serious concern and offered to help find the dogs other fosters and permanent homes.

I next consulted family and friends, who were split on the issue. Some suggested that I keep quiet; these dogs may not be in a perfect place, but at least they're still alive, and this woman had played a critical role in saving Blue's life. I owed her a pass. Others urged me to make a phone call immediately, lest my silence lead to innocent dogs suffering further stress or possible harm. I owed the dogs at least that much.

During the previous thirteen years of my life, I'd have ultimately come to a decision by talking things over with my husband. With the divorce, though, our "speaking" had become limited to e-mail exchanges that usually ended by me telling him to go, well, do things that aren't fit to print here. I tossed and turned in bed, looking over at the empty pillow next to me, and often ended up clicking on the television to ease my insomnia. I found myself watching all-night marathons of "Confessions: Animal Hoarding" on cable. The more I watched, the more I realized that what I'd seen in Turner's house looked really similar to what I was seeing on the TV. I researched the backgrounds of hoarders and learned that they usually had suffered some kind of severe trauma, which fit Turner's life story like a puzzle's key corner piece. I came to understand that reporting someone who appears to be hoarding dogs is actually helping not just the dogs, but also the person. A lot of good people who mean well—as I believed she did—end up trying to save a lot more dogs than they can actually handle.

I happened to be wading karma-deep in all of this moral vacillation right before the tenth anniversary of the 9/11 terrorist attacks. My home is in the New York City media region, and the authorities were on high alert. The week that I returned from North Carolina, my local television and radio programs were consumed by a marketing campaign that urged citizens to help police avoid another tragedy. Advertisement after advertisement urged: "If you see something, say something." The phrase began to echo like the chorus of a catchy tune that I could not get out of my mind.

Beyond the question of whether to say anything at all was the question of whom I might actually say something to. My instinct was to make the phone call, but the local authority on the matter was Person County Animal Control. The building was just a few minutes' drive from Turner's property, standing at the ready with a gas chamber and a 95-percent kill rate. I didn't want any of the dogs going right back to that shelter where they'd started, and I could never live with myself if I became the person who caused them to be killed by asphyxiation. I was sure they didn't deserve to be there or to die that way any more than my boy Blue did.

I picked up the telephone on September 7, 2011, and dialed the North Carolina chapter of the Humane Society of the United States. I was on guard from the moment I heard the line ring on the other end. I'd listened repeatedly to local-level rescuers nationwide tell me that they do not trust large charities when it comes to saving actual dogs on a day-to-day basis. There is a shared opinion—which, right or wrong, is common among rescuers and regularly reported in the media—that big organizations collect an awful lot of donations by showing pictures and videos of dogs in distress, but then put that money toward efforts that help animals in general, and not always shelter dogs in particular.

Even given this information, it seemed to me that a prominent, nationally funded organization was my best bet, and the truth was that I wanted to interview somebody from the HSUS in North Carolina for this book, anyway. A representative answered my call, and we spent about twenty minutes talking about the turnaround at Robeson County's animal shelter. She seemed every bit as professional and smart as activists in North Carolina had told me she was, even while they criticized the organization for which she worked. I had the Turner situation in the back of my mind the entire time we spoke, and as I was winding up the interview, I told her there was something else I wanted to discuss, something about Person County.

I explained that I'd seen something troubling while I was in North Carolina doing research, and I wanted to know if one thing in particular that I'd been told was actually true. I then repeated what Turner had said, so matter-of-factly while sitting next to me in her golf cart, about being able to keep as many as sixty dogs at one time on her land.

"The legal limit for adoptable dogs in a home that are part of a rescue is actually nine," the representative answered.

Nine, I thought. I'd counted twenty-seven. I'd written their locations in my notebook—yard, bedroom, kitchen—and then added them up to be sure. And I'd heard what sounded like even more dogs behind the covered doors and blacked-out windows. Even if the dogs were spread across two properties, there were a heck of a lot more than nine. Or even eighteen. And on top of the numbers, the place just hadn't felt right to me, for whatever that was worth.

I took a deep breath, and I told the representative everything. While I'd been asking her open-ended questions just moments before, she now began extracting information from me with the sharp beats of a criminal prosecutor. She asked me exactly what I had seen and precisely where I had seen it. She listened while I looked at Google Maps on my computer and tried to remember how I'd driven to Turner's place. I felt incredibly nervous and talked about all the shelter statistics I'd verified, making sure she understood that I did not want the dogs ending up in the local gas chamber. She soothed my fears by telling me the Humane Society of the United States is a well-funded organization that can offer everything from temporary shelters to assistance with getting the dogs adopted through proper channels. She assured me that I'd done the right thing by providing the information so an expert could go and take a look. I hadn't filed a police report or accused anyone of a crime. I'd simply seen dogs who appeared to be in a questionable situation, and I'd reached out to people with more experience so they could verify what was actually happening.

By the time we hung up, I had a clear vision of what I thought was going to happen next. An HSUS representative would go to Turner's homes to look around. If things seemed okay, they would leave Turner and the dogs alone. If things didn't seem okay and a large number of dogs had to be seized, the HSUS would step in and make sure they didn't go straight to local animal control and get killed.

That sounded right to me. It sounded reasonable and responsible. I won't say that I slept well that night, but I did sleep better than I had the previous few nights. Making the call seemed to have been the right thing to do. If Blue had still been in one of those houses, I'd have wanted somebody else to make the call for him.

Less than twenty-four hours later, the representative e-mailed to give me an update. An officer had been sent to take a look around. Whatever he'd seen appeared to be part of an investigation that was already under way. Enforcement agencies in neighboring counties had been contacted. The representative instructed me not to speak to anyone else in the state of North Carolina about what I'd seen. She didn't want the investigation being compromised. She said she'd be back in touch soon. That was all.

Enforcement agencies in neighboring counties? I thought. *What on earth could involve dogs like Blue and an investigation in neighboring counties?*

I flipped back through my notebooks and remembered what an activist had told me about Robeson County: She was now turning her attention from the conditions at the shelter to the growing problem of dogfighting, which seemed to be a serious and emerging threat. A Person County shelter official had mentioned dogfighting, too, when he told me that gang members had once cracked a shelter window trying to get inside to retrieve pit bulls who had been seized. A Robeson County shelter employee had also mentioned dogfighting, when she told me that men wearing matching colors and tattoos used to enter the facility and bang on all the cages, trying to determine which dogs were the most vicious. There was a reason that both Person County and Robeson County animal shelters were surrounded by tall chain-link fences topped with barbed wire. It wasn't to keep the good dogs in. It was to keep the bad people out.

The ding of realization might as well have been a game-show buzzer in my mind. I felt my back stiffen. I felt my pulse race. I thought about all of the cash that changes hands whenever a dog gets rescued. I imagined ways that some people might want to enhance that cash flow by, say, using a rescue organization as a cover for something sinister.

It occurred to me that a scared, little, freshly neutered dog like Blue might be somewhat valuable to people like me looking for a new pet, but might in fact be far more valuable to people who wanted a large number of small dogs as bait.

I didn't come to this conclusion without thinking seriously through the numbers. The economics of dog rescue, I'd learned, do not make anybody rich. The economics of acquiring dogs for purposes other than rescue, however, sometimes do.

Where rescue is concerned, the money trail starts with the shelter where a dog like Blue is found. Most shelters charge an adoption fee. It's usually a low fee at a shelter where officials actually want to see dogs go to homes. In Person County, where Blue is from, the fee is $25 after a refund when the person gets the dog spayed or neutered. Otherwise, the cost is $100.

Once a rescue acquires a dog from a shelter, the rescue pays to get him a rabies vaccine plus basic shots. The rescue also pays to get the dog spayed or neutered. Whether a Northern or Southern rescue is funding the care, it's almost always done in the South. Up North where I live, such care costs hundreds upon hundreds of dollars. But in the South, the same needs can often be met at a sharply discounted rate. In some cases, dogs may be diagnosed with mange, heartworm, parvo, or other illnesses that cost hundreds of additional dollars to cure, but for a dog like Blue, the basic investment by the initial rescue group is usually somewhere between $100 and $125. The rescue puts that money into the dog's care knowing that an adopter like me will then pay to take the dog once he is "adoption-ready."

Sometimes, a Southern rescue moving dogs into the care of a Northern rescue will add an upcharge, an amount that depends on the rescue group itself. Generally speaking, a dog like Blue can be acquired from a North Carolina rescue for anywhere from $150 to $250—an amount that is consistent with basic, initial vetting. If a group is charging more, it can get a reputation for being "in it for the money" instead of "in it for the dogs." Northern rescues will stop working with Southern rescues if they feel this is the case, which helps to keep prices in check.

Next comes the transport, which, if done by RV, averages about $100 per dog. So for a pooch like Blue, the total investment in care and transport is somewhere between $250 and $350. If an adopter has not been found by the time the dog arrives up North, the dog goes into a foster home or a kennel at additional expense to the Northern rescue. In Blue's case, no kennel was needed. I was standing at the end of the rescue pipeline with a $400 check, so the Northern rescue pocketed the difference and applied it toward saving more dogs.

A lot of this money is changing hands in cash—not to mention under the tax shield of charity status. When a rescue truly is putting every possible nickel toward saving more dogs, the profit margins are small, if they exist at all. That's especially true when you add in things such as collars, leashes, flea and tick prevention, and heartworm medication. Rescuing shelter dogs into good homes is a lot of work for little to no money.

By comparison, there is a great deal of quick cash that can be made by selling shelter dogs to people with different motives. Dogs sold into pharmaceutical trials and other forms of experimentation, for instance, require far less initial investment. Dogs sold into illegal fighting operations, too, can create a far bigger stream of income. Some dogfights have deep-pocketed investors.

Once you understand that math, it's easy to imagine a scenario in which a person establishes a rescue charity for the ultimate purpose of gaining unfiltered access to a constant stream of cheap shelter dogs. It's also easy to imagine that person moving a handful of dogs each year into homes to keep his tax status as a charity intact, all the while selling the majority of dogs out the back door at far higher prices for pure profit.

And so, while dutifully keeping my mouth closed about whatever the Humane Society had discovered at Turner's house, I couldn't help but let my mind run wild. I thought about dogfighting and pharmaceutical experiments and all the ways a shelter dog could be bought and put into harm's way, all of the kinds of things that might involve a multicounty investigation. I felt physically ill at the thought that Blue, or any of the dogs I'd seen, may have been destined for such a fate.

The only thing I failed to imagine in the case of the dogs at Turner's house is what actually happened.

A week after my initial report, I spoke with the representative by telephone again. She told me not to worry about dogfighting—though a logical conclusion, it was not true in this particular case—and said the situation was under control. She had personally taken the initiative, she assured me, to contact Person County Animal Control on the day that I originally talked with her.

"What the hell are you talking about!" I blurted into the telephone. "I thought I was very clear in telling you the local animal-control department has a gas chamber and a 95 percent kill rate. I called you, and not them, for a reason."

She said her job required her to follow the rules of legal jurisdiction, and that's what she'd done. While the HSUS could offer assistance, it was not actually in charge of anything. She'd been in touch daily with an animal-cruelty officer under Person County Shelter Director Ron Shaw's command, an officer who had been knocking on Turner's door for a week without being able to get inside and investigate further. But at the end of the day, the dogs at Turner's house could very well find themselves right back in the local shelter's cages and, ultimately, inside the gas chamber. The HSUS would only actually offer assistance depending on how the situation unfolded, if it decided to offer assistance at all.

I felt like screaming, but I tried to return to reason. "Person County Animal Control," I said, "is going to kill all of those dogs. They have nowhere to put them."

"That's not true," she said as if batting away a confused idiot.

"It's absolutely true," I insisted, with anger now rising in my voice. "I've just spent months documenting that it's true. I'm writing an entire book about how it's true. The shelter director himself gave me the paperwork that proves it's true. I have it here on my desk. I'll fax it to you, right now, if you still don't believe it."

She took a moment to collect her thoughts, which probably included my reminder that she might see this story in print someday. She then told me that it was her hope, since the HSUS had become involved, that Person County Animal Control would contact her for assistance if a large number of dogs had to be seized. That was the best she could do. She thanked me again for my information and assured me that I'd done the right thing by calling her.

I hung up the telephone, stood up next to my desk, and bent over with sharp pains in my stomach. Blue heard me moaning and wandered into my office to see what was happening. Izzy and Summer followed him. I was certain that I'd just caused at least thirty dogs like them to be killed in a gas chamber.

I sat down on the floor, let Blue crawl into my lap, and began to cry.

Later that night, I joined friends for dinner at a restaurant in Summit, New Jersey. It was a tiny little Italian place with home-made pasta and outdoor tables that attracted wealthy celebrities like CNBC stock guru Jim Cramer, who wandered past our table just before our appetizers arrived. I completely hijacked the evening's conversation with my friends, neither of whom had any background in dog rescue, but both of whom tried to help me figure out what, if anything, I could do to undo the nightmare I'd apparently set in motion. My elbows were on the table and my head was in my hands. I was pale-faced and inconsolable, like someone who had just witnessed a bloody crime.

"Excuse me," I heard a voice say from the table next to ours.

I spun in my chair to see a woman with long brown hair and gentle, wise eyes. She reached out her hand to shake mine.

"I couldn't help but overhear you," she said. "I'm ToniAnn from Home for Good Dog Rescue here in Summit. I've saved more than six hundred dogs from Georgia in the past couple of years."

This woman sailed into my day like a life raft for my conscience, which had not only become untethered but now felt long lost at sea.

"Can you tell me," I practically begged her, "what on earth I can do to make sure these dogs are okay?"

She smiled knowingly. She had the face of a mother who realizes her child has been cut from the football team before the kid figures it out for himself. She shook her head, and she slowly adjusted the napkin in her lap.

"You can't do anything," she said. "And nobody is going to help you. The big organizations are useless. They collect a lot of money, but they don't actually save the dogs. That's why we're all driving back and forth to the South on the weekends. We take off our jewelry, put on our shabbiest jeans, find a beat-up old car that won't draw any attention, and go into these places to get the dogs out. That's what you can do—drive down there, get the dogs out, and find them good homes up here."

I asked her if she thought I'd done the right thing in calling the Humane Society.

"Those dogs had a better chance of staying alive at that woman's house," she said. "Even if she's a hoarder, sometimes a hoarder is the only chance these dogs have. The rescuers have to be hoarders to get as many of them out of the shelters as they can. I would never have made that phone call. You only made the situation worse for all of those dogs you saw."

Needless to say, I did not order dessert. I barely was able to keep down the dinner I'd just eaten. I drove home in a panic and spent the rest of the night trying to figure out what I could do to actually achieve the goal of helping those dogs. I realized that I had quite a lot in common with Annie Turner at that point. I would have hoarded the dogs in my own house until adopters could be found if I thought it might keep them out of the gas chamber.

By morning, I'd decided that I could at least try to hold the HSUS to what the representative had initially implied, that the group would offer assistance to Person County Animal Control should a large number of dogs need to be seized. Director Ron Shaw had generously given me his personal cell phone number when I was in North Carolina in case I needed help while I was there, what with my New Jersey license plates and all. I'd never dialed it—until now. I called at precisely 9:01 A.M., hoping to catch the ex-Marine right after he came on duty for the day.

He picked up on the second ring and seemed surprised to hear from me. He also seemed surprised when I told him that I was the person who had told the Humane Society about the dogs at Turner's house. He immediately said, and rightly so, that he could not comment on an ongoing investigation.

"I understand, but that's not why I'm calling you," I told him. "Do you remember in your office, when we talked about how some rescue groups are good, and some seem to be not so good, and there seems to be a lot of room for error? I just want to make sure you're being given the same information that I'm being given. I want to make sure the Humane Society has told you that they have funding available to provide assistance like makeshift shelters should a large number of dogs need to be seized. I want to make sure you are aware that you don't have to simply kill all of those dogs for lack of space if they end up being brought in."

Shaw went silent for a few moments before saying, "I have not been given that information."

I thanked him for his time and hung up. It would not have surprised me to see actual steam blowing out of my ears like I was a cartoon train speeding over a cliff. I sent a strongly worded, though carefully polite, e-mail to the HSUS representative. I cc'd Shaw so that he would know how to reach her directly. I wrote that I wanted the representative to make sure Shaw knew all of the resources that the HSUS had available, because I felt personally responsible for making sure these dogs would be all right. I wrote that I wanted the representative to understand that Person County Animal Control already has a 95-percent kill rate and no extra space for more dogs, and that Shaw himself had verified that information for me.

The representative replied immediately. She said that she had been in constant contact with the officer working under Shaw's jurisdiction, and that the officer was well aware of how the HSUS could help.

However, she added, none of that mattered anymore. The officer had gone back the night before to try yet again to get inside Turner's house, but it appeared that Turner had been tipped off about the investigation. The representative implied that the tip-off may have been my fault, because I'd asked Lulu's Rescue and Rhonda Beach what to do about what I'd seen, and to help find homes for any dogs who needed to be seized. Small rescue groups, she told me, talk to one another. They are not always to be trusted. Word can spread faster than an oil slick, and sometimes it's awfully hard to tell which people are more slippery than solid.

No matter the reason for the tip-off, the representative said, the investigation was now stalled. When the officer had tried once again to get into Turner's house, he'd arrived to find an entirely new situation. Turner would remain on their watch list, as well as on the radar of Person County Animal Control, in case she actually was hoarding or doing something else dangerous to dogs. But as for what I'd seen, there was really nothing else that anyone could do.

The dogs, the representative told me, were inexplicably gone.

Safe Haven

~

Sometimes in dog rescue, well-intentioned people just get in over their heads. I'd certainly managed to do exactly that with a single phone call about some pups I thought might need help. Annie Turner may have done it after spending so many years trying to save dogs from her local gas chamber that she simply couldn't stop taking more in. But in some cases, it doesn't take grand ambitions to find yourself in a situation you can't resolve. In at least one case, it took only a few cute puppies for a woman to look beyond the rescue world as I understood it—and to introduce me to what I can only describe as the promised land.

That woman's name is Jodi Pope. She explained to me by telephone that she once found a couple of Labrador puppies near her home in Burke County, Georgia. The pups were just four weeks old, adorable as all get out, and perfectly healthy. She figured she'd bring them home as fosters and that, like Izzy and Summer, they'd be requested by adopters inside of a week or ten days.

"We ended up having them for six months," she told me. "We went every weekend to adoption days, posted them on the Internet, did everything we could think of—and we could not find homes for these dogs. We even drove to the nearest city, Augusta, which is forty miles away. And do you know what we found? About twenty rescue groups showing up there every weekend, and not enough people to adopt all the dogs."

After half a year had passed, Pope was looking for a better solution. She spent that summer working the Web to make connections, and eventually, she found several shelters up North that were willing to work with her.

"There were three of us who had started Old Fella Rescue here in Georgia, and we brought up eight dogs the first time, including those Lab puppies," she recalls. "The next transport, we had thirteen dogs. Then it was twenty-one. Now, in 2010, we're averaging thirty-five dogs a month. We've probably sent almost five hundred dogs up North, because we realized that the county above ours is killing about fourteen thousand dogs a year. So now I'm coordinating transports for other rescues in our area, too. We work with a lot of great shelters, especially Northeast Animal Shelter in Massachusetts, where they promote the dogs like crazy. I've driven there and seen people standing in line to see which dogs we're bringing. We've had near fistfights by people trying to adopt our dogs, there's such a desire for them up North, for these dogs and puppies that people in our part of Georgia leave in Dumpsters."

When Pope mentioned Northeast Animal Shelter to me, my ears perked up. It was as if somebody had just asked me whether I wanted to go for a walk at the p-a-r-k. I had heard again and again about this particular shelter in Massachusetts that rescuers all across the South feel is *the* example of the gold-standard way station for dogs like Blue who are in transit to permanent homes.

And it came to exist, I learned in a telephone call, because a woman named Cindi Shapiro happened to read *The Wall Street Journal* on Thursday, March 6, 1970.

Shapiro was just twenty-five years old, a recent graduate of Harvard Business School whose entire education had revolved around preparing her to run a health organization. But she loved animals, so her eyes gravitated naturally toward one particular front-page headline. "With Right Tactics, It's Easy to Market A Three-Legged Cat: Little Animal Shelter Succeeds By Imitating Big Business."

The article, by staff reporter William Mathewson, told the story of Alexander Lewyt (pronounced LOO-it). At the time, the resident of Long Island, New York, was sixty-six years old and best known for having invented the Lewyt vacuum cleaner. It was sold door-to-door following World War II with a promise to homemakers that it would not interfere with the reception on their big-box radios or black-and-white televisions. This was a huge marketing hook in its day. Lewyt's vacuum cleaner was no small shakes. He was featured in the 1952 book *America's Twelve Master Salesmen* alongside Conrad Hilton, who founded the hotel chain that bears his name; James Farley, who is credited with turning Coca-Cola into a global brand with help from the U.S. military; and Max Hess, Jr., who would eventually sell his family's Hess department store chain to Dillard's, Bon-Ton, and May Department Stores (now part of Macy's).

The *Journal* article explained how Lewyt became involved with North Shore Animal League on Long Island in 1969, when his wife talked him into donating $100 after receiving a funding request. Lewyt got curious about how his money would be spent, so he paid a visit to the twenty-five-year-old shelter. It was open only two hours a day on five days of the week, had one full-time employee, and barely had enough cash flow to keep the lights on. "They were also acting as the local dogcatcher," Lewyt told the *Journal*, "and they were losing money on every dog they'd catch."

Lewyt thought that was a pretty dumb way to run an operation, so he taught the shelter's directors about direct-mail campaigns. Working with Publishers Clearing House, which was near his home and the shelter on Long Island, Lewyt produced a letter featuring a photograph of a puppy and a kitten. The letter asked its 28,000 recipients, "Would you give a dollar—just $1—TO SAVE THEIR LIVES?" Lewyt got a celebrity endorser to donate his signature, too. It was singer Perry Como, whose Christmas specials were as much an annual television event in the late 1960s as the all-day marathons of little Ralphie on *A Christmas Story* are now.

That mailing brought in $11,000, which is the equivalent of about $67,000 today. Within the next five years, the shelter's staff grew from one to twenty-five employees, its hours of operation increased to every day of the year, and its advertising budget alone was earmarked at $50,000 (about $125,000 in current dollars). That's why *The Wall Street Journal* had taken notice. Lewyt was running the shelter as if it were a corporation—work he would continue until his death in 1988. "We have the same concept as bringing any product to the public," Lewyt told the *Journal* in 1975. "We have our receivables, our inventories. And if a product doesn't move, we have a promotion. . . . Most animal shelters are run by well-intentioned people who don't know anything about fund-raising or running the place like a business. The only reason they don't go broke is that a little old lady dies every year and leaves them something."

That was all that Cindi Shapiro needed to read.

"This article was an epiphany for me," she recalls. "It put together everything that I wanted to do with everything I'd been trained to do."

Shapiro found Lewyt's number in a thick printed phone book, called him unannounced, and said she wanted to do what he was doing near Manhattan, only up in Massachusetts. He spent the next forty-five minutes berating her from his end of the phone line—the way a father might snap at a daughter who says she wants to turn down a corporate job offer and instead become a painter of abstract expressionist art. Lewyt told Shapiro that rescuing animals was a lifelong commitment, and that the work could be absolutely heartbreaking. He tried to scare off the fresh-faced college graduate by insisting there wasn't a darn nickel of money to be made.

"When he was done, maybe just because I was still on the line after all that, he invited me to Long Island to see what he was doing," Shapiro told me. "I met his wife. I stayed at their home for a weekend. I visited his shelter. I tried to write down everything I saw to learn how things worked. At the end of the weekend, he told me he'd always wanted to know whether his concept could be duplicated, and that I was the first person he'd met who had a shot at succeeding. He told me, 'I'm going to give you the ten trials of Hercules, make you do things like a financial projection and a marketing study, to see if you can do it.'"

She went home, took out her typewriter, and did everything he'd asked. The business logistics he demanded for the creation of a sustainable shelter were a far cry from the criteria placed on the majority of animal-control centers in the United States today, but then again, Shapiro was not the type of person to don canvas work gloves and toss a sweet puppy like Blue into a gas chamber. Her heart told her there was a better way, and her Ivy League education, along with Lewyt's example, gave her the skills to find it.

Not long after Shapiro completed Lewyt's feats of mental strength, he sent her a check for $5,000. She rented the basement of a veterinarian's office with room for just ten cages. In the early months, when she couldn't place dogs quickly enough, she fostered them at her own home. "We'd have orphaned puppies at the dining-room table during dinner parties, dogs giving birth in the living room," she recalls. "Bless my husband's heart, he supported me."

That was in 1976, a full thirty-five years before I stepped foot into the current incarnation of Northeast Animal Shelter in Salem, Massachusetts. I drove along the New York-to-Boston corridor on Interstate 95 just as so many rescue groups do with dogs like Blue, only instead of puppies in my passenger seat, I had a notebook filled with questions. As I pulled into the parking lot, I saw not a single hint of the organization's humble roots. The building wasn't exactly a glimmering skyscraper, but it sure was a heck of a lot bigger and nicer than any other shelter I'd seen so far.

Today, Northeast Animal Shelter is located inside an old Honda dealership that Shapiro and her sister, Executive Director Randi Cohen, raised funds to convert into a facility that can accommodate more than a hundred dogs and cats at a time. The renovations took two full years, with Cohen overseeing the project by learning everything from local zoning laws to the ins and outs of air-handling systems. In her previous careers, Cohen had been a remedial reading teacher and a travel agent. Like Shapiro, she simply did what needed to be done to make the shelter vision a reality.

The doors opened at the new facility on May 21, 2008, with supporters cheering all the way down the red brick walkway and into the asphalt parking lot. By August 2010, Northeast Animal Shelter was celebrating its 100,000th adoption. Less than a year later, it would experience its biggest moment of success, finding permanent homes for forty-three dogs and cats in a single day. There are now fifty-three full- and part-time workers along with more than two hundred volunteers supporting the New England shelter, where some 90 percent of the dogs arrive every month from rescue groups in Virginia, West Virginia, Georgia, Tennessee, California, Indiana, South Carolina, and Puerto Rico. The shelter's budget—all of it privately generated through direct-mail campaigns, online donations, fund-raisers, and adoption fees of about $295 to $395 per dog—has grown from Lewyt's original $5,000 check to some $2 million per year.

Although Shapiro started out saving local dogs in the 1970s, she began transporting rescued dogs from across the country in 1993. She got the idea after an attorney friend called her about a shelter that the friend's parents ran in Nebraska. They had more dogs than they knew how to handle, and puppies were going to be killed for space. This was before cellular telephones and fax machines, so Shapiro sorted things out by snail mail and landline telephone. She arranged for fifteen puppies to arrive from Nebraska by way of a commercial airline's cargo hold, and she personally met them at the airport at nine o'clock at night, with her three children in tow. Within two days, she had found homes for every last one of the pups who had previously been slated to die.

In that moment on the tarmac at Boston Logan International Airport, Shapiro became one of the first Americans to lay the groundwork for today's nationwide rescue network. In its first five years, the effort that Shapiro dubbed Puppies Across America saved five thousand dogs. As of 2010, her shelter was saving more than four thousand dogs each year.

It's an effort that the local rescue community in New England now appreciates and even celebrates, but that, in its early days, was met with intense scorn.

"We'd go to rescue seminars and have to sit alone. Nobody would talk to us," recalls Betty Bilton, a member of Northeast Animal Shelter's Board of Directors and a twenty-five-year veteran of the organization. "They thought there were dogs dying in the Massachusetts pounds while we were bringing in more dogs from out of state. Well, the only dogs that were dying here were vicious or so sick that they couldn't go back into the community. We didn't care where the dogs came from, but at first, we were the only people who thought that way."

Bilton, in working with Shapiro, was among the first Northern shelter workers to approach shelters in the South about creating rescue partnerships. She initially met with resistance and distrust that seemed ridiculous to her, but that she soon came to expect as standard.

"I was in Kentucky once, and I went to a shelter where they were going to put a bunch of puppies down, and they wouldn't give them to me," she recalls. "They said, 'You're from Massachusetts? Near Boston? You're just going to sell them to the universities there for medical experiments.' They weren't finding homes for them, but they wouldn't give them to me, either. And it's not just Kentucky. I remember a lady from West Virginia driving all the way up here with a van full of dogs that she had saved, and she sat in that van crying in our parking lot. Just absolutely weeping. She was afraid that we sounded too good to be true. She was exhausted. She had fought to rescue those dogs. She had driven all that way. For her, giving those dogs over to us required a massive leap of faith."

Today, the primary criticism Northeast Animal Shelter faces is that it does not accept every dog who needs a home. Shapiro says no-kill facilities that accept every dog in need would be ideal, but that her shelter—like many rescue operations nationwide—is not equipped to do so. She cannot, for instance, take a dog who has bitten a child in the face. It's not a dog who can be adopted back into the community safely, so it is not a dog Northeast Animal Shelter will accept into its program. Other dogs who are routinely denied include pit bulls, since they are so difficult to place with families because of stereotypes about the breed.

Being able to make that choice is a luxury that is not available to public facilities like the one where Blue, Izzy, and Summer were found. They have to make room for every dog who comes in, if not by finding adopters, then by killing the dogs already in the cages.

Even still, Bilton says, it is just as psychologically challenging for her to choose which dogs to accept into the Northeast Animal Shelter program as it is for volunteers in Blue's home state of North Carolina to choose which dogs to save from the gas chambers.

"I have this dream, this horrible dream," Bilton told me, her eyes gazing at the floor as she gently laid her hands in her lap. "I'm in the woods, and I'm standing in a river, and there's this waterfall up ahead. A puppy is in a cardboard box, and he's about to go over that waterfall. And I look at him, right into his eyes, and he looks at me, and he talks. That little puppy talks. He looks right at me and says, 'But you promised.' And then I wake up. After all these years, after all the dogs we've saved, I just can't get rid of that dream."

The fact that a shy dog like Blue made it out of a shelter like Person County's and all the way to a safe home with me is evidence that the longtime work of people like Shapiro, Cohen, and Bilton is beginning to make a real difference for desperate dogs across America. Northeast Animal Shelter is no longer alone in its nationwide efforts, with smaller groups like Lulu's Rescue in Pennsylvania now rising up to help the cause. In years past, a dog like Blue wouldn't even have had a chance. Today, the actual process of his cross-country adoption was practically routine for the people involved.

And yet, as thankful as I am to be able to give Blue a safe and loving home, some activists are still opposed to the changing national landscape that brought him into my life. Jenny Stephens of North Penn Puppy Mill Watch in Pennsylvania, for instance, told me by telephone that even today, she shares a lot of the same concerns that Bilton says her team encountered in Massachusetts several decades ago. As great as I think it is that Blue was saved, and as fascinating as I find the growing movement that is saving dogs like him every day, there are some advocates and critics who say rescues should focus on their own backyards instead of following the nationwide-transport model.

"In 2009 alone, we had more than 70,000 dogs entering the shelters in Pennsylvania," Stephens told me, unable to hide the frustration in her voice. "Now, if we already have 70,000 homeless dogs in Pennsylvania, then why the hell are these rescue groups bringing more into the state? Not every one of these rescue groups is reputable. They're in it to make money, and lots of money. They go down South and bring back pregnant dogs and puppies because they know most people want a puppy, and they can sell them for the highest fees. They're leaving perfectly adoptable three- and five- and seven-year-old dogs to die in the shelters up here because they're harder to sell. These dogs from the South have heartworm. They have medical problems that we didn't used to see up North, but that are now spreading to the dogs up here. People think the problem is just in the South, but it's not just there. Pennsylvania is in the North, and these overcrowded shelters are a problem here, too. We have so many puppy mills in states like Pennsylvania and Ohio whose dogs end up in these shelters. The average family that goes on a site like Petfinder is trying to do a good thing and adopt a dog, but they have no idea what's going on behind the pictures. There are serious issues behind these pictures, issues that are convoluted by multiple states and really powerful lobbying groups and cash being paid for puppies and all kinds of money being funneled to politicians."

It is of course hard for me to hear activists like Stephens talk with such disdain for groups like Northeast Animal Shelter, which has saved so many dogs. Michele Armstrong hears similar criticisms directed toward Lulu's Rescue about dogs like Blue, Izzy, and Summer, and she always replies by telling detractors that the need in the South is quite simply much greater than it is in the North.

To me, it seems clear-cut that everything Stephens says is rooted in fact, but that even still, if not for the efforts of such groups, then hundreds of thousands of dogs like Blue would not be safe in homes today. I really don't care where Blue was born or found. And I'd have no problem with a transport moving in the opposite direction, if a person from Oklahoma were willing to adopt a dog from New Hampshire. Blue is learning new tricks at school, going for walks to the park every day, and cuddling on my lap as we sit on the sofa together. Without the work of cross-country rescue volunteers, he would be a lifeless carcass in a trash heap.

One thing upon which activists like Shapiro, Armstrong, and Stephens all agree is that shelter dogs have been unfairly maligned for many years as less valuable or less worthy than purebreds, when in fact they are often wonderful dogs like Blue who have simply found themselves in a tragic situation. The idea that shelter dogs are worth paying for, and worth saving no matter their origins, is a good thing—and it's an idea that is continuing to spread across the country as more and more dog lovers become educated about stories like Blue's. I know that I, for one, will never again question the validity of paying $400 for a shelter dog. Knowing what a great dog Blue is, I'd have been stupid not to pay $1,000.

"I've noticed a real change, especially in the past few years," Shapiro told me. "North Shore Animal League on Long Island was doing transports with vans all those years ago, and we were the first to ever use commercial airplanes starting about fifteen years ago. Today, you have lots of transports of all kinds going back and forth, including private jets and RVs. Now, while all of that was evolving, things haven't changed so much up here. People still get up every day, brush their teeth, take their kids to school, and spay and neuter their dogs. It's automatic. And things haven't changed much in the South, either, where the lack of spaying and neutering is still a real problem. But what I'm starting to see now, just in the past few years, is that when I walk on the beach up North the majority of dogs are no longer purebreds. Most of them are mixed breeds, and when I ask where they're from, the owners say out of state. It was not that way when I started in 1976. Transports would never have worked then on the scale that they are working today because all of the people wanted purebreds. We haven't solved the cultural, religious, and economic problems that these dogs face in the South, but we are starting to see some changes in attitude there just like we have seen in the North. There are rescues opening down there, too. It used to be people from the North who moved down there and started rescues, but now people who are from there are opening rescues. That's new. And we also seem to have reached critical mass in the North with our message that shelter dogs can be excellent pets. The affluent people up here who used to only have purebreds now have an awareness that mixed breeds are sometimes just unfortunate victims, and that they can be absolutely terrific."

After several hours spent talking with Shapiro and her team while touring Northeast Animal Shelter, I realized that the very building where we were standing had a lot to do with their success. It took me a while to notice, but I felt different than I had at any of the publicly funded facilities I visited. I felt calm and relaxed, and I had a genuine sense that any problems the dogs faced were completely under control. When I realized how this feeling came over me, I started thinking about the building itself. It conveyed an incredibly different presence than the publicly funded facilities I'd visited, starting at the front door.

The first thing I noticed when I walked up to Northeast Animal Shelter's gray building with green trim was the hours of operation, posted clearly next to the entrance. While Person County Animal Control had hours from 9 A.M. till 4 P.M. Monday through Friday when Blue was there, Northeast Animal Shelter is open from 10 A.M. till 8 P.M. Monday through Friday and from 10 A.M. till 6 P.M. on Saturday and Sunday. The hours are intended to make it easy for working people with school-age children to come inside and adopt dogs at their convenience, as opposed to at the convenience of a strict forty-hour-per-work-week staff.

The second thing I noticed was that immediately after I walked through the front door, I was inside a bright foyer with wall-size windows on all sides. To my right were windows into two rooms, one with dogs for adoption and the other with cats. The puppies had plush beds to lie on, lots of toys to play with, and plenty of room to romp if they felt frisky. To my left was a wall-sized window into another room where I saw decorations being hung for a child's birthday party. This, I would learn, is the shelter's Humane Education Room. It's where senior groups, school groups, Girl Scouts, Boy Scouts, and friends gathering for parties can learn about the shelter's mission, meet the dogs available for adoption, and play with dogs or cats for as long as they like.

I had to remind myself that I was seeing all of this while standing in the entry foyer. I wasn't even inside the actual shelter yet. I hadn't even stepped foot into the lobby, and I was already smiling at the cute, happy dogs available for adoption.

The lobby itself was topped by a large rectangular skylight that filtered in so much sunshine that regular lights weren't even needed. The desk that welcomed visitors was low enough for virtually anyone to see over. I watched a girl no older than ten, wearing her auburn ponytail through the back of a pink baseball cap, lean comfortably on the desk while listening to her mother ask a shelter worker about the criteria for adoption. The child felt intimately involved in the process from the moment she entered the shelter, too. Behind that family were a few cages holding puppies and kittens, each with a handwritten note posted about the animal's age, where he was from, and what his personality was like. Potential adopters were talking to the dogs in these cages the way people casually approach a bank teller at a local branch. There were zero barriers to completing the business of falling in love with a puppy and asking to take him home.

And this was just the lobby. For the next two hours, Cohen would show me all the rooms in the shelter, each of them filled with cages and runs where dogs had plenty of room to relax, move around, and feel comfortable. The walls in each room were painted shades of pale yellow, blue, and beige, all of it cheerful and inviting for the countless potential adopters who walk through every day. Not a speck of dirt, food, or even dog hair was on the floor. There was some barking, of course, but no howling or wailing or crying to indicate that the dogs were stressed in any way. And the air I breathed as I walked through the dog and cat areas seemed remarkably clean and fresh—which is really saying something, since I have a severe allergy to cats that flares up at even the hint of one being near me.

"We installed a system that makes sure the air circulates out of each room ten to twelve times an hour," Cohen told me. "It helps with everything from cat dander to diseases like kennel cough. Everything airborne stays in the room where it should and doesn't get into the rest of the building."

It wasn't until about halfway through my tour that I also realized I'd been listening to classical music the entire time.

"Do you pipe that in so potential adopters will feel more relaxed?" I asked.

"No," Cohen replied. "I read somewhere that it helps the dogs feel calm. It's nice for the people, too, but it's really there so the dogs feel at home."

The most remarkable thing I saw during my tour of Northeast Animal Shelter was not just the exceptional facility itself, but the effect that it had on the people who entered it. Would-be adopters arrived with baby strollers, toddlers, teenagers, and spouses. The kids skipped through the front door with the same eagerness and smiles that they might have at an amusement park. Senior citizens wandered about as if they were at the local community center, chatting up the dogs they'd known for a few weeks and saying hello to newcomers in need of a friendly, welcoming voice. The place felt cheerful, like a supermarket candy aisle with lots of great treats there for the taking. There was only one dog with a brindle coat like Blue's, and I couldn't help but notice how quickly he bounded up to the front of his cage to meet me. He was in no way cowering in the back, terrified, the way Blue had been when Rhonda Beach found him at Person County Animal Control. The dogs at this shelter had an easy way about them and seemed happy, whether they were sniffing my hand through their cages or playing with one another in one of the three outdoor play areas where visitors could watch.

"Does each dog get taken outside at least once a day?" I asked, watching a couple of dogs romping the way Blue does with his canine pals at our local dog park.

"Oh heavens no," Cohen answered, showing me a log sheet that volunteers had been dutifully filling in that entire afternoon. "Each of the dogs we have gets outside at least a few times a day, sometimes six or seven times a day if we can manage it."

Cohen also showed me the behind-the-scenes areas that make the shelter's massive operation possible. For instance, one large room is dedicated to adoption counseling services by a number of trained professionals. That space is across from four private rooms where people can spend one-on-one time with a pup they're thinking about taking home. "This is one of the only places where anything is left from the old car dealership," Cohen said. "These round tables where our counselors talk with the adopters, these came from the dealership's salesmen. They used to use them to try to get people to buy cars. I kept them because I think they're better than square tables, where people are on opposite sides. These make people feel like we're all working together."

Farther in the back, behind electronic door locks, Cohen took me to see the shelter's veterinary and isolation rooms. Massachusetts law requires dogs entering from across state lines to be held in quarantine for forty-eight hours—with dogs from different states being held in different rooms, to prevent any possible transfer of regional diseases. Northeast Animal Shelter has four quarantine rooms with a total of fifty spaces, which means fifty is the number of out-of-state dogs who can enter the shelter's program in any two-day period. An erasable white board in the staff lounge keeps track of which rescue groups are planning drop-offs throughout the month, to ensure that enough quarantine rooms will be available at any given time.

"There aren't any transports that move even close to fifty dogs at a time to us," Shapiro told me, "so unless something unexpected happens, the system we have in place works well."

The last thing I saw before I left the shelter was a computer in the lobby, placed there specifically for use by the public. Northeast Animal Shelter takes great pride in the photographs and videos it posts online of the dogs it has available for adoption, going so far as to photograph the dogs in front of blue backgrounds because research showed that they stood out more and generated more interest. The shelter also works regularly with Petfinder.com and is happy to direct potential adopters there instead of having them walk out of the building without a rescue dog at all.

"We figure that if people can't find a dog they like here, then they can sit down, log on, and find another shelter that has whatever they want," Cohen told me. "It works both ways. We've had people drive from as far away as Vermont to adopt dogs from us that they found on Petfinder. We really do try to do all we can to solve the problem for as many dogs as we can."

The rise of online pet adoptions is key, she and Shapiro told me, because it makes the process a heck of a lot simpler than building a facility like theirs. When Shapiro first approached

Alexander Lewyt in the mid-1970s, she said she wanted to learn how to replicate everything he'd done at North Shore Animal League in New York. Today, it's Shapiro who receives requests from people wanting to copy what Northeast Animal Shelter has achieved in Massachusetts.

And ironically, she now reacts to the telephone calls the same way that Lewyt did when she first dialed his number.

"It's always somebody who is trying to rescue dogs out of the goodness of their hearts, and I talk to them the same way that Mr. Lewyt talked to me," she says. "I tell them that to be successful at this scale, you need either a business degree or real-life business experience. You need a lot of common sense. You need to know about marketing. You need to be able to absorb a financial loss for at least the first five years, just as with any startup business. You need the type of personality that can give a hundred and ten percent, working nights, weekends, and when dogs need help on Christmas Day. You have to be able to manage a staff. You have to be able to interact with the public. And you have to be able to steel yourself against heartbreak. There will be a dog that comes through the front door, that will be standing right there staring at you, that you will have to turn away. A lot of people can't take that kind of heartache, even if they have all the other qualities for success."

After a half hour on the phone, Shapiro hangs up. "I never hear from them again," she says. "They have good hearts, but not the rest."

I asked Shapiro how a place like Northeast Animal Shelter can exist, almost like the fabled city of Oz, in the same country where taxpayers are funding a shelter like the one where Blue was found. The difference is so dramatic that they seem like opposite poles of the world. Obviously, there are many kinds of shelters in between, and there are many reasons Northeast Animal Shelter succeeds where some of the worst public facilities fail—including having a different mandate. Northeast Animal Shelter is able to focus solely on adoptions, while public facilities are supposed to do them in addition to many other things, including protecting the public's safety. Public facilities also have to accept every dog who is brought in, while Northeast Animal Shelter chooses to take the ones who seem most likely to find a home.

But in Shapiro's mind, there is also something else at play. "The mind-set in a lot of these shelters is not to rescue," Shapiro says. "It's to kill. It's that these dogs are a problem, and the job is to eliminate the problem."

A lot of the tension between rescuers and shelter directors arises because rescuers see facilities like Shapiro's succeeding on private donations alone. There is great public support for the cause. People are putting their money where their mouths are. When the directors of taxpayer-funded shelters say this type of work can't be done even with hundreds of thousands of dollars a year in public money—when they use gas chambers with the regularity of washing machines, trying to cleanse their communities of homeless dogs instead of working harder to help them—it frustrates the activists even more. Nobody, including me, believes that a publicly funded facility will ever have a perfect record of saving every dog. But when the ratio saved is just one in twenty, it's hard not to wonder why those shelters are not employing at least some of the techniques that places like Northeast Animal Shelter have proved so successful.

Of course I wish Blue had ended up in a place like Northeast Animal Shelter, where people would have held him and talked to him and made him feel safe as opposed to scheduling his death without so much as a walk. It's incredibly frustrating that shelters with kill rates as high as the one in Person County even exist, especially since the road map for giving every possible dog a home has been available in print since at least 1975, since the day *The Wall Street Journal* printed the article about Alexander Lewyt that so inspired Cindi Shapiro. In that article, Lewyt talks about how he can find a home for virtually any animal, even ones who are blind, deaf, or missing a leg. He told the newspaper that "unadoptable" dogs simply need to be treated as special cases and marketed in a way that makes their disadvantages seem like attributes. In Blue's case, a bio might have read: "I have a few scabs from a skin rash, but I'm otherwise a happy, healthy puppy whose heart is full of love. I can be shy at first, but once I get to know you, I will be loyal forever. I just need somebody to give me a bath and a few hugs in a place where I feel safe while I wait for the rest of my fur to grow back."

That same *Journal* article also quotes John Hoyt, then-president of the Humane Society of the United States, who says that American shelters in the mid-1970s were killing an estimated 85 percent of the dogs and cats who came into their care. By his guess, that was nearly fifteen million would-be pets a year.

Our nation's current estimates, of as many as five million dogs and cats being killed every year, are a step in the right direction—and are a credit to the people who run excellent shelters that save far more dogs than they kill. But it's wrenching to learn that taxpayer-funded shelters like the one where Blue found himself are still moving backward. If you don't count the help of rescue groups, they're killing dogs at an even higher rate than dogs were dying across America thirty-five years ago.

The ultimate solution to this now generations-old problem in America, according to every single advocate I met, requires a focus not just on supporting good shelters and finding homes for the dogs in their care, but also on creating inexpensive ways for the public to spay and neuter the dogs who already exist. Public shelters are never all going to be like the private one that I visited in Massachusetts, so change has to come from the pet population itself. Yes, some dogs are brought to shelters for real behavioral problems. And yes, some are dropped off by people who have failed to train their dogs and then get upset when they act, like, well, *dogs*. But the far bigger problem according to every advocate I met is people who let their dogs breed again and again without any intention of finding homes for the puppies. The flow of these dogs into the shelters has to be eased, and spaying and neutering is the way to do it.

"Even with all that we have done and continue to do, it's a drop in the bucket," Shapiro says of the more than 100,000 animals Northeast Animal Shelter has saved. "It's a Band-Aid on the real problem. Until people in these areas start to spay and neuter their dogs, it is not going to stop. It's going to remain a tidal wave of dogs that never ends."

Many rescue advocates from all across America agree. As one told me: "The problem is ultimately that dogs are treated as a commodity. We've had puppy mill[10] owners refer to them as a cash crop. If there were cows being bred and then left to wander loose on the streets of America, the problem would be solved, but because dogs can be big business, the animal rights issues get confused with the business interests, and the problem remains. Until this country adopts a mandatory spay/neuter law, we are never going to see an end to this problem. It's like trying to move an entire beach with a colander."

In parts of the Northeast where the message of spaying and neutering has gotten through to the general public, the number of healthy dogs and puppies being killed in shelters has plummeted. And the success these shelters are enjoying thanks to spaying and neutering has contributed in great part to the rise of cross-country transports, too. The shelters where the problem is under control have the time and resources to help the shelters where problems remain. Since about 2007, national experts say, this type of interstate assistance has become noteworthy.

One of the most ambitious spay/neuter programs in America is based in Asheville, North Carolina—ironically, perhaps, just four hours west of where Blue was found in Person County. It's called the Humane Alliance, and its entire existence is devoted to offering low-cost, high-volume, high-quality sterilizations.

[10] According to the ASPCA, a puppy mill is a large-scale breeding operation where profit is placed above the well-being of dogs. Many purebred dogs from puppy mills are sold at pet stores and later found to have diseases, genetic illnesses, fearful behaviors, and a lack of socialization. Some female dogs at puppy mills are bred at every possible opportunity, never allowed to see the sun, and killed as soon as they are physically depleted.

The group does this not only in its own facility, but also by training others to use its methods all across the United States.

The more I learned about spay/neuter as an ultimate solution to the problem, the more I realized that I needed to pay a visit there, too. I was emotionally exhausted from seeing so many dogs who I knew were going to die needlessly. I felt positively buoyed with faith after seeing Northeast Animal Shelter and realizing that in some places, people were starting to get a handle on the problem. What I initially learned about the Humane Alliance made me feel as though it, too, might be a facility filled with promise of a better future. I needed to know it was true on an almost visceral level. I'd seen so much sadness, and I needed more hope.

I got back into my car, left the rescue organizations in my rearview mirror for the time being, and went to get the perspective of some surgeons. As I stepped inside the Humane Alliance building and looked around, I actually heard myself think, *Well, Toto, we're not in Person County anymore.* This animal hospital was nicer than some doctors' offices I've been inside—and it was being used in one of the most creative ways ever attempted in America, let alone ever even imagined in places like the one where Blue was found.

Turning Off
the Faucet

~

"That thing you just did, that thing with your shoulders? I have to tell you, we see that a lot."

Marianne Luft was watching me at the same time I was watching the Humane Alliance veterinarians at work. She's the longtime assistant to the group's director, and mine was one of countless tours she's given during the years. We were standing in the center of six glass-walled surgical suites where dogs are spayed and neutered at a pace that tops even the diligent hands of Dr. Wendy Royce, who sterilized Blue in the POP-NC mobile clinic. In the span of about five minutes, I saw more than a half dozen dogs being prepped for surgery, another six on the operating tables, and, lying next to them, three or four dogs in each of the six suites waiting to come out of post-op anesthesia and have their breathing tubes removed.

I had arrived at the Humane Alliance with a brain full of desperate dogs' faces and a heart filling day by day with despair about the scope of what needed to be done. Seeing what was happening at the great shelter in Massachusetts had taught me just how distant that reality was from the one that so many dogs like Blue continue to face every day. The enormity of the task required to right this ship was subconsciously stressing me out. I hadn't realized how tense my back had become, nor how my shoulders were now swinging from a location freakishly close to my earlobes.

"A lot of the folks who work here have worked in shelters like the worst ones you've seen," Luft told me. "They see the need for what we're doing. We can see a palpable sense of relief in them, just like you relaxing your shoulders. Every day, they come here and they realize that there is a way—that they can actually make a huge difference."

The Humane Alliance was founded in 1994 inside a space just two thousand square feet in size. It was a spay/neuter clinic, nothing more or less, and the workers spent their entire first day sterilizing just five animals. "It took them something like twelve hours that first day," Luft says with a chuckle. "They were exhausted and felt like they'd saved the world."

In 2000, the transports began. The Humane Alliance realized that it had a state-of-the-art facility for performing spay/neuter operations, but it didn't have the volume of clients that it needed locally. Asheville is the largest city in western North Carolina, nestled in the stunning Blue Ridge Mountains with a population just shy of 85,000. The Alliance thought it could make a bigger difference, and stay financially afloat, if it increased the client base by adding twenty-two neighboring counties and their hundreds of thousands of residents. Drivers began leaving the facility at dawn, collecting dogs from as far as 150 miles away, and bringing them back for the operation plus an overnight stay. By the time the incoming dogs are unloaded, it's time for the transports to turn around and return the previous day's sterilized dogs to their owners. The facility's box truck can hold eighty animals, and the van can hold another thirty. Each of the vehicles, Luft told me, averages about sixty thousand miles of driving every year.

About 20 percent of the dogs sterilized in the Asheville facility are from local homes, while about 80 percent arrive by way of the transports. Almost nine in ten of the dogs have owners, as opposed to being in the care of rescue groups. Demand for these transport services turned out to be so great that, in 2009, the Humane Alliance moved into its current facility—a 13,000-square-foot space where about 120 animals are spayed and neutered during operating days. It's about half and half, dogs and cats, which means a total of about 11,000 dogs a year. And the facility is once again preparing to expand to meet increasing demand, not only from the public, but also from animal activists and veterinarians who want to learn how to export the business model nationwide.

The ultimate goal is to achieve in the neighboring counties, and across America, what the Humane Alliance has been able to document in its home base of Buncombe County—a 75-percent decrease in euthanasia rates at the local shelters since the spay/neuter services became available in a low-cost, high-volume, high-quality way.

"Most of the people who come here to learn our model are animal rescuers who have been trying to re-home dogs in their own communities, and who at some point realized they weren't making a dent in the problem," Luft says. "They realized that spay/neuter is the ultimate answer, so they decide to focus on that."

There are actually three programs that fall beneath the Humane Alliance banner. The first is the spay/neuter clinic, which means the surgeries along with the transports. The second program is continuing education for veterinarians as well as externships for veterinary students. The third program is called the National Spay Neuter Response Team, which is where people from all across America can learn how to start a similar facility in their own community. In September 2011, the Humane Alliance trained its one hundredth team as part of NSNRT. All but one has succeeded in re-creating the business model in their own neighborhoods, which are located in states as far away as Oregon and Massachusetts.

I scratched my head for a moment when I heard that, and I tried to think of something else, anything else, that had a 99-percent success rate when trying to deal with the question of shelter dogs. My first thought was that the people creating these outposts must be seriously committed to the cause.

"Typically," Luft told me, "the groups that want to be trained approach us. And they almost never are led by veterinarians. It's almost always rescue groups, or groups created specifically to open a spay/neuter clinic. They are often people who come from the middle of nowhere, who have mortgaged their homes, who have begged, borrowed, and stolen to try to save animals from the shelters and then decided to move into spay/neuter as the answer."

Generally, after being accepted into the program, the applying group takes about a year to get logistics in place. This means everything from finding a local space for their future clinic to ordering equipment and figuring out staff. Grants from PetSmart Charities and the ASPCA are available to fully fund this part of the process, Luft says.

Next, the applying group must show that it has at least $35,000 cash on hand. Without this cushion, Luft says, most new clinics—like most new businesses—will not be able to cover operating expenses during the start-up phase.

"Even if you have a great veterinarian on your team," Luft says, "they right now may be able to do about fifteen sterilizations a day. Well, they need to get it to at least thirty a day to be a financially stable nonprofit. Now, if an angel gives you a building and you have no mortgage to pay, you might be able to ease up on that number a little. But generally speaking, new teams need that cash on hand to succeed."

After that, the Humane Alliance considers the new facility ready to open and invites the group for a week's worth of training in Asheville. In the second week of training, two members of the Asheville team go to the group's new clinic to help them get up and running. The third week of training usually occurs sometime within the first three to six months of a new clinic being open, when a specific location's unique needs become more apparent. The Humane Alliance sends people back out to the clinic once more, to help the new team surmount whatever hurdles exist.

"There are PetSmart grants to cover all of this travel, too," Luft told me. "And then, if a new clinic expands by adding a new veterinarian, they can start the process all over again, also with a PetSmart grant. So the costs of starting up are greatly alleviated, and then we at the Humane Alliance stay in touch with all of the groups that went through the program. They stay in touch with each other, too. It's meant to be a system of continuing support all across the country."

And word is spreading about it, fast. In March 2011, the Humane Alliance organized a national conference for spay/neuter best practices in Asheville. They were hoping like lottery players that they might luck out and get 600 attendees.

They ended up with 850 and ran out of room in the hotel ballroom for more people who wanted to participate.

"Something has happened, especially just in the past couple of years, where there is a groundswell of knowledge about making spay/neuter the solution," Luft says. "And I don't just mean the rescuers and vets. I stand at our entrance some days, and we have people come in here with their animals. They say, 'Okay, I get it, I want the surgery done. But please don't cash my check until Friday, because that's when I get paid.' Now, that's a person making serious choices in life, and we've reached an education level where they're doing the right thing anyway. They are no longer going to be the people bringing boxes of puppies every six months to the shelter. Whenever I'm having a bad day, I just go and stand at our counter, and I wait for that person to walk in. It makes me feel so much better that they're starting to walk in almost every single day. What we do here is not sexy. We can't put a picture of a puppy on a mailer and ask people to donate money for vaccines. We're telling people to do something to prevent something else from happening. It's so encouraging to me that more and more of the general public are getting it."

As a member of that general public, I couldn't help but recall my own reaction when I was first told that Blue had been neutered "in the back of a van." I had been horrified and disgusted at the thought. I had bought right into the stereotype. I'd been completely ignorant of the great lengths to which Dr. Wendy Royce at POP-NC had gone to make the procedure safe, accessible, and affordable inside her thoroughly professional mobile clinic. At the time, I could not begin to imagine a mobile facility like hers, nor like this building where I now stood as a guest of the Humane Alliance. The phrase "back of a van" had left me with ridiculous visions of tattered Led Zeppelin posters and a sputtering fog machine where anesthesia devices and sanitized tools should be.

The ASPCA often hears people react just as I did when they first encounter its mobile spay/neuter clinics in Manhattan. The stereotype is nationwide. It stems from benign ignorance, from the simple fact that so many people with the means to pay for their dogs to be sterilized typically have the surgery done in a standard, full-service veterinarian's office.

"We are so very touchy about that," Aimee Christian, vice president of spay/neuter operations for the ASPCA, told me by telephone. "We started with one van in 1997 in New York City. It really was small, with the capacity for about fourteen animals a day, and people still call our mobile units vans because of that. But in 2001, we had a company in Texas design a custom mobile clinic that is a box truck. It's a forty-foot-long hospital on wheels with state-of-the-art equipment and the ability to do sterile surgeries. We now have five of them going out seven days a week in New York City to provide services to low-income residents, and we have a sixth mobile clinic that goes even one step further. That thing is a tank. It's a freight liner that can go clear across the country to support small rescue groups and people who want to learn how to do high-quality, high-volume spay/neuter. I really can't stand it when people call it just a van. It's so much more than that."

And when the ASPCA is using it, the purpose is not just to perform sterilizations. It's to take yet another step toward solving the problem of homeless dogs—by gathering what may be the first-ever reliable documentation about the financial and statistical difference that spay/neuter programs can make to shelters all across America.

In order to collect this data, the ASPCA's mobile clinics work regularly with the Mayor's Alliance for NYC Animals. New York City passed a law in 2000 requiring all dogs who enter shelters to be spayed or neutered before they go to homes. Two years later, the Mayor's Alliance was founded in part to broaden the effort. It's a coalition of more than one hundred fifty rescue groups and is the parent of the Maddie's Spay/Neuter Project, which provides low-cost or free services in all five boroughs. While I would have to fork over several hundred dollars to get a dog like Blue neutered at my local veterinarian's office in New Jersey, the Maddie's Project offers the service with co-pays as low as twenty bucks in New York City—and for free if you are a dog owner who receives public assistance such as welfare, food stamps, or public housing.

As of December 2010, working in cooperation with the ASPCA, Humane Society of New York, The Toby Project[11], and New York City's own Animal Care and Control shelters, the Maddie's Project was helping to perform a little more than 52,000 sterilizations each year—and just as the Humane Alliance documented in North Carolina, the New York City operations were directly correlating to big-time changes inside the local shelters.

"In the year before we started our spay/neuter program, in 2002, they were killing 74 percent of shelter animals in New York City," says Jane Hoffman, president of the Mayor's Alliance for NYC Animals. "By the end of 2010, we had it down to 33 percent, and we expect it to go to 28 percent by the end of 2011. That's because of a confluence of things, and spay/neuter is a huge part of it. That, plus marketing these great dogs to get them homes, plus educating people that they should adopt dogs instead of buying them."

The ASPCA is also now rushing its mobile clinics to any New York City neighborhood where shelter intake numbers spike.

[11] The Toby Project provides free and low-cost spay/neuter services throughout New York City. A graphic on its website, www.tobyproject.org, shows how a single, unaltered female dog and her puppies, if also left unaltered, can give birth to 67,000 additional dogs in just six years.

The hope is to use sophisticated mapping software to determine precisely how many spay and neuter surgeries need to be performed in "hot spots" before the balance tips back.

"It's never been proven how many spay/neuters need to be done and how long that pace has to last before you see a significant difference in the shelters," Christian says. "The only previous study that was done was proved not so scientific. So we are gathering the data now, to back up what we already know from many years of anecdotal evidence."

Once the ASPCA has the data compiled, it plans to make it available to counties and cities nationwide. A shelter like the one where Blue was found would be able to see—say, at the time the county's annual budget is being allocated—what it is spending to kill dogs versus what would likely be achieved if the same number of taxpayer dollars went toward a local spay/neuter project.

"You have to change attitudes about this not just in the public, but also in the shelter system and even among veterinarians in a lot of places," Hoffman told me. "You need somebody in charge of the shelter who sees himself as more than just the dogcatcher-in-charge. You need somebody who's going to change the culture at that shelter, somebody who will look at the costs of killing dogs and disposing of their bodies, and then look at the similar cost of holding an adoption event to save them, and then look at the cost of spay/neuter in the big picture, and then check their own attitude. These places that have gas chambers—that, to me, should be embarrassing to any community that still has one. It is a stain and it is a shame. These gas chambers are barbaric.

There are resources out there to help you change, if you actually want to change."

Millions of dollars in resources, actually. A number of organizations make substantial financial grants to help shelters start spay/neuter programs. PetSmart Charities alone budgeted nearly $12 million in 2011 for spay/neuter initiatives.[12] The Petco Foundation provides similar financial grants to shelters and rescue groups, and works with Spay USA to provide low-cost sterilizations nationwide.[13] The ASPCA gives grants as well as business plans and training to shelters that want to improve spay/neuter services.

None of these organizations have a problem with rescue groups transporting dogs like Blue hundreds of miles into homes, but they do believe those groups also have a moral responsibility to assist with spay/neuter initiatives—so there will be fewer dogs needing transport overall.

"It can be true that, if you just work on the transports, then all you are doing is exploiting the problem," Hoffman says. "Unless you are also involved in spay/neuter, you are not actually solving the problem. You never turn off the faucet that is flooding the shelters in the first place."

When I adopted Blue, I was actually pleased to see that he had already been neutered. By the time I met him, the surgery was long since a memory and I only had to worry about routine shots going forward. To me, it's just plain crazy to believe that

---

[12] According to the PetSmart Charities 2010 annual report, the spay/neuter funding was part of nearly $40 million the organization planned to give in 2011 for projects including adoption and transport.

[13] Visit www.Petco.com/foundation for a state-by-state list of places where you can receive low-cost spay/neuter surgeries.

spaying or neutering a dog will do anything but prevent him from procreating. I have seen no evidence, with any dogs I've known, that spaying and neutering changes a dog's personality or causes him health problems beyond minor post-operative discomfort.[14] I had my Beagle mix Floyd neutered, and he lived to be nearly sixteen. I got Stella spayed right after I adopted her, and she was just as hyper after the surgery as she was before it. If Blue was any different before he got neutered, well, then I need to go thank the veterinarian for yet another job well done. Blue's personality is absolutely dynamite. He could not be a better dog.

The same is true of my foster dogs Izzy and Summer. The people who eventually adopted them appreciated the fact that they had already been sterilized. The adopters also appreciated how beautiful they were, how friendly they were, and how much love they wanted to share—all of which left me with tears in my eyes as I dropped both of them off at their new homes.

---

[14] And researchers are now working to eliminate that, too, along with the cost and training required to perform spay and neuter surgeries in the first place. As of August 2011, the Michelson Prize and Grants program had given more than $6 million in funding to applicants with ideas for nonsurgical spaying and neutering techniques. The first researcher to succeed in creating a pill or other easy-to-use sterilizer for dogs and cats will win a $25 million prize. Details are at www.michelson.foundanimals.org. Another group working toward this future is www.600million.org, which was started by a cofounder of PETA. That group takes its name from estimates that 600 million stray dogs worldwide give birth to as many as three billion puppies every year.

A Better Life

~

Summer went first. I was surprised, actually, because compared to Izzy she seemed less likely to find a home fast. Like Blue, she was a little skittish. She wore life's hard knocks on her face the way gangsters wear brass knuckles on their fingers. She wasn't jumpy and bubbly, like Izzy. She was a little older and couldn't be advertised as young, let alone as a puppy. She was calm and sweet and most content if she could just find a safe place to take a well-earned nap. She was the kind of dog who seems to have had the odds piled sky-high against her from the day she was born.

The family across town who applied to adopt Summer after seeing her on Facebook didn't care that some people might find her less than perfect. They thought she was beautiful, and they wanted to give her a good home. They'd always had pure-bred Golden Retrievers, including their four-year-old Golden,

Abbey, who was just as much a part of their family as their college-age son and high-school-age daughter. But they'd recently learned about the crisis in America's shelters, and this time, they wanted to adopt a rescue dog instead of buying a purebred. I happened to post Summer's photograph online pretty much to the exact day that they decided they were ready to make a difference.

I drove to their house with Summer in the backseat, and, if I'm being honest, prepared to hate these friends-of-a-Facebook-friend. Even though Summer had been with me for less than two weeks, I'd already come to love her and felt fiercely protective of her. Blue loved her, too, and I secretly hoped that the adoption wouldn't work out. I was ready to keep her and make sure she was safe forever. I was fully prepared to become what rescuers call a "failed foster"—somebody who tries to say good-bye to a dog only to realize what she really wants to do is adopt him.

I sat for a few moments after turning off my engine in the family's driveway, trying to find something—anything—wrong with everything around me. But the neighborhood was so quiet that I could hear birds chirping. Norman Rockwell might as well have painted the scene, it was so gosh-darn picture-perfect. I knew I had no choice but to get out of the car and take Summer inside.

When I knocked on the door and was invited in with a smile, I saw tons of room for dogs to romp and play. I saw dog toys on the floor and a water bowl nearby, just as in my own home. Their Golden Retriever, Abbey, seemed as healthy, friendly, and content as any dog in my own family. She seemed to like Summer immediately, too, going right up to her with a feverishly wagging tail.

Then I shook hands with the mom and dad. They briefly looked at me, but they couldn't take their eyes off Summer. As I was looking up and around their house, they were looking down at her frail little body with love.

"She's a bit shy," I said, making excuses as Summer slowly made her way inside. She at first didn't seem interested in getting to know their dog Abbey at all, and instead sniffed all around the kitchen to check the house out.

"That's okay," the dad said—and then he lay down on the kitchen floor. The mom sat down next to him, as did their daughter. "Summer will come to us when she's ready," the dad said as we all patiently waited.

It was like somebody was feeding this guy lines from a script, his attitude was so perfect. The whole family might as well have been a figment of my imagination. They were, quite simply, awesome.

And sure enough, after a few minutes, Summer did go to them. She played with them, she sniffed around Abbey, and she figured out where the water bowl was so that she could take a few gulps. I spent a solid hour making sure Summer was in good hands before I felt comfortable enough to say good-bye. I drew out the process of leaving the way a three-year-old hems and haws when she doesn't want to go to bed.

As I walked out the door, leaving Summer behind, I started to cry just the same way Rhonda Beach had when she'd handed

Summer over to me in the diner parking lot in North Carolina. I was so happy and sad, all at the same time. I drove down their street and had to pause for a few minutes at the first stop sign. I cursed myself for failing to have tissues in the car. I had to use my sleeve to wipe away the tears streaming down my cheeks.

Later that night, while sitting on my sofa with Blue and Izzy, I got a phone call from Summer's new mom.

"I saw how worried you were when you left," she told me, "so I wanted you to know that Summer and Abbey have been wrestling like old friends. They love each other. And we love her, too. She's going to sleep with our daughter tonight, curled up in bed. She's doing great. We're thrilled to have her in our family."

Yes, of course, I started weeping all over again, like I do at the movies when that rousing orchestral music starts playing during a happy ending. Blue and Izzy, sitting there staring at me on the sofa, must have thought I was ready for a straitjacket.

A few days later, it was Izzy's turn to go home. I followed the directions to a neighborhood in Pennsylvania that turned out to be just as nice as the one where I'd left Summer. This family's house was also on a cul-de-sac, also with a grassy yard.

I rang the front doorbell with Izzy standing next to me on her leash, and when the door opened, she leaped inside as if she owned the joint. The dad and teenage brother stood over to the side while the mom and teenage daughter sat on the foyer steps, cooing and coaxing Izzy to go over and give them a kiss.

"She's just so gorgeous!" the mom exclaimed, petting Izzy as if she were a priceless stallion won at auction. "I can't believe she's ours. This is really our lucky day."

I made sure that Izzy had everything she needed. I'd brought along her favorite toy, her veterinary papers, and even the phone number of her first foster family, back in North Carolina, in case anything came up that required all of us to help. I'd also brought Izzy's collar, which, of course, I said the family could keep.

"Oh no," the teenage daughter said. "I already picked out Izzy's new collar."

The girl walked over to the kitchen counter and produced a brand-new collar with matching leash. Her mom and I helped her adjust them so they would fit perfectly. Both were hot pink and covered in black zebra stripes.

All in all, I spent about forty-five minutes that day helping Izzy to feel settled in. The mom's cell phone rang at least five times while I was there.

"It's just the family," she told me, silencing the ring tone again and again. "They all want to know what our new girl is like. Do you think she can swim? Because we go to a house at the shore in the summer. Do you think she'll like the beach? Everybody wants to know if she'll like the beach house."

Yes, indeed, it seemed that both of my foster dogs were going to have better lives than I do.

A Puppy's Potential

~~

After Izzy and Summer were gone from my home, Blue seemed a little bit lonely. I offered to foster more dogs for Lulu's Rescue, but until the next one arrived, I made sure to take Blue on many trips to our local dog park and to Top Dog, which is our nearby obedience school. Blue loves to spend time with other pooches, and he's a fast learner who has a lot of fun in class. He went on to earn his AKC Canine Good Citizen certificate on the very first try, following some pretty impressive turns at puppy kindergarten.

For those who have never attended, I can say that puppy kindergarten is not unlike your average day on a youth soccer field. There's the coach, standing in the middle and trying to give instructions whether the kids are listening or not. There are the parents, technically not playing the game but still intensely engaged, constantly shouting commands, and seriously hoping their kid isn't the one who screws it up for the rest of the players. And then there are the kids themselves, who really don't seem to understand all the effort that has gone into creating their day's fun. They're pretty much just excited to be around lots of other kids, and they're willing to follow a ball wherever it's kicked.

The difference with puppy kindergarten is that, while every dog is part of the same group, the ultimate goal is to achieve individual success. There is a lot of repetition and practicing commands such as "sit," "stay," "lie down," and "come." Some dogs listen, some dogs don't, and some owners get bored and give up way too soon in the training process. So just to drill home the point of the whole exercise, the Top Dog trainers traipse out one of their seasoned graduates at the beginning of each eight-week session. They tell him to sit and stay, and then they gleefully take turns trying to distract him by clapping in his face, offering him food, and shouting other commands. The dog—usually a Border Collie who possesses more award ribbons than Lassie had endorsement deals—never moves a muscle, except perhaps to yawn at these silly, silly humans. The dog's unfettered obedience to his master's most recent command of course impresses all of the newly enrolled people, most of whom ooh and aah while scooping their own puppies into their arms to prevent them from peeing on the floor.

As the weeks went on at obedience school, Blue got to know every dog in our class and loved them all. During playtime, he romped equally well with the spunky, three-pound Yorkshire Terrier named Bella as he did with the lanky, twenty-five pound

Spaniel named Laslo. Blue became a rock star when working on basic skills, too. He sat when told. He walked on a leash without pulling. He came when I called him, flying across the ring and into my arms as if I, personally, were made of bacon and peanut butter.

I was, without question, the proudest mom in the entire ring, beaming as if my kid had just won the National Spelling Bee. And while I know all dog owners think their new puppy is the cutest thing since their first teddy bear, mine actually seemed to be, with the trainers coming over to tell me so and trying to determine Blue's mix of breeds the entire two months that puppy class lasted. These are professionals who see upward of a hundred dogs every week. They'd coo over Blue and cuddle with him while all of the other dogs watched like wallflowers at the prom. One trainer even offered to dog-sit for Blue if I ever went on vacation, and she warned me, with a chuckle, that I might not get him back.

The last day of puppy kindergarten is the big finale, the Puppy Olympiad, as they call it in the alternate universe that is dog-training school. The day's schedule includes games that test what the dogs have learned, injecting a little fun into the experience after so many weeks of rote drills. In one game, each of the pups is given thirty seconds alone in the ring with his handler, to sit and lie down on command as many times as he can. The teacher holds a stopwatch, tells you when to start, and then watches alongside all the other people in class, who cheer you with their out-loud voices while thinking silently about how to beat your score when their turn comes.

Xena, a gorgeous Weimaraner named for television's warrior princess, was first to stride into the ring that day. Her gangly legs were still growing, which left her a little off balance when she attempted to move too quickly, but she tried hard and did her best to listen, and her owner seemed happy with their score of seven. Laslo the Spaniel, on the other hand, positively blew it and barely earned a three. We clapped for him, anyway, because he seemed so happy just to be in the game. Most of the rest of the puppies earned respectable scores in the vicinity of nine or ten. I cheered for them all and encouraged Blue to watch, secretly hoping he might pick up a few tips that we could use to our advantage.

Then came Bella the Yorkie—or, shall we call her, Bella the Ringer. Her tiny body stood barely three inches off the floor. This, I would soon learn, gave her a distinct advantage in this particular Puppy Olympiad event. For a bigger dog like Xena to go from sitting to standing position and then back to sitting or lying down took a few seconds, at least, because of sheer physics. A Weimaraner has a lot of body to move. But Bella? She could move from standing to sitting with less effort than it takes most humans to clench their butt cheeks. A stiff breeze could blow this little dog's rear end onto the ground. And she was well trained, too, watching her owner intently and responding to every single command. "Sit!" "Lie down!" "Sit!" "Lie down!" And she would, the little bugger, every darn time. Her score, when the trainer called time after thirty seconds, was an impressive eighteen.

Bella was still striding out of the ring with her precious plastic barrette atop her proudly raised head when the trainer called

Blue and me as the day's final contestants. I am embarrassed to say that I actually took a deep breath before I walked him into the center position to start. No three-pound pooch wearing pink hair accessories was going to whip my boy after all he'd been through in life.

"Aaaaand.... Go!" the instructor said.

My strategy was to keep Blue moving constantly, so he had time only to react to the commands instead of to think about them. Most of the other puppies had seemed confused by the idea that they had to move from sitting to lying down and then go right back to sitting, which is something we'd never practiced in class. Usually, our drills went from sitting to lying down, and then the puppies were told they could get up altogether. So, instead of telling Blue to sit and lie down, sit and lie down, in rapid succession, I decided instead to have him sit, lie down, and then walk a step or two toward me by telling him to come. Then I'd start again with sit and lie down, and then get him on his feet with "Come!" before telling him to sit and lie down again.

He thought this was one of the greatest experiences of his life, a mesmerizing new dance that we were doing together in the rhythm of synchronized swimmers. For about the first twenty seconds, Blue followed me around that ring as if he were a college kid chasing a dropped dollar bill in the wind. His eyes were focused on mine, his ears were perked and listening at all times, and his reaction to my every command was immediate. The teacher counted aloud as we approached Bella's score of eighteen. "That's fifteen for Blue!" "Sixteen!" "That's seventeen for Blue with five seconds to go!"

I was sweating. I was breathing heavily. I was working desperately to concentrate and maintain the pace. I might as well have been trying to juggle apples while running on a treadmill at the gym.

And then I said, "Lie down," and Blue looked at me like I was from Mars.

The entire room went silent. It was if everyone gasped at once, sucking the very walls of the place in.

"Lie down!" I cried. "Lie down!" My decibel level grew alarmingly high, as if I were trying to coax a child out of a burning building. All the people around us, who had been cheering just a moment earlier, no doubt thought to themselves, "They lost it! Blue lost it! He choked at the end!"

We had only two or three seconds left. Our score was seventeen. We needed nineteen to win, and Blue was just sitting there, staring at me.

"Okay, then come!" I screamed. "If you won't lie down then come! Come now for the love of all that is holy in this world!"

It was not exactly a command that we had practiced, but for some reason, he did. And then he sat. And then he lay down—just in time to score nineteen before time ran out.

Bella's owner smiled politely. The rest of our classmates beamed and cheered. Blue looked up at me waiting for my next command, confused as to why all of the fun had suddenly stopped.

It was all I could do to walk out of the ring without raising my arms over my head and humming the theme song to *Chariots of Fire*.

Our days at Top Dog were almost always a delight, but getting to and from school each week slowly but surely became a disaster. Blue's fear of cars, which had seemed minor when he first came home, was growing like a star destined for a cosmic explosion. Pretty much every time that Blue got into my Jeep, he vomited. Sometimes more than once. It didn't matter whether we were going to school, to the vet, or for our daily walk at one of the five parks within ten miles of our house. Something about getting into that vehicle made Blue react like a condemned man being forced into a guillotine.

The trainers at first told me that lots of dogs are afraid of cars because there's a window of time, when they're quite young, that is ideal for introducing them to the feeling of being inside a moving vehicle. Breeders, for instance, will put puppies into cars and drive them around the block to get them used to the experience of the ride. In Blue's case, we had no idea if he'd ever even seen a car as a baby. For all we knew, he'd been born on the side of a road where cars whizzed by like terrifying dog-crushers. Heck, he could have been tossed out of a car or even grazed by one in oncoming traffic. At a minimum, it was certainly possible that he'd missed his window of learning time and was having the same normal reaction that a lot of dogs face when they get into a car for the first time at an older age.

But as the weeks went by, the trainers' shared opinion changed. The pivotal day in their thinking was the one when we learned the skill of having the dog stay inside when you open the door to your house. The idea is that, if somebody rings your doorbell, you should be able to open your front door without the puppy scampering out and into the street. We practiced by having each dog on a leash, telling him to sit, and then opening the door to the Top Dog parking lot.

Each of the puppies in our class, the minute the door opened, tried to rush out into the fresh air. Their owners dutifully pulled them back inside, leashes intact, and made a second attempt. Usually, the puppies tried to run outside again. This was normal, the trainers said, and it's why we all should practice this skill at home using our leashes until the puppies got the message.

When Blue's turn came, things seemed to begin just fine. I checked his leash, told him to sit, and then reached out and opened the door. I was ready for him to dash outside like all of the other puppies had, but instead, he bolted backward. He pulled as hard as he could against his leash, yanking desperately to get away from the door.

We settled him down and tried again, only to experience the same result. The third time we tried, he wouldn't even go near the door. He pulled to the center of the ring, sat down, and let his ears droop so low that he looked as if he'd just been beaten with a stick.

I stood there puzzled, his leash dangling from my hand, trying to make sense of his bizarre reaction.

Then the trainer said, "Oh, I know what it is. He can see your Jeep right outside that door. Boy, I wonder if something really bad happened to this dog inside of a car."

Back at home, his fears got worse and worse. On days when I would open the door from the house to the garage, Blue absolutely, positively would not follow me into the Jeep. And after he realized that the only reason we went into the garage was to get into the Jeep, he began refusing to go into the garage at all.

I tried a few times to carry him into the garage, holding him close and telling him in my most soothing, aloe-vera voice that nobody would ever hurt him again, but whenever I put him down to open the door to the Jeep, he pressed his belly flat against the concrete garage floor and made himself dead weight. When he realized that I would then pick him up off the floor and put him into the Jeep, anyway, he started dashing to hide under it, where I couldn't reach him. Then he got smart enough to run around inside the house when he saw me grab his leash, so that I couldn't pick him up to take him into the garage in the first place.

Our trainers at Top Dog told me that Blue's level of fear was something they'd rarely seen. It was deeper than normal, even for a puppy who had not been properly exposed to cars early in life.

"The only way to break his bad association with cars is to create a new, happy association," one trainer told me. "And there's no easier way to create a happy association than by giving a puppy treats and food."

Thus, twice a day for about three weeks, I created a treasure trail of treats across my den and into my garage—right before Blue's breakfast and dinner times, when he was likely to be hungriest. And slowly but surely, he began to follow the trail, sucking up each treat like a Hoover on high speed and inching his way closer and closer to the garage. Once or twice, he looked up from his treats, realized how close he was to entering the garage, and fled back to the safety of the kitchen. But for the most part the plan was working, so the trainers had me take it up a notch.

Now that I could get Blue to the garage without fear, it was time to get him into the Jeep itself. I'd let him follow his trail of treats, and I'd be waiting at the end to scoop him into my arms. I'd then carry him across the garage and place him in the Jeep, where he would find his bowl full of dog food waiting on the seat. This confused him at first, but by the second or third day, it became a standard part of our daily routine. He no longer tucked his tail or flashed panicked eyes upon entering the garage. Around the middle of week two, he started walking across the garage and hopping up into the Jeep by himself, without me having to do anything but tell him "good boy" as he downed his breakfast and dinner.

Soon, all it took was a treat or two to get him ready for a ride, and then no food at all. Blue finally accepted that when he was with me, he was safe and good things would happen.

A lot of good things, actually, way bigger than him and me both.

The Days to Come

~

One of my favorite things about Blue is that he's a snuggler. Floyd was a snuggler, and Stella was not. When Floyd died after sharing nearly sixteen years of my life, it wasn't just the loss of his companionship that crushed me. It was also the loss of his warm ears and paws cuddled up against me on the sofa at night. While Stella always stuck to her spot on the ottoman, Blue took immediately to sitting in Floyd's old seat next to me on the sofa, sometimes snuggling even closer. And to this day, Blue is funny about the way he does it. He likes to "air things out," shall we say, flopping upside down with his head on my lap and his, well, you know, dangling in the breeze below the ceiling fan.

It's these kinds of quirky characteristics that you remember when a dog you love dies. It's these kinds of things that help you smile again. I'm not yet sure what memories will stay with me after Blue is gone, since he's not even two years old as I write this. Hopefully, he has at least another decade worth of memories yet to make.

I do know Blue well enough already to know that there will be plenty of happy memories, like him winning the Puppy Olympiad at dog school. There will be some funny memories, like the day that he came barreling through the doggy door covered in mud and jumped with absolute glee into my arms, slathering me in the stuff along with his kisses. There will be countless inspiring memories, like all the times he has found just a little bit more confidence to say hello to new people while forgetting whatever human unkindness so frightened him in the past.

At the same time, I also know that my love for Blue will make his death just as difficult for me as Floyd's was. The ride to the veterinarian with Floyd cradled in my arms, unable to hold up his own head, was unbearable. Floyd's heart beating weakly against my thigh as the vet inserted the needle, and then the moment when I felt his heartbeat stop, was devastating. I could barely let go of Floyd's lifeless body, I was crying so hard. The only saving grace was knowing that I had kept him as safe and made sure he had as good a life as I could until his very last breath, just as I now plan to do with my little boy Blue.

Floyd's death was an actual act of euthanasia—helping a living creature to die with mercy, to end incurable pain and suffering. That's what the word euthanasia means. Floyd was so old and frail that on the morning we finally made the hard decision to put him down, he could no longer stand without wobbling or drink more than a few sips of water from my fingertips. The deed barely took fifteen seconds from start to finish, and he didn't appear to feel a thing beyond the comfort of my arms and the relief of no longer wheezing to get air into his dying lungs. It was the opposite of the gas chambers that kill so many dogs like Blue—inside buildings called shelters that are not in any way places of refuge. Too many of those dogs experience scary, painful asphyxiation punctuated by their bodies being shoveled into a pile of puppies at a garbage dump. The contrast is absolutely staggering. It takes my own breath away.

Just as paralyzing to me is the realization that, instead of working primarily to save the lives of healthy, adoptable puppies and dogs, so many people still have to fight to ensure that they at least die peacefully, without pain or torture. That certain regions of the United States continue to argue about gas chambers versus lethal injection, well, to me that's just ridiculous. The conversation should long ago have moved on to how best we can find homes for dogs like Blue while enhancing spay and neuter operations—not remain stuck in the mire of the least-offensive way to kill them en masse.

I recognize that to a lot of folks, I'm one of "those people" when it comes to dogs. I know that I don't treat my own like animals. I spoil them rotten and let them sleep in my bed and ask them to give me kisses on my face. They are my family. I would step in front of a moving car to protect my dogs, or to save my parents' dog, or to guard my sister's dog, just the same way I would for my parents or my sister themselves. For me, it would be instinctual. I'd have shattered ankles and elbows from oncoming traffic before my brain fully engaged, and even after my synapses fired, they'd never register the message "it's only a dog." If anyone ever tried to hurt Blue again, they would most definitely have to deal with me first. And man, would they have to shed blood and break bones to even try to get past me.

I've noticed my protective instincts growing even stronger with Blue than with any other dog I've known. It's because of his personality, which is so loving and sweet once he knows a person, but so cautious and timid until he feels safe. Dogs don't bury the traumas of their childhoods deep down in their souls the way people do, letting them fester and ooze out later in life with cruelty or violence toward others. Dogs instead wear their histories on their faces and in their movements every day. Whenever Blue sees a stranger and crouches instead of wagging his tail immediately, his personal life story is on display. The details of his journey become almost irrelevant. The desire to soothe him is as natural to me as the impulse to seek shelter from a powerful storm.

What gives me the most hope for all the great shelter dogs like him is not just the inspiring number of volunteers now working nationwide to help as many pooches as possible, but the fact that so many everyday people who meet Blue—people who know nothing of gas chambers or transports—are visibly moved by his character. They may not be as nuts as I am in their love for dogs, but their own natural instinct is to show him kindness and love, too. Blue has an innate quality that just plain brings out the best in people. If he's friendly and happy when he meets them, then they're friendly and happy in response. If he's a little shy and reserved at first, then they calm their personality a notch or two to put him at ease. If for some reason a person spooks him—most often a man carrying a walking stick, umbrella, or cane—then the person typically stops moving altogether and looks to me for guidance.

"He's very sweet and loving," I say to those people, "but he's a little cautious around people because of whatever happened to him before he came to live with me."

Almost every time, the person will sigh with disgust, say something like, "What the heck is wrong with some people?" and crouch down to Blue's level so he can sniff and say hello. If the person is physically able, he will gently place his walking stick or cane behind his back, so Blue no longer has to even look at it. "See that?" the person usually says to Blue as the entire world shrinks away and leaves only the trusting gaze between them. "Nobody is going to hurt you here, fella. You have my personal word on that."

One of the best ways to help a puppy learn confidence is to put him into situations where he is likely to meet friendly people. The more people who pet him and show him love, the more likely he is to trust humans in the future. I thus was happy to take Blue with me on the day that I went to cheer a friend in a triathlon in a cute little New Jersey enclave called Tuckerton. It's a small borough in Ocean County that is best known for being home to Tuckerton Seaport, a living-history museum that tells the story of the region's clamming and boating heritage. While most people think of places like nearby Atlantic City as being the real New Jersey—filled with flashing and tacky lights, rowdy teenagers causing trouble on the boardwalk, and the occasional mobster humming a Bruce Springsteen tune in between visits to the kinds of strip clubs made famous on *The Sopranos*—I know places like Tuckerton to be the true backbone of my home state. It's a quiet little place that gets inundated during the summer months by tourists from New York City and beyond, but that most of the year is brought to life by everyday working people who spend their afternoons reveling in their good fortune to have such a picturesque view of the Atlantic Ocean. Tuckerton is Americana as painted by nature in seaside style, with the endless tide washing away yesterday's footprints and offering a new canvas beneath every sunrise.

We traveled there so that I could cheer at the finish line when my friend completed his first triathlon. I was excited about the day, but horribly nervous about the two-hour drive south along the Garden State Parkway. Blue was still wrestling with his fear of cars, and though my friend offered to drive, we would be inside my Jeep. I knew that Blue would be sitting on my lap in the passenger seat throughout the entire ride, and that if he got carsick as usual, it would be all over my pants.

As it turned out, my belly was more nervous than Blue's. I spent the first fifteen or so miles of the drive petting him gently and telling him that he was a good boy so constantly that my voice sounded like Muzak being piped into an elevator at a health spa. Around mile thirty, I caught myself watching him as he stared at the cars ahead of us through the windshield, cocking his noggin occasionally when he heard a horn or a radio blaring.

By mile sixty, he was napping on my lap, his six-month-old head cradled into my elbow for a pillow. We might as well have been snuggling on his favorite cushion at home, he was so content.

The triathlon course in Tuckerton is right alongside the beach, so the first thing I did when we arrived was take Blue for a walk on the sand. While other dogs tend to barrel into the lapping surf like a Big Kahuna on Maui, Blue, always so cautious with new things, took his time figuring out the ways of the water. He'd try to sniff the salty stuff when it flooded toward him, and then he would yip and yelp when it receded. It was as if the tides were taunting him the way a big bully keeps a shiny toy out of a smaller child's grasp. Blue delighted in chasing the waves for a few minutes, not quite finding the courage to wade in deep enough to swim, but absolutely thrilled to be part of the fun. It seemed he was going to feel right at home in New Jersey, after all.

I'm pretty sure there's no such thing as sand crabs in Person County, North Carolina, which is landlocked just shy of two hundred miles from the Atlantic Ocean. The odds are thus good that this day was the first time Blue ever encountered the critters, which would explain why the scent of them just below the surface made him explode with excitement. These crustaceans are no bigger than the average human thumb, and they spend much of their time buried just deep enough to camouflage themselves safely in the sand, but not so deep that they'll miss out on whatever nourishment the tide washes in. Blue spotted his first sand crab about ten minutes after we stepped foot on the beach, when it skedaddled past him like a flash of lightning.

He whipped his head around, stiffened himself on all four feet, and somehow intuited that he was standing atop a gold mine of fun. He then began digging for more sand crabs with the fervor of an obsessive-compulsive mole trying to plow straight through the middle of the planet and then back out the other side to China.

It took me more than a few minutes to fill in the deepest holes that Blue dug that morning. He would have happily continued his personal journey to the center of the earth had all of the triathletes not descended upon the beach as if it were Normandy. I was pretty sure there were no remaining sand holes where a competitor might break an ankle, but I'd been so focused on letting Blue discover a new joy in life that I'd accidentally let him decimate part of the triathlon course itself. After filling in all of the holes I could see and hoping for high tide to arrive early that day, I moved with Blue into the spectators' area near the sand dunes and tall grass. When I cheered at the start of the race, it was as much with relief as it was to spur the competitors on. They leaped safely off the sand and into the water in a matter of seconds.

The thing about cheering at a triathlon is that the clapping and rooting come in quick spurts. Each race includes a swim course, a bicycle course, and a run course with a transition area in the middle for the competitors to switch out of their swim goggles and into their sneakers, usually taking about a minute for each transition. Spectators stand near this transition area, cheering the athletes as they zip from one course to the next. If you're there as a fan, then you get maybe a total of four or five minutes' time to clap and hoot and holler throughout the entire race. For the bulk of the event, which can last an hour or two, the competitors are off on the various courses, far out of sight and well beyond hearing distance. The spectators end up milling about and making small talk with one another while awaiting the big finale at the finish line.

Dogs tend to be people magnets at these events, and puppies, well, they might as well be holding a sign that reads "Get Some Free Money Here." The slowest competitors were barely out of sight when adults and kids alike began sidling toward me and asking if they could please, oh pretty please, pet Blue. We had drawn a crowd of ten or fifteen people inside of as many minutes, most of them just as curious about Blue's looks as they were happy to partake in a bit of early morning puppy love.

"What breed is he?" one man asked as his son stroked Blue's backside.

"I'm not sure," I answered. "He's a shelter dog from the South, and he has the looks of everything from a Beagle to a Boxer to a Coonhound."

The man brushed aside my answer like a gnat on a hot summer's day.

"You should tell people he's a Breagle," he said. "You know, for brindled Beagle. Tell them he's a new type of designer dog, like a Puggle. You could make a fortune breeding that cute little guy with those awesome tiger stripes and floppy Hound ears."

I smiled politely, knowing that the man was trying to be complimentary. And then I heard myself say, before I stopped to think, "You know, he only cost a few hundred dollars, since he was a shelter mutt without a home. There are lots more great dogs like him who need homes and are still sitting in cages at the shelters, if you think he's cool."

The man's son stopped petting Blue and looked up at his father with begging eyes. The dad looked back at me as if he wished I were a commercial that he could turn off with a flick of his television remote control.

About a half hour later, a group of kids around ten years old came over to ask if they could play with Blue. A few of them knew about dogs and waited for me to say it was okay, but two or three of the kids didn't know how to act around dogs, and they reached toward Blue all at the same time, trying to pet his head without giving him a chance to first sniff their hands. The flurry of fingers so quickly approaching his face made Blue jump back with fear. He rolled onto his back to show submission and just lay there, frozen, until I made him feel safe again.

One of the kids asked me, "What's wrong with your dog?"

"There's nothing wrong with him," I said, squatting next to Blue to keep him at ease. "It's just that when you raised your hand above his head like that, he thought you were going to hit him." I stood my tallest and raised my hand above the child's head, to demonstrate what I meant, and the kid got the point right quick. I then lowered my hand, squatted back down between the child and puppy, and continued, "Somebody may have hit Blue before he came to live with me. That's why he got scared. But with all dogs, you have to say hello in a way that the dog understands so that he doesn't feel afraid."

The kid thought this over for a moment and then asked, "Why would anybody hit a dog?"

"Some people are mean to dogs," answered another kid who was wearing a green baseball cap atop his short brown locks. "We have a dog that somebody was mean to, too. He was kinda like this dog at first, but now he's really happy. This dog is just shy. You have to go slow."

And then I watched that young boy in the green ball cap plop himself down and sit cross-legged on the grass, waiting for Blue to go to him. I didn't utter a word. I simply sat down, too, and let Blue inch past me toward the kid.

"See?" the boy in the green ball cap asked his friend. "That's the way you do it." He sounded like he was teaching a magic trick, making all the other kids really want to watch.

The next thing I knew, all the kids were sitting cross-legged around me as if I were a camp counselor with some kind of coveted badge for them to earn. This caught the attention of other kids at the race, who came bounding over with their moms and dads to ask if they could play with the puppy, too.

"You can play with him, but you have to go slow and not scare him," the boy in the green ball cap answered, not even giving me a chance to reply. He was now Blue's self-appointed defender, explaining quite clearly the way that things were going to be done on his watch. "Somebody was mean to Blue, so we have to be extra nice to him now. You can pet him, but you have to hold your hand like this, and not like this, because he'll think you are going to hit him."

The kids around him all practiced the correct way to hold their hands when meeting Blue. It was like watching an elementary-school flash mob breaking into its own version of the Macarena.

As the children all gently played with Blue, I couldn't take my eyes off the kid with the green ball cap. He was like a miniature animal-welfare activist in the making, the kind of person who would grow up and slam a backhoe into a gas chamber without asking for opinions or tolerating questions. All that this kid had needed to do was assert himself as that little group's leader when it came to the treatment of Blue, and all of the other kids had fallen in behind him, knowing instinctively that it was the right thing to do.

If only it were so easy with adults, I thought. *But there sure is great hope for the future.*

For the rest of that morning's race, I let Blue sniff his way around the grass and sand. He eventually started to grow tired from all the excitement of new people and new smells, and he wanted to sit instead of walk. It took us a few tries to find a quiet spot in the shade, and I noticed that in every place we stopped for a break, Blue positioned himself with something against his back. Sometimes, he leaned against the tall tufts of grass on the sand dunes. Other times, he sat back against large logs of driftwood. I watched him sit with his back pressed to a car tire in a parking lot, and I felt him perch himself in front of me, with my ankles serving as a wall behind him.

It wasn't until our drive home after the triathlon, when Blue once again made it all the way without getting carsick, that I realized our ride to Tuckerton was the first time Blue had ever sat in the passenger seat on my lap. It was the first time I wasn't driving the Jeep, the first time he didn't have to sit in the passenger seat by himself. I hadn't realized it during the drive down to the race, but I saw it now as I took a moment to enjoy the breeze blowing through our hair and the sun shining on our faces. Blue let his ears flap as he pushed his nose up as high as he could get it toward the clear blue sky, as if trying to inhale the day itself. He was sitting on my lap in a precise way, with his spine firmly burrowed into my belly.

Blue, I realized, finally felt safe. His stomach was okay because, for the first time in his young life, he knew that somebody had his back—and for good.

Epilogue

~

In its first two years of operation, Lulu's Rescue helped to place at least 575 rescued shelter dogs from the South into permanent, loving homes in the North. I began volunteering with Lulu's not long after adopting Blue. I started by checking the references of, and doing the home visits for, many of my fellow New Jersey residents who applied to adopt dogs. I now continue to foster puppies as Lulu's is working to find them permanent homes. So far, I've helped at least twenty-five shelter dogs from the South end up with loving families in the North. Twelve of them including Izzy and Summer have lived with Blue and me as fosters.

Rhonda Beach's new rescue group Chances Angel Rescue and Education, between its creation in 2010 and autumn 2011, found homes for 391 dogs. Most of them would likely have been killed inside Person County Animal Control had she not intervened. When I met Beach in August 2011, I donated about one hundred fifty collars for her to place around the necks of the next dogs to be saved. Dr. Wendy Royce in the POP-NC mobile clinic told me that she would look for the collars and think of Blue every time another dog from Person County arrived to get spayed or neutered.

Annie Turner remains president of Canine Volunteer Rescue in Person County. The dogs I saw at her house have yet to be located.

In January 2012, North Carolina officials inspected the gas chamber at Person County Animal Control and issued a state license certification for the year. As of this writing, the gas chamber continues to be used regularly.

Ron Shaw remains director of Person County Animal Control, which changed its hours of operation. They used to be 9 A.M. till 4 P.M. Monday through Friday. The facility is now open 9 A.M. till 4 P.M. Monday through Thursday, 9 A.M. till 7 P.M. Friday, and 11 A.M. till 2 P.M. Saturday. The hope is that the new hours will make it easier for working people to meet dogs available for adoption.

Because I volunteered to take Summer and Izzy as foster dogs, their foster families in North Carolina were able to welcome two more dogs who were on death row at Person County Animal Control. They were a Golden Retriever mix named Cal and a Hound/Shepherd mix named Luke. Rhonda Beach and her volunteers at CARE found homes for them both.

Not long after Blue came to live with me, I finally, after thirteen years and nearly two hundred thousand miles, traded in my Jeep Wrangler for a new car. Blue jumps willingly, and sometimes eagerly, into the Honda CR-V, which offers a much smoother and quieter ride. He seems to especially enjoy looking at the road ahead while warming his rear end on the heated upholstery.

What You Can Do

~

If you spent three days reading this book, then in the time it took you to reach this page, as many as 42,000 companion animals died in American shelters. This book tells the story of where Blue came from, in North Carolina, but there are many shelters nationwide that struggle daily to help great dogs just like him. Please pass your copy of *Little Boy Blue* to a friend so more people can understand the scope of the crisis. Change begins with education.

If you want to bring a dog home, then please adopt one from a local shelter or through a rescue group on a website like Petfinder.com. Puppies and purebreds are almost always the first to find homes, so if you are willing, then consider adopting a dog who is at least two years old or is a mixed breed.

Dogs who have been in foster care after being pulled from shelters often have well-known temperaments, including testing with children and cats. It is reasonable to ask any rescue to put you in direct contact with a dog's foster family so you can get additional information. It is also reasonable to ask the rescue what behavioral tests were done to determine the dog's temperament. If a rescued dog is in a kennel or shelter, it is reasonable to ask the rescue if you can meet the dog there to evaluate him yourself. If you are meeting a rescued dog the day of his transport, it is your right to evaluate the dog upon arrival and decide whether to go through with the adoption or not.

If you want to help a dog but cannot adopt one permanently, then please consider fostering. The number of dogs that rescue groups can pull from the worst shelters is directly correlated to the number of homes where those dogs can be temporarily housed.

If your local shelter is killing more dogs than it saves, especially by means such as a gas chamber, then please seek out local advocates and ask how you can add your voice to the chorus for change. The typical path toward success includes hiring shelter personnel who believe in rescue versus killing, appropriating funds to follow that philosophy, and reaching out for help and grants from national organizations. If you cannot get access to your local shelter's kill-rate statistics to determine what's happening inside, then look at the shelter's hours of operation. Shelters trying to save dogs are usually open at least some nights and weekends, when potential adopters are able to visit.

If you have old towels and blankets, unused dog food and supplies, or anything else that a hardworking shelter or rescue group can use, then please donate. Some shelters will not allow rescuers to remove dogs without leashes and collars, so the dogs die even when rescuers have room for them. The donation of an old dog collar that has been sitting for a year in your basement could save the life of a dog like Blue who is scheduled to die in a gas chamber tomorrow.

If you would prefer to give money instead of supplies or time, then please donate to rescue groups and shelters, or to spay/neuter clinics, that are working tirelessly to save dogs' lives and stop more homeless puppies from being born. Many of these groups are recognized with 501(c)(3) charity status, so your donation will be tax deductible. Donations may be made online, through the mail, or even at the checkout counter of major pet stores such as PetSmart and Petco. Some groups, including the ASPCA, allow you to make a gift in memoriam of a beloved family pet who was lucky enough to die with compassion after living a long and wonderful life.

Acknowledgments

~

My literary agent, Jessica Faust of Bookends, Inc., believed in this book exactly as I envisioned it, helped to shape its proposal for a maximum chance of success, found the book a home with a publisher who shared my vision, and guided me exquisitely through the publishing process.

Literary agent Brandi Bowles of Foundry Media helped me to see my concept clearly and follow my original instincts even if it meant taking *Little Boy Blue* to another agency.

Editor Angela Tartaro at Barron's was helpful to me and supportive of the *Little Boy Blue* project from the day it landed on her desk. She also helped me to handle legal issues that arose with everyone from shelter directors to national advocacy organizations that attempted to control the book's content. Tartaro's edits and guidance made the final draft of this book far better than the first. Thanks also to everyone else at Barron's who dedicated their time and efforts to help make *Little Boy Blue* a success.

Jim Gorant wrote a beautiful foreword with every bit of the talent that made his own book *The Lost Dogs* a best seller on *The New York Times* list. I am honored to have my work appear alongside his.

Countless people in multiple states graciously shared their knowledge, forwarded me information, and helped me dig up records. Some who provided great help behind the scenes include reporter Grey Pentecost at *The Courier-Times*, tireless cross-poster Cathy Restorick, reference librarian Vickie Clayton and the entire staff at Person County Library, and numerous rescue advocates from SPCAs, Humane Societies, and independent organizations across America.

The Brian Dean Book Club reviewed an early draft of the manuscript and provided thoughtful, helpful comments about how to make the book more interesting for a general-interest audience.

Trainers Anita Zack, Dianne Posteraro, and especially Shelley Clawson of Top Dog in Flanders, New Jersey, gave hours upon hours of their time to help Blue learn basic skills, overcome early fears, and earn the AKC Canine Good Citizen Certificate for obedience. Clawson continues to help Blue at her new facility, K-9 Coaching, in Lafayette, New Jersey.

Dr. Allison Milne and her staff at Mendham Animal Hospital have been dedicated in their care for Blue's health from Day One. He loves them and trusts them so much, he actually wags his tail when going for routine shots.

Jeanne Craig helped me conceive the title *Little Boy Blue* over artichoke dip that turned out to be well worth every calorie. Michelle

George kindly listened to the entire book outline even though Blue's story made her cry at my kitchen table. Stacy, Eric, Erika, Andrew, and Rocky Weiss continue to be Blue's favorite playmates in the neighborhood and welcome him regularly into their home. Brandi Bartolomeo, Adam Machala, and Avery Machala helped Blue learn to be around young children, and to share toys and food in their home. Janice, Vaughan, Jordan, Sean, and Lauren Abel helped Blue learn to feel comfortable around older kids, even when they're yelling while kickboxing against the XBox. Copper Abel taught Blue how to respect older dogs with aplomb.

Patti Storm and her staff at Well Bred in Chester, New Jersey, as well as the staff of PetSmart in Mount Olive, New Jersey, continue to help Blue learn confidence with strangers. They give him treats and allow us to hang out in their store aisles, where other patrons pet Blue to teach him that most people are kind.

Almost everyone who visits the Long Valley Dog Park in Washington Township, New Jersey, and especially the park president, Harriett Chomen, has helped Blue to feel safe, happy, and loved. They are among his most vociferous champions.

My parents, Marc and Donna Kavin, and my sister, Michelle Kavin, immediately welcomed Blue into our family and continue to give him all the love in their hearts. Their dogs, Quincy and Sadie May, also adore Blue no matter how often he tries to steal the bones from their mouths.

Rhonda Beach and Annie Turner pulled Blue out of the cages for "non-preferred dogs" at Person County Animal Control. He would have been dead before he turned four months old had they not intervened.

Michele Armstrong and Jane Zeolla marketed Blue for adoption, coordinated his transport to New Jersey, and chose my application from among several that they received from people who wanted to give Blue a good life. They are the reason that he and I are together.

Blue is a wonderful dog who brings many smiles to many faces, including mine every single day. I am most thankful to have him in my life, lest anyone think he's the only lucky soul in this story.

"If I have any kind of belief or philosophy, it is that hope is not a strategy."
—Ken Mehlman

Petfinder
FOUNDATION

The Petfinder Foundation, a nonprofit 501(c)(3) public charity,
saves homeless pets by helping shelters increase adoptions,
prepare for and recover from disaster, and become more sustainable.
Its mission is to ensure that no adoptable pet is euthanized
for lack of a home.

Since 2003, the foundation has provided over $20 million
in grants to Petfinder.com shelters and rescue groups.

Visit
petfinderfoundation.com
to learn more or to donate.

The Petfinder Foundation
4729 East Sunrise Drive #119
Tucson, AZ 85718
(520) 207-0626
foundation@petfinder.com

Help a homeless pet like Blue!

Text 4PETS and your email address to 20222
to donate $10 to the Petfinder Foundation.

Join us on social media.

Like our Facebook page, *facebook. com/petfinderfoundation,*
to learn about the newest ways we're helping pets, see success stories
and photos and interact with like-minded animal advocates.
Join our Causes.com community at *causes. com/petfinder* for updates
on how you can take action to help homeless pets nationwide.

Looking for your new furry friend?

Visit Petfinder.com, the largest database of adoptable pets
on the Web, to browse the photos and profiles of more than 300,000
pets at more than 13,500 shelters and rescue groups.

North Shore Animal League America is the world's largest no-kill animal rescue and adoption organization. The non-profit group conducts hands-on rescue missions throughout the United States and internationally, saving dogs and cats from death.

Since its founding in 1944, Animal League America has rescued and found loving homes for more than 1,000,000 dogs, cats, puppies, and kittens. Each animal is given the extensive support, care, and individual medical attention it needs to live a long and healthy life. It is estimated that 8 million dogs and cats are brought to shelters each year, and tragically, about 4 million are euthanized.

Animal League America is leading the way in promoting the adoption of dogs and cats in shelters through the Mutt-i-grees® Movement. The Movement elevates the status of shelter pets, which encourages the public to adopt "Mutt-i-grees"—rescued shelter animals, whether mixed or purebred, canine or feline.

Animal League America pioneered the concept of mobile adoptions, using state-of-the-art Mobile Adoption Units to bring shelter animals into high-traffic areas where potential adopters can meet them face to face. The success of that program led to the creation of several national adoption tours, done in cooperation with shelters, rescue organizations, and animal welfare groups. These events result in the rescue and adoption of many thousands of animals around the country every year.

The Mutt-i-grees Movement also includes the Mutt-i-grees Curriculum, a unique educational approach in Pre-K through high school that builds on children's connection with animals through lessons and activities that teach empathy, compassion, and responsible decision-making. The Curriculum, now in more than 1,300 schools, represents a new research-based approach to humane education.

The Animal League also promotes educational initiatives to increase spay/neuter programs, reduce animal cruelty, and advance the highest standards in animal welfare.

To learn more visit _www. animalleague. org_ or _www. facebook. com/theanimalleague_.

North Shore Animal League America
25 Davis Avenue
Port Washington, NY 11050
516-883-7575